# Praise for Text and Tech

*Kristin has magnificently connected the instructional practices and beliefs of classroom teachers as they bring together both physical and digital texts. The stories that they tell are inspiring and bring to light the ways that students can connect with each other and through story by the careful and deliberate decisions they make when determining the story as well as the format. This book is the perfect addition to any collection that seeks to examine literacy and reading in the digital age.*

—Bill Bass, Innovation Coordinator, Parkway School District (MO)

*This book will expand educators' understanding of literacy, particularly digital literacy, and its role in deepening students' engagement with the text. It challenges traditional notions of how technology can be used in the classroom, providing practical strategies for leveraging digital tools to foster student agency and critical thinking. What stands out most is how the book centers students by showcasing the stories of reflective practitioners, offering invaluable insights, reflections, and modifications that encourage educators to prioritize the humanity of every student. It is a must-read for educators seeking to incorporate digital literacy to empower their students and support their learning journeys.*

—Dr. Towanda Harris, Professor, Consultant, Author

*In* Text and Tech: Reading All Ways in K–8, *Kristin reminds us that teachers are learners first and foremost who learn every day from watching their kids. She champions the value of both digital and print reading. Thank goodness! Because both are essential but may require different strategies and instructional approaches. She shares powerful and inspirational stories from a host of passionate, committed, skilled teachers who engage kids with high-quality images and texts of all sorts. We peer into their classrooms to witness a plethora of active learning lessons that spark curiosity—lessons that drive kids to understand more deeply, build knowledge, and come to care about what they are learning. Such joy in these classrooms. Such joy in this book! Run, don't walk, to grab a copy!*

—Stephanie Harvey, Educator and Bestselling Author of *Strategies That Work*

*In* Text and Tech: Reading All Ways in K–8, *Kristin Ziemke expertly weaves together stories and snapshots from a community of practitioners whose classrooms embody the purposeful use of technology with young people. Each chapter is overflowing with examples of mindful engagement, emphasizing technology use that fosters empathy, imagination, and connection—all while helping kids develop healthy relationships with the tools and platforms that play such a big role in all of our lives. This book is a must read, both for the practical tools and ideas that educators will be able to implement right away and for the inspiration provided by Ziemke, whose wisdom and expertise reminds us all why this work matters now more than ever.*

—Jennifer LaGarde, Digital Teaching and Learning Specialist and Library-Literacy Mentor; Coauthor of *Developing Digital Detectives*

*The wonderful collection of articles will invite readers to "visit" classrooms with Kristin. The thoughtful pieces by educators provide a variety of ways to include digital literacy in the classroom. The student-centered pedagogy and practices go in depth in a clear and concise way. Combined with Kristin's expertise, this book will challenge and inspire educators to try new ideas.*

—Anita Stratton, Elementary Teacher, Dublin, Ohio

# TEXT AND TECH

# TEXT AND TECH

*Reading All Ways in K-8*

## Kristin Ziemke

National Council of
Teachers of English®

1 E. Main St., #260
Champaign, Illinois 61820
www.ncte.org

Staff Editor: Jon Reigelman
Developmental Editor: Franki Sibberson
Copy Editor: Michael Ryan
Interior Design: Zachary Selter
Cover Design: Adrian Morgan
Cover Image: Kristin Ziemke

ISBN (print): 978-0-8141-0259-6; ISBN (epub): 978-0-8141-0260-2; ISBN (PDF): 978-0-8141-0261-9

©2025 by the National Council of Teachers of English. All rights reserved. No part of this publication may be reproduced or transmitted in any form or by any means, electronic or mechanical, including photocopy, or any information storage and retrieval system, without permission from the copyright holder. Printed in the United States of America.

It is the policy of NCTE in its journals and other publications to provide a forum for the open discussion of ideas concerning the content and the teaching of English and the language arts. Publicity accorded to any particular point of view does not imply endorsement by the Executive Committee, the Board of Directors, or the membership at large, except in announcements of policy, where such endorsement is clearly specified.

The following training content may contain the trade names or trademarks of various third parties, and if so, any such use is for illustrative purposes only. All product and company names are trademarks™ or registered® trademarks of their respective holders. Use of them does not imply any affiliation with, endorsement by, or association of any kind between them and NCTE.

NCTE provides equal employment opportunity to all staff members and applicants for employment without regard to race, color, religion, sex, national origin, age, physical, mental or perceived handicap/disability, sexual orientation including gender identity or expression, ancestry, genetic information, marital status, military status, unfavorable discharge from military service, pregnancy, citizenship status, personal appearance, matriculation or political affiliation, or any other protected status under applicable federal, state, and local laws.

Every effort has been made to provide current URLs and email addresses, but, because of the rapidly changing nature of the web, some sites and addresses may no longer be accessible.

Library of Congress Control Number: 2025936252

# Contents

Acknowledgments . . . . . . . . . . . . . . . . . . . . . . . . . . . . . . . . . . . . . . . . . . . . . . . . . . . . . . . . . . . . . 2

Introduction . . . . . . . . . . . . . . . . . . . . . . . . . . . . . . . . . . . . . . . . . . . . . . . . . . . . . . . . . . . . . . . . . . 5

**Chapter 1: Text and Tech: Defining Literacy Today** . . . . . . . . . . . . . . . . . . . . . . . 13

**Chapter 2: Weaving Digital into the Literacy Classroom** . . . . . . . . . . . . . . . . . . 35
    Shameer Bismilla – Embracing the Passion for Reading: Knowing Oneself through Books . . . . . 38
    Clare Landrigan – Creating a Digital Classroom Library . . . . . . . . . . . . . . . . . . . . . . . . . . 46
    Franki Sibberson – Pairing Powerful Picturebooks with Digital Texts for Deeper Reading . . . . . 53
    Kathleen Fox – Audiobooks in the Middle School Classroom . . . . . . . . . . . . . . . . . . . . . . . 59
    Nessy Moos – Leveraging Technology to Monitor and Support Independent Reading . . . . . . . . 63

**Chapter 3: Agency and Action: Tracking Thinking and Learning** . . . . . . . . . . . . . . 73
    Chrissy Moore – Structuring for Student Agency . . . . . . . . . . . . . . . . . . . . . . . . . . . . . . 76
    Lynsey Burkins – Annotation as a Liberatory Experience . . . . . . . . . . . . . . . . . . . . . . . . . 84
    Sophia Garcia-Smith – A Look into Student Learning . . . . . . . . . . . . . . . . . . . . . . . . . . . 91
    Carrie Baughcum – One of My Favorite Days of the Year: Introducing Sketchnoting . . . . . . . . 96
    Katie Keier – Turning Documentation Over to the Children . . . . . . . . . . . . . . . . . . . . . . 104

**Chapter 4: Embedding Digital Tools to Enhance Conversation, Collaboration, and Comprehension** . . . . . . . . . . . . . . . . . . . . . . . . . . . . . . . . . . . 111
    Stella Villalba – Using Photos as a Bridge . . . . . . . . . . . . . . . . . . . . . . . . . . . . . . . . 116
    Ann Marie Corgill – Enhancing Read-Alouds with Digital Tools . . . . . . . . . . . . . . . . . . . 122
    Shameer Bismilla – Digital Tools for Comprehension . . . . . . . . . . . . . . . . . . . . . . . . . . 127
    Gary R. Gray Jr. – Beyond the Rhyme: Teaching Poetry for Liberation . . . . . . . . . . . . . . . 132
    Angelique Trevino – Conversations with Care: Guidance for Online Interactions . . . . . . . . . 137

**Chapter 5: Reading across Content** . . . . . . . . . . . . . . . . . . . . . . . . . . . . . . . . . . 143
    Debbie Plemons – Reading Video for New Information . . . . . . . . . . . . . . . . . . . . . . . . . 150
    Angelique Trevino – Evaluating Sources . . . . . . . . . . . . . . . . . . . . . . . . . . . . . . . . . 154
    Stacy Hansen – Animation to Support Science Learning . . . . . . . . . . . . . . . . . . . . . . . . 158
    Stacy Hansen – Podcasting for Understanding in Social Studies . . . . . . . . . . . . . . . . . . . 162
    Sara K. Ahmed – Click, Capture, Convert: A Science Conversation . . . . . . . . . . . . . . . . . 168
    Katie Muhtaris – Planning for Content: Going Down the Rabbit Hole . . . . . . . . . . . . . . . . 175

Conclusion . . . . . . . . . . . . . . . . . . . . . . . . . . . . . . . . . . . . . . . . . . . . . . . . . . . . . . . . . . . . . 189

References . . . . . . . . . . . . . . . . . . . . . . . . . . . . . . . . . . . . . . . . . . . . . . . . . . . . . . . . . . . . 191

Biographies . . . . . . . . . . . . . . . . . . . . . . . . . . . . . . . . . . . . . . . . . . . . . . . . . . . . . . . . . . . 199

# Acknowledgments

**Contributing Authors of *Text and Tech*:** Thank you for sharing your stories! Your practice is inspiring, and the world needs your voices leading the conversation as we redefine literacy today. We are privileged to learn from you.

**Brittany Bonanno, Kristina Labadie, Ed Renas, and Bernardo Wilson:** Thank you for allowing readers a glimpse into your classroom to see all your students can do.

**Franki Sibberson:** There is no way I could've done this project without you. Your vision for what this could be, your insightful feedback, and your positive energy made it possible. In every text, you pushed my thinking or made me laugh. Thank you for organizing all the details so I could write. The best part of this process was spending time with you.

**Mom and Dad:** Thank you for raising me to be a reader. I've had countless adventures that began with a book. Thank you for working with me when I struggled and for liberating me through literacy.

**Marko Dumlija:** Thank you for being such a wonderful think partner as I wrote this book. Your background in design criticism shone through as you helped me to iterate and create. You held all the pieces of my life together so I could focus on this project. Hvala.

**Kirk Ziemke:** I won the sibling lottery. Thank you for always being in my corner. Your responsive timing on when to offer coaching, comedic relief, or a good hang is always appreciated. It's an honor to be your sister.

**Kimberly Querrey:** Thank you for always believing in me. You uplift all that I do and cheer for me to charge forward. You make it possible for me to do this work and your generosity knows no bounds.

**Nate:** You are my favorite six-year-old. Thank you for your smart thinking and for being a part of my book. I love you.

**Jon and the team at NCTE:** Thank you for believing this book could come to fruition in a matter of months. I am beyond grateful for your push to get this into the hands of teachers.

**Josh, Rebecca, Eliza, and Liz:** Thank you for all you do to support students and teachers in Chicago and Northwest Indiana. Your passion for this work fuels the world. Thank you for always supporting me. Para los niños!

**Big Shoulders Fund Students:** Thank you for allowing me to lean in and learn beside you. You give me hope for a brighter tomorrow.

**Big Shoulders Fund Principals and Teachers:** You inspire! Each day, I witness the love and care you bring to your classrooms to ensure your students have every opportunity to learn. Thank you for all you do for young people. Thank you to all the principals who have welcomed me into your buildings. Special shout-out to Bonnie Hall, Kathleen Fox, Sally Santellano, Damani McClellan, Nicole Mundt and Our Lady of Guadalupe, St. Ann, St. John de la Salle, and Visitation for contributing to this book.

**Principal Johnson and Alcott Elementary:** Thank you for inviting me to learn with you. Your effort to support learners is unmatched. I'm honored to stand alongside you and so proud of the work we've done together.

**Stephanie Harvey and Smokey Daniels:** Thank you for being the shoulders that I stand upon. You raised me to recognize that nothing matters more than student thinking. I continue to learn from you and carry you with me every day.

**Sara Ahmed:** From Burley to Bangkok, we've learned and laughed together. I can't wait for the next adventure! Grateful to be on this journey with you.

**Katie Muhtaris:** So many times while writing, I stopped and thought, What would Katie do? I missed you on this one.

**Nancy Mangum, Darren Hudgins, and Teresa Gibson:** You continually push me to grow. Thank you for the ongoing collaboration and laughter. Darren, thank you for the website design!

**Carolyn Skibba:** Technology coordinator extraordinaire, it all started with you. Thank you for guiding me to see the power and potential of digital learning.

**Barbara Kent:** Thank you for creating the conditions for teachers to thrive. What I learned teaching at Burley School is the foundation of the work I do each day.

**Julio Coiro:** Thanks for always pushing me to think about what's next. On behalf of educators, thank you for your research.

# Introduction

The best teacher is a student.

As educators, we keep learning to improve our craft. We stay abreast of the latest research and instructional practices. We gather information about our students and their needs. As Don Graves attested, the teacher is the chief learner in the classroom. We learn about our content, the latest and greatest books, new technologies, and what our students may need to be healthy, informed citizens of the world. We keep learning so that we can be the best educators we can be for ourselves and for our students.

We also need to recognize that students are our best teachers. After twenty-plus years in education, this is the most important thing I've learned. Every day, the students teach me. I feel incredibly lucky to listen, observe, and interact with young people. Their curiosity fuels new questions, new research, new understanding, and new learning. They share with their peers and recognize that learning is a process. They test and try ideas, fail, and try again. They adapt to new lessons and new tools and make plans for what they hope to learn next. They teach me far more than I could ever teach them.

Futurist Alvin Toffler said the illiterate of the twenty-first century will not be those who cannot read and write, but those who cannot learn, unlearn, and relearn (1970).

We recognize that literacy is a living and evolving practice. How we capture and communicate ideas, information, stories, and important events has changed and will continue to change. Throughout history, literacy practices have evolved as people gained skills, had a need to share with new audiences, and as new tools of technology became available. Today, with the rapid acceleration of technology and seemingly unlimited access to information, we continue to adapt and adopt a new understanding of literacy. As conditions change in this literacy ecosystem and our knowledge expands, we learn, sometimes unlearn, and relearn on our journey to lifelong literacy.

Students model this for us every day. They try a new skill, make mistakes, unlearn what they used to do, and then relearn in order to have another go and grow. As educators, we can look to our students as teachers and adopt their stance of learn, unlearn, and relearn to adjust to the evolving needs of the literacy ecosystem. Throughout this book, I invite you to learn something new. Maybe you'll find a new strategy or learn of a book you might want to read aloud. Perhaps you'll hear a new idea, like collective annotation, and try that with students. Or maybe you'll gain insight into how to know your students even better. As teachers and librarians, we learn.

Along the way, you may have to do a bit of unlearning. Maybe there's new research that sheds light on a better way of assessing students, and you step away from a practice that is less effective. Perhaps you can unlearn the dated mantra that listening to an audiobook is not real reading. Maybe you step away from a book that you used to love because you've learned about a problematic theme. Or, possibly, you abandon the phrase, "We've always done it this way . . . " and try something new. Sometimes, we have to unlearn today the practices we've been taught in order to find a better tomorrow.

After you've unlearned, you relearn and get excited about new breakthroughs in literacy instruction. You immerse yourself in cognitive science to understand just how powerful the brain can be. You find new websites, build new content units, leverage AI, and discover a whole new way of engaging with texts. You've learned from and with other educators, are energized, and want to share this new learning. You experience that sense of agency and joy that we hope to instill in our students.

The educators featured in this book have spent their careers as students. They have learned, unlearned, and relearned across years and decades to become the most effective teachers they can be for the young people they work with. They've taken risks, experienced successes and failures, and committed to grow. They are curious learners and masterful kid-watchers. They value print and digital text and celebrate reading in every format. All ways, always.

## About the Educators in This Book

I'm incredibly honored to have twenty-one classroom stories featured in this book! You'll hear from educators across the US and around the world who layer text and tech throughout their teaching and learning days. Their experiences will help you craft a vision for what this learning looks like in many types of classrooms and with many types of students. Recognizing that young people will need to be skilled in traditional and digital literacies, they use all the resources available to craft lessons, increase access, and build knowledge. They'll share the routines, strategies, and practices that support their students to use, understand, and find joy in all types of text. Throughout the book, they'll share what has worked for them with the hope that it might also work for you and your students.

This book was designed to share and showcase the work of educators in the field who are doing incredible things with students. Each day, teachers are innovating for young people, making unbelievable things happen in challenging conditions, yet most never get to share their stories. This is a small attempt to change that. In this book, you'll hear many new voices that we can learn from. You'll also hear veteran voices as they explore new ideas as literacy evolves. Together, these educators bring deep knowledge of students, digital know-how, and a commitment to lifelong literacy. We celebrate their contributions as we craft a text and tech continuum.

## Contributors

- Sara K. Ahmed
- Carrie Baughcum
- Shameer Bismilla
- Lynsey Burkins
- Ann Marie Corgill
- Kathleen Fox
- Sophia Garcia-Smith
- Gary R. Gray Jr.
- Stacy Hansen
- Katie Keier
- Clare Landrigan
- Chrissy Moore
- Nessy Moos
- Katie Muhtaris
- Debbie Plemons
- Franki Sibberson
- Angelique Trevino
- Stella Villalba

I am lucky that I get to learn with students and teachers and hear their stories every day. I spend part of my time in classrooms as a resident teacher for the Big Shoulders Fund and the other portion of my time coaching teachers on best and emergent practices in digital education. Big Shoulders Fund believes every child deserves a high-quality education and supports 25,000 students across a range of ethnic, economic, and religious backgrounds in Chicago and Northwest Indiana. Additionally, I provide staff development and school-based residencies across the US and around the world. Time spent in a diverse range of schools informs my thinking as I plan for what students need now and what they need to know next. It is critical to know how others are supporting literacy and technology initiatives as we seek equitable learning conditions for students.

I spent my formative years teaching in the Chicago Public Schools and was "raised" by a community of exceptional literacy educators. My former principal was a literacy leader and would push teacher practice to grow every child into a reader. As a community of teachers, we read professional texts together and authored our curriculum by picking the best-of-the-best ideas and making them our own. "A little Penny Kittle here, and some Alfred Tatum there. . . . " With a focus on literacy and writing and an ongoing commitment to learning, our students achieved. As a result, we were given a tremendous amount of freedom to keep innovating. I worked with a wonderful technology coordinator who brought digital learning to life. Early on, she showed me how students could create a podcast to summarize their learning; when I heard their voices and saw their faces as their thinking was published for the world to hear, I was hooked! From one classroom iMac to two (one of which I had to start with a paper clip because the power button broke), technology entered the chat.

With just two desktop devices and my teacher computer, we captured thinking and shared with the world. Because we had limited devices, students always worked with a buddy, and I discovered that this was the perfect partnership for learning and thinking. In a team of two, young people could support each other as they constructed meaning. When they weren't sure how to use the technology, they worked together to figure it out. It was true; two heads were better than one! I still believe this is a perfect match-up and encourage this in classrooms today.

In 2010, my school wrote a grant request to pilot thirty-two iPad devices for Apple in a shared device setting across first and second grades. Even before the iPad had a camera and before there were apps for students, I could see the tremendous power of the tool. Kids want to know, and digital tools helped them build background knowledge and increase vocabulary and offered access to information as they worked to become proficient readers. I believed then, as I believe now, that these devices have the most significant impact on developing readers and writers.

With technology, I'm always looking through the lens of literacy and thinking about how a device or app will promote reading and writing development. I think that's what makes the work I do different; for me, literacy and technology have always been intertwined, and the purpose has always been to gain access to information so students can keep learning and keep thinking. I strive to position students so that they no longer need me to be the gatekeeper to their curiosity.

I started to share our technology work online and at conferences. My students continued to innovate with iPad devices, and Chicago Public Schools and Apple enriched our learning with the second generation iPad. The addition of a camera changed everything! Now students could photograph their work, make videos, capture their thinking, and so much more. Apple shared my work globally, schools asked me to support their educators as they embarked on their digital journey, and nearly twenty years later, I'm still excited about digital learning, and I recognize its potential.

The best part of my work is that I get to learn alongside educators and students in a variety of settings. Every time I walk into a classroom and listen to a read-aloud, join a book club conversation, or support student research, I learn something new.

Observing other educators expands our understanding of instructional practices, the resources available to learners, what students are capable of, and how we might support a diverse range of learning needs. While we can't jump on an airplane and visit all the classrooms you'll read about, this book was designed to offer readers a window into those classrooms and the opportunity to hear new perspectives on traditional and digital literacy practices. From Alabama to Texas, Connecticut to Singapore, these stories offer new insight, amplify instructional practices, and equalize understanding of what young people need, have access to, and are learning.

## What You'll Find in This Book

The format of *Text and Tech: Reading All Ways in K–8* invites you to dip in and dip out of the articles as you choose what you need to know right now. It was designed this way so you can read an article whenever you have the chance—over lunch, at a grade-level planning meeting, or during a staff development session. My hope is for you to read a section of the book and gain a teaching strategy or idea you could implement the next day with students.

Throughout this book, we honor and respect the unique teacher voices featured and celebrate their writing style, instructional decision making, and the snapshot of learning they share, just as we celebrate the diverse lenses our students bring into our classroom.

As you embark on your reading journey, you'll see the big ideas of the book addressed across five chapters.

### Chapter 1: Text and Tech: Defining Literacy Today

Chapter 1 builds background knowledge for the evolution of literacy. It addresses the importance of print and digital texts, the need for explicit instruction in how to read on devices, and shares new research on digital literacy. This chapter expands the definition of literacy and celebrates new resources for learning.

### Chapter 2: Weaving Digital into the Literacy Classroom

Chapter 2 explores the marriage of digital and print resources to enhance literacy learning. From multimodal engagement to promoting reading joy, this chapter offers ideas for building reading identities, digital classroom libraries, audiobooks to support reading, and using technology to monitor reading progress.

### Chapter 3: Agency and Action: Tracking Thinking and Learning

Chapter 3 offers strategies to cultivate student agency by empowering young people to take ownership of their learning journeys. With traditional and digital tools, student thinking is made visible through annotation, video and audio recordings, and sketchnoting.

### Chapter 4: Embedding Digital Tools to Enhance Conversation, Collaboration, and Comprehension

Chapter 4 provides strategies to enhance student conversation, collaboration, and comprehension with traditional and digital tools. Contributing authors share practical strategies for using digital bulletin boards and enlarged texts during read-alouds to promote conversation and comprehension. It highlights how understanding students' stories and needs fosters meaningful connections and allows educators to tailor instruction effectively.

### Chapter 5: Reading across Content

Chapter 5 amplifies strategies and tools for enhancing student learning by reading in the content areas. It emphasizes building background knowledge, evaluating sources, and fostering critical thinking using traditional and digital resources. Chapter 5 guides teachers to leverage video as a means to share new information, design experiences for students to create to learn, and to leverage AI to personalize resources and instruction.

### Putting It into Practice

Each chapter ends with a section called "Putting It into Practice." Here, you'll find lessons built upon ideas shared in the chapter that are easy to implement and designed to use right away with students.

### Multimodal Reading Engagement

Throughout the text, you'll find QR codes that link to additional content, places for you to write and reflect, and space for you to sketch your thinking as you read. Please mark up this book and visit the links, as there are additional spaces for you to share online. We know that literacy today requires multimodal interactions and the opportunity to leverage print and digital sources; we invite you to engage in this practice as you read.

### Online Content

Visit the website to hear more from Kristin or to access thinksheets, slide decks, and reproducibles to support your teaching. Scan the QR code in each chapter or visit the website at https://www.kristinziemke.com/text-and-tech. The password to access the content is **KZTandT**.

bit.ly/4dz16gl
Visit the website for more content and resources.
(Password: **KZTandT**)

## Equity and Access

I acknowledge and identify that all young people have not had the same access to quality education. I recognize that literacy is a first step to equity and works to change learning conditions for students in communities who have been historically marginalized.

This work honors the voices of students, caregivers, and the community; understanding the knowledge they have is invaluable (Qarooni, 2024). Through an asset-based stance, I support learners by building upon their cognitive development and lived experiences as they grow into thriving readers and writers (Hammond, 2015). I recognize that students are constantly making sense of who they are and that classroom instruction needs to be responsive to their identities (Muhammad, 2020). I acknowledge the "potentials and perils" (Shelton & Lanier, 2024) of digital access and provide instruction so that students can read, comprehend, and build new knowledge.

In this book, you'll find a collection of educators from diverse backgrounds utilizing strategies to encourage equity through literacy. With high-quality practices, tools, and resources that are accessible, inclusive, and engaging, we build upon children's curiosity and develop thinking routines that promote independence and agency, support instruction, and foster belonging. Active literacy and multimodal learning are promoted to invite learners to enter and extend the thinking experience wherever they are able. Throughout, there is the intentional drive to enhance background knowledge, develop vocabulary, decode information, and build comprehension skills.

The commitment to equity and access is ongoing; as educators, we continuously work to improve the educational experience for all learners. As part of this effort, 50 percent of author royalties from this book are being donated to the National Council of Teachers of English (NCTE) Annual Convention Scholarship fund, providing educators of color access to the largest annual gathering of ELA educators in the US.

# Text and Tech

- leaving digital into literacy
- Make literacy evolves
- tools transform
- show your work
- Agency & Action
- new strategies needed!
- More
- sketch
- Thinking
- word wealth
- More talk on similarities & differences books + screens
- Thinking evolves
- Teach equity
- READ JOY
- Reading
- multimodal students 1st
- active literacy
- print vs digital
- video, graphics, audio, eText, books, AI, audiobooks, podcasts
- Print AND Digital
- AI to personalize, device agnostic
- engage, Yes and
- build fluency w/ digital
- identity
- text + tech matters!
- layers of interaction
- Learn, Unlearn, Relearn
- 4 E's of Cognition
- students as teachers
- Ways new cognitive ecosystems
- embodied, embedded, enacted, extended
- text sets + access
- tech matters!
- Comprehension
- background knowledge
- conversation, collaboration
- AGENCY!!
- Books ♥ enable
- tech sets!
- CREATE 2 LEARN
- construct knowledge
- Content
- Reading

# CHAPTER 1

# Text and Tech: Defining Literacy Today

## A Brief History of Multimodal Communication

More than 35,000 years ago, humans created the first paintings inside a cave. Using charcoal and ochre to sketch, they depicted horses, mammoths, bears, lions, leopards, and rhinoceroses. They painted scenes where animals interacted with each other, butting heads, and predators running down prey. They rubbed ochre on their hands and pressed them to walls to include themselves in the work. To show their existence. These paintings, found in the south of France, depicted the life of the people who painted them. They showcased what they valued, what scared them, their struggles, and how they passed their time.

Their paintings told stories.

From the first paintings at Chauvet, it took more than 30,000 years for what is considered the earliest form of writing to originate in Mesopotamia. This early form of writing, called cuneiform, consisted of wedge-shaped symbols written on clay tablets. These early pictographs were used in trade and business as lists and ledgers to record transactions. Around 3000 BCE, Egyptian hieroglyphs emerged, and the desire to capture information and records endured. Shortly after (2568 BCE), the first scrolls were created to capture ancient text.

Scrolls were cumbersome and expensive, so the Romans replaced it with the codex. The codex was the first iteration of what we know today as a book—a series of pages bound together on one side by boards or cloth. In the Middle Ages, books were copied by hand to match an original manuscript. This was a time-consuming process that only slightly increased access to texts. Paintings, tapestry, and other forms of art played significant roles in how information was shared. Nonliterate people could read the imagery and interpret a scene from history, religion, or daily life.

Meanwhile, in China, the first printing press was invented around 860 CE, and the oldest print book dates back to 868 CE. Movable type was introduced at the end of the first millennium. Nearly 400 years before Gutenberg invented the printing press in Europe, printed books were prevalent in Chinese society.

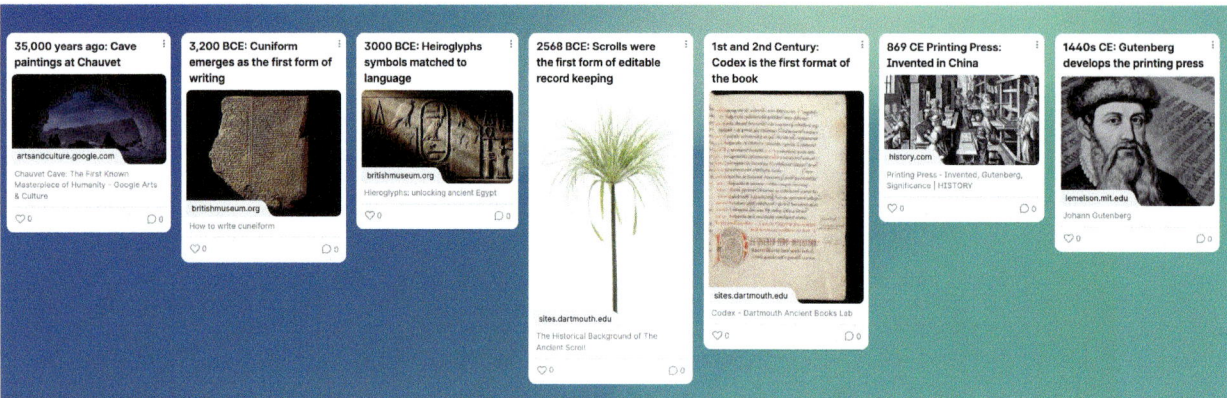

**Figure 1.1:** Literacy timeline.

bit.ly/4dz16gl

To learn more about the evolution of literacy, visit the Padlet on the website. (Password: **KZTandT**)

When the printing press was invented in the 1440s, only 30 percent of the European population was thought to be literate. Gutenberg's printing press completely changed how knowledge was spread from Europe to other parts of the world. Information was easier to share. Because of quicker production rates and lower costs to create, text became more available. In 2020, UNESCO data showed nearly 87 percent of the adult global population to be literate.

So, why the history lesson?

To showcase that literacy is a living and evolving practice. How we capture ideas, information, stories, and events has and continues to change. Throughout history, humans have sought new modalities for communication and have updated their technologies along the way. The examples shared are all thought to be mind-blowing inventions and technologies that changed literacy by providing new ways to transfer information. Humans desire to share our experiences and learn from the experiences of others. We crave information. And we will continue finding new modes for crafting, telling, and sharing our learning.

The National Council of Teachers of English (NCTE) has studied and stewarded the definition of what literacy is as it has changed over time. Its position statement on the *Definition of Literacy in a Digital Age* detailed the evolution of literacy and the new skills,

**Figure 1.2:** Students annotate an image on an iPad to document their learning.

**Figure 1.3:** After reading, a student uses a thinksheet and a video recording on Seesaw to explain what they learned about deep sea creatures.

competencies, and dispositions needed to be literate today. NCTE stated, "As society and technology change, so does literacy" (2019). As we look back on the innovations in literacy through the years, it is clear that we can expect continued change.

## The Evolution of Literacy

As literacy evolves, cognitive dissonance occurs.

> How do we accommodate this new format for literacy?
> Print books are a more effective format for reading development.
> But I love books and I want my students to love books, too!
> I don't think reading on a device is healthy for young people.

As conditions change, we naturally experience discomfort when we attempt to conceptualize how this change may impact our values, beliefs, or attitudes (Festinger, 1962). We may ignore the new innovation. We may discount it and share how it does not align with our beliefs. We may compare the new to the old and name the differences. We may question to learn more. We may seek additional information. Ideally, we commit to learn and grow.

bit.ly/3rmmHoi
NCTE position statement: *Definition of Literacy in a Digital Age*

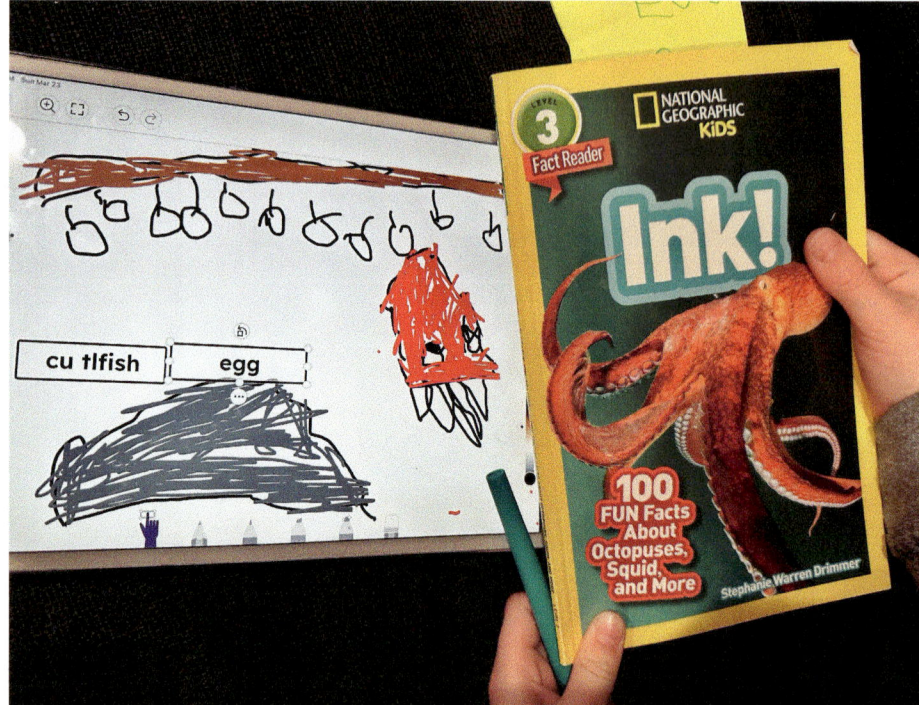

**Figure 1.4:** A student uses drawing and labels to document his understanding of the book *Ink!* Later, he adds an audio recording to share what he learned and what questions he has. The drawing paired with the audio recording allows the teacher to assess his comprehension of the text and plan for next steps in learning.

## This Is Not an Either/Or Conversation

Too frequently, change comes slowly to schools. Educators have been framing literacy as a "print-versus-digital" standoff for more than a decade. We've determined it's high noon in the land of books, and we're heading to a duel.

But it doesn't have to be that way. Books do not have to become extinct to access the benefits of digital literacy, nor does technology have to be vilified so we can continue to value printed books. Today's educators must recognize that we are in a "yes, and" scenario. Taking a mindset approach from theater and improv, we adopt a "yes, and" principle in which we say yes to print and celebrate all it offers our students while also saying "and" to digital because we acknowledge that these texts can build upon what we do with books and offer new ideas, accessibility, and opportunities. Lifelong literacy is not a binary either/or scenario; we do not have to make a choice between print and digital offerings (Coiro, 2020). Instead, we should celebrate the additional options for students and invite them to use all the tools available as they develop their literate lives. Literacy is not a zero-sum game.

Today, as our world expands, so too must our definition of literacy. Previous, narrow definitions of literacy no longer fit the expansive options we have for telling, hearing, and acting upon stories. Our definition of literacy stretches to include digital literacy, media literacy, critical literacy, information literacy, and so much more, broadening the concept of what it means to be "literate." A quick inventory of the myriad ways we connect with information can illustrate this point. Take 60 seconds and jot down all the things you have read in the past week. Go ahead! It's okay to write in this book.

**Things I've read this week:**
_____    _____
_____    _____
_____    _____
_____    _____
_____    _____
_____    _____
_____    _____

How'd it go? Did you notice the wide variety of what you read in a week? Did your list include things that span beyond a traditional definition of reading? Chances are, you notice how we read print *and* we read e-text, video, graphics, code, art, environments, emotions, maps, virtual reality, closed captions, AI-created content, and more!

**Figure 1.5:** Examples of the many things we might read across the course of the week.

TEXT AND TECH: DEFINING LITERACY TODAY

Here's an example of what I read in one week while working on this book:

> **Things Kristin read in a week:**
> - Email
> - Books in class
> - Student work
> - Text messages
> - Recipes
> - Videos
> - Instagram posts
> - News websites
> - Traffic signs
> - Menu
> - Books on Kindle
> - National Geographic
> - Weather reports
> - Audible books
> - Social media chats
> - Research articles
> - Bills
> - Facial expressions
> - AI-created content

Paulo Freire said we read the word and the world (Freire & Macedo, 1987). We guide students to access, craft, create, and comprehend all types of information and coach them to be adaptable and open to continued change. We show them what that looks like by also embracing these attributes and seeking opportunities to model these behaviors in front of them. In doing so, we grow and travel down the path of lifelong literacy right beside our students.

### You Are Here

As we broaden our understanding of lifelong literacy, we find ourselves and our students experiencing new cognitive ecologies where the conditions in which we think and learn are ever changing.

**Figure 1.6:** Students work with devices, print books and articles, markers, pens, and sticky notes as they build new knowledge.

Our ability to think is not only determined by our brain and the physical structures and systems that are innate but also by the interactions we have with others, the technology and tools we have access to, our cultural influences, and the environments in which we live. Thinking does not happen in isolation inside our heads but in collaboration with tools, technologies, and other people.

The 4 E's of Cognition framework (Figure 1.7) helps us better understand how there are many factors that play a role in cognition. As we learn more about the cognitive outcomes of reading, we explore reading as a multisensory human-technology interaction (van der Weel & Mangen, 2022).

| | | Definition | Example |
|---|---|---|---|
| **The 4 E's of Cognition Framework** | **Embodied** | Cognition is tied to the body and its physical interactions with the environment | Problem-solving often involves gestures or physical manipulation, such as counting on fingers or modeling with the hands. |
| | **Embedded** | Cultural and environmental contexts shape how we think offering both resources and constraints | A DJ needs an understanding of the crowd's background and musical preferences, and a deep knowledge of popular songs across time and cultures to successfully determine what she plays next. |
| | **Enacted** | Cognition emerges from or is cued by purposeful and active engagement with the world | Learning to speak another language requires active practice and interaction with others, not merely abstract theorization. |
| | **Extended** | Cognitive processes are not confined to the brain but span through tools and technologies | A photo app on a smartphone acts as an external memory device, influencing how people remember events, time periods and information. |

**Figure 1.7:** The 4 E's of Cognition framework shows us how cognition spans beyond our brain and body, and is influenced by cultural and environmental contexts, active engagement with the world, and the technologies we interact with.

As new technologies emerge, we refresh our cognitive ecosystem to keep pace with the modalities in which information is shared (Clowes, 2018). The human mind evolves in tandem with technological advancements. Tools don't just aid cognition—they transform it. New technologies redefine how we think, remember, and solve problems. For example, I no longer stress if I left my wallet at home because I have a pay app on my phone. Instead of making a note on a scrap of paper, if I want to remember to purchase a book I saw on Instagram, I save the post. Today, I can watch a video on YouTube to help me complete tasks like installing a new TV, brining a chicken, or updating my smart thermostat.

If we want our classrooms, libraries and learning spaces to be fertile cognitive ecosystems, we must be intentional in creating the conditions that make expansive literacy possible. If we want our students to be literate in all ways, always, we must update our instruction with new lessons on how to choose and use tools effectively and we must provide our students the time needed to practice and build fluency. If we want our lessons to reflect the authentic ways humans tell, hear, and act on stories, we must continue to pursue new and evolving understandings of literacy.

**What We Need to Know Now**

As classroom teachers, it's challenging to stay on top of all the burgeoning reading research. There's so much to do each day that there's never enough time to find, sift through, and process dense research papers. Of all the new information out there on digital reading, here are a few pieces of research you may be interested in:

1. **Reading strategies for analog reading do not seamlessly transfer to digital reading. New strategies are needed (Muhtaris & Ziemke, 2015).**

   One of the major findings in the last few years is that the instruction we provide is not meeting the needs of students living in an ever-changing world. Substituting the literacy instruction we offer students using books and replacing it with the same type of lessons in digital contexts is like forcing a square peg into a round hole. Some of the strategies we offer do transfer into digital reading; however, many new strategies are needed to support how young people access information, document their thinking while reading, link to additional information, and research (Mangen, 2016). All of these skills require explicit instruction for digital and multimodal texts. Gone are the times when we assume young people "know" how to use the tools simply because they grew up with them. Today, we need to teach, model, and monitor students so that they know how to use these new offerings as tools for thinking.

2. **Digital natives do not display superior screen reading performance (Singer Trakhman et al., 2018).**

   Contrary to popular belief, digital natives are not experts at or deeply skilled when reading on a device. However, they think they are. Research from Singer Trakhman et al. (2018) shows that digital natives prefer to read on a device. They're overconfident and believe that they are more successful readers on a device than on paper. In reality, their actual comprehension performance was significantly better on paper than on screen.

   > "Students know more about these devices than I do."
   > "I simply ask my students to do it for me."
   > "What can I teach them? They already know how to use it."

   These generalizations are the result of observation. As we see kids touch, type, or manipulate devices without fear or hesitation, we interpret this willingness to test and experiment as a deeper understanding than what actually exists. As learners discover how to capture photos and video and move fluidly through applications, we see their preferences in action. But what many fail to consider is that what learners prefer is not necessarily what they need for successful learning (Støle, 2018).

   Blanket assumptions people make about students under the umbrella use of "digital natives" are highly inequitable. Access to technology requires resources. Assuming that all kids know how to use tech also assumes that they've had access to these tools at home. Technology and internet access are still unaffordable for many students and their caregivers. In other cases, young people have limited access to devices, and so they play, swipe, and click as fast as they can, knowing their access is, at best, fleeting. The ability to manipulate a device quickly can also be a red flag; a child "devicing" is very different from a child learning. Either scenario prompts us to caution our assumptions.

I have always been a firm believer that while some students may know how to use the device, that doesn't mean they know how to use it as a tool for thinking. We've seen a lot of device use with the absence of instruction. Young people need explicit instruction on how to use devices as tools for thinking. They need to be taught how to slow their reading down so that cognition can catch up as they ask questions to formulate deep understanding. They need to learn how to find quality sources and reflect upon what they're reading on a device. They need to learn to support their thinking by jotting notes and ideas on paper or in a notebook, embracing a multisensory approach. The "active body, the pencil, the text, and the device all become parts of the extended cognition process" (Malafouris, 2013).

This type of learning requires practice. And practice requires time. When we teach students the skills they need to think deeply, we must give them plenty of time to experiment, to fail, and to try again. Just like with print reading, students need time to build fluency for reading on a device. They need to practice the new strategies we've taught them and test how multimodal resources can work together. They need time to refine their new skills and apply them across many contexts.

We are the mentor models in so much of what we do in the classroom. We can mentor students in digital reading by watching how they interact with devices, asking questions about their new learning, or addressing challenges they're having with the text. We can act responsively and provide the just-in-time teaching they need right now. We can sit down and learn about digital reading right beside them, which may be the most important modeling we ever do.

We have the opportunity to change the direction of reading for the next generation of learners. Together, let's do so.

bit.ly/4japmH0
Read Erstad et al.'s "Reading in the Digital Age."

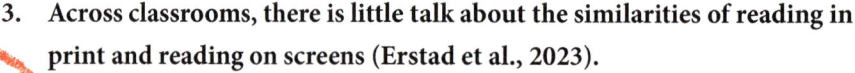

3. **Across classrooms, there is little talk about the similarities of reading in print and reading on screens (Erstad et al., 2023).**
One of the major findings that relates directly to our interactions with our students is documented by Ola Erstad and colleagues; they have found "there is little talk about the differences or similarities in reading on paper versus screen, and little attention to what kind of reading strategies and reading habits you may benefit from in one format versus the other" (2023).

We haven't talked enough (or maybe at all!) about how we approach reading in these diverse formats.

Awareness is the first step toward understanding. To help students monitor their comprehension, we need to make them aware of how the tools work for them.

Simple mini-lessons on how to navigate on a device, where to go to conduct research, and how to tap to access the definition of a word are easy starting points. Then, we observe our students to see where they might need support and respond to their needs with modeling and instruction. Most importantly, we name and notice the similarities and differences between paper and screen as we learn across the year.

| How We Read in Books | How We Read on Screens |
| --- | --- |
| We turn the pages. | We tap or swipe to move forward. |
| We read the words and pictures and think about what makes sense. | We read the words, pictures, and videos and listen to audio to build new knowledge. |
| We save our page with a sticky note or a bookmark. | Sometimes we click links to learn more. |
| We use stickies, thinksheets, or notebooks to hold our thinking as we read. | We use notebooks, thinksheets, digital sticky notes, digital markers, and annotation tools to hold our thinking as we read. |
| We turn the pages to go backward to reread something. | We swipe or scroll to look back at something we read. |

## Accessibility and Joy for All Learners

One of the great benefits of supporting digital text in the classroom is the increased amount of text, images, graphics, information, audio, and visuals that become a part of our teaching repertoire. We now have so many resources to excite learners and engage them in deep thinking work.

For the students I have taught, the most significant digital benefit has been information that is more accessible in a number of ways. For learners who have accessibility needs, the ability to enhance the size of text, use voiceover, or switch device controls allows them to access the content alongside their peers. With an iPad, any print content can be spoken with a swipe or a touch and the device can be controlled by one's voice.

For multilingual learners, digital tools can support language acquisition with a variety of accessibility features. Text and audio translation scaffold instruction by offering guidance in a child's home language. Immersive Reader allows digital text to be translated into one hundred different languages. It also offers an audio option to read the digital text in the translated language to students. New AI tools promote interaction through speech-to-text, text-to-speech, video, and will even translate at the click of a button.

For years as an early elementary teacher, I had students who wanted to learn about video game design. Unfortunately, there wasn't a print text heavily supported with visuals written at a guided reading Level B for them to explore. My students were curious, but the information simply wasn't available to them. Today, when a student wants to learn more about a topic, we can do a quick internet search and find an article on how video games are made. With tools like Brisk, I can quickly adapt the article to a first-grade reading level and add images to support comprehension. I can also copy the article into a Word document so students can access Immersive Reader and have the text read to them, just as if listening to a read-aloud.

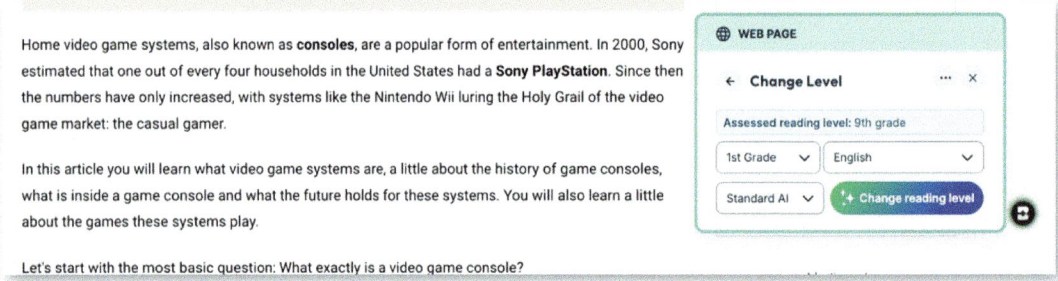

**Figure 1.8:** A tool like Brisk can adapt content on many websites. When you tap the Brisk button, you can adjust the reading level and language to tailor the content to your students' needs. Brisk will adjust the content and paste it into a Google Doc; from there, you can personalize it even more or share it with students.

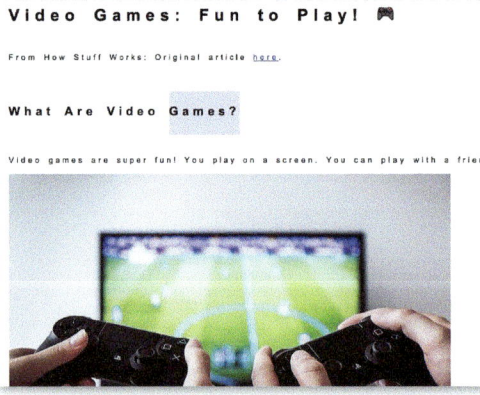

**Figure 1.9:** Immersive Reader is a fabulous tool available with Microsoft 365. At the click of a button, the text can be read aloud, adjusted for visual ease and text preference, identified by part of speech, supported with a picture dictionary, or translated into over a hundred languages. Some websites also build Immersive Reader into their site to increase access for readers of all ages.

Another quick search leads us to a short video about game development. Together, students can watch the video and document in a notebook their new understanding about video game design. From the video, they may gain new questions, which lead to further curiosity and more research. As they research, we can direct them to books and digital content, and thus, the reading and thinking continues.

Alongside teaching students phonemic awareness and decoding, we use digital content as the carrot to lead them to deeper thinking. We build comprehension skills by accessing audio or video to develop background knowledge and enrich vocabulary. We teach students to ask questions about topics they didn't even know they were curious about. And as their reading skills develop, they have a wealth of topics they want to read more about.

**More Resources Equal New Lessons**

To effectively access multimodal literacies, we craft new lessons that scaffold and support student learning. We build lessons that teach students how to "read" a video effectively, how to listen to audio with purpose, and how to balance a device, physical book, and notebook to maximize learning. We give students access to reliable tools and teach them to be device agnostic, as we know that the tools and platforms will change. We coach students to move between print, digital, and multimodal text, and we provide various options for them to hold and share their thinking. Notebooks, chart paper, digital discussion boards, video platforms, infographics, animation tools, audio recording sites, and stapled-together paper books are all terrific options for student response. Why limit our learners when there are so many ways for them to show their thinking?

**Ways to Show Thinking**
- Write a paper book
- Make a video
- Paint a mural
- Create a sketchnote
- Make a diagram

We hold on to research-based principles like active literacy, the significance of choice, and student agency. Multimodal text and response options offer additional layers for active literacy, as now students can read, listen, and view with ease and archive their learning by sketching, writing, or speaking. We invite students to choose their tools regularly and nudge them to increase their repertoire as they go.

In Ed Renas's middle school classroom at Our Lady of Guadalupe school in South Chicago, Ed recognized that his students needed more time to practice reading digitally. He realized that while he offered students access to a wide variety of print texts during the ELA block, he did not offer the same type of access to texts that students could read on a device. Initially, he tried having students go online and find a news source, ebook, or blog that they would like to read. After observing how students searched for text online, he identified that an open internet search was not working for his students. He saw students searching for a topic and then getting distracted by the number of results they found. Students clicked on several results before they selected content to read; often, the text was too difficult, so they would attempt another internet search, which would lead to the same path of searching but not finding the right content to read. Instead of gaining time to practice reading, students lost minutes with text because they couldn't access digital text effectively.

**TIP:** If I didn't have access to Padlet, I would use Google Slides.

1. Take a screenshot of each site you want students to access or download the site logo.
2. Link the web address to the corresponding image. Now the slide is a clickable visual that links students to a variety of digital text.
3. Share with students via link or QR code.

bit.ly/4dz16gl
You can view this Padlet on the website.
(Password: **KZTandT**)

Ed knew he needed to find another approach. Together, we brainstormed and decided that we could source quality sites for students and help kids locate these sites with ease. We decided to use Padlet, a digital bulletin board site, to house eight to twelve websites with content that was appropriate, at-level for middle school readers, and contained information they wanted to read. Now, students had a curated list of sites they could read to practice their digital reading skills. Ed posted a link to his Google Classroom, and throughout the week, students gained access to digital reading content through the Padlet link. Ed continues to curate this list,

**Figure 1.10:** A digital bulletin board for choice digital reading. We can curate a list of options for students that offers readability and choice of content. This scaffolds students' reading selections as they learn how to effectively search for content on the open internet.

adding and removing resources as student needs and interests evolve. Unlike the open internet searches he began with, this new iteration allows Ed to be responsive to the needs of his learners.

Just as we would with print text, we offer students choice. Sometimes, learners can select any type of multimodal text they want to read. Frequently, we scaffold choice and offer a selection of text sets and titles from which they can choose. Similar to what we do in print book clubs or article circles, we organize digital text sets that guide students to text that they are able to read, teaches them something new, or elicits curiosity. We offer students many choices in print text and need to ensure that we are offering them the same opportunity for digital text as well. It might be as simple as creating a digital bulletin board linking to websites that offer quality content for a specific grade level. A curated digital choice reading board will give students lots of opportunities to choose what they want to read without an open internet search that often guides students to difficult text too complicated for them to comprehend deeply. Curated spaces like this also allow us to differentiate and scaffold by grouping texts for specific learner needs.

And when we give students the choice, we help them develop the sense of agency that fosters motivation, engagement, and self-confidence. When we invite students to make strong choices, we help them navigate and practice how to make appropriate instructional decisions based on their learning needs. We teach them to reflect on their reading with a few guiding questions, including:

- How'd it go with my reading today?
- What did I learn?
- What questions do I have?
- What can I work on next time?

With a little bit of practice, students become cognizant of their reading habits and behaviors.

**Reality Check: Mandates, Minutes, and Funding**

Too often, we see kids in classrooms using district-issued devices to log a set number of minutes on a program. Typically, students in this setting work in isolation with little focus on the quality of what they are doing or the purpose behind the time spent on the device.

We are very aware of curriculum mandates, testing mandates, device and software mandates, blocked sites, and a lack of funding for tech subscriptions and classroom books and materials. We know many of you must teach each subject for a specific number of minutes daily. We know that others are required to be on page 246 of the teacher's manual by March 20. We recognize that in many places, it feels like teachers have lost the right to plan for instruction, choose resources that address what their students need, and embrace creativity. But it doesn't have to feel that way for our students.

Even though students may be required to spend minutes on their device—reading practice, math practice, reading assessment, math assessment, read their science text, and much more—we can safeguard the little time that we do have to offer them something different. With the time that we have with students, we can move away from the "skills and drills" or "fill-in-the-blank" practices used by many of the companies that value capital over what's best for young people and balance our kids' learning opportunities with choice. Students have excessive access to low-level instructional practices; they don't need more of that. Instead, we can offer choice in the tools they have access to, the way they collaborate with peers, and the mode in which they share their learning.

Kids deserve more. They need more time on devices using tools that help them show what they know. They need time to create content and the opportunity to have conversations with their peers—both online and in person. They need to understand the purpose behind their work and recognize their growth over time. Our students need access to all the materials available that will help them to read, write, communicate, connect, and create. And so, when we have a minute to offer them that, we do.

**Controlling the Controllables**

We can't fix everything, but we can control the small moments within our classrooms. When we have five or ten minutes, seek opportunities for students to choose and create. Balance out the low-level tech interactions with enriched opportunities to create using traditional or digital tools. For too many kids, school feels like something that is being done to them. Look for opportunities to use tech to empower kids to guide their own learning. Think about how you might give kids more time to engage joyfully and less time to trudge through the school day. Here are a few ideas you might try:

| MORE | LESS |
| --- | --- |
| Student-created videos to show understanding | Worksheets |
| Collaboration between students | Working in isolation with a device and headphones |
| Make something to show what you know | Online assessment |
| Independence | Teacher directed |
| Projects | Skill and drill |
|  |  |

*Add your ideas here!*

You'll find additional ideas for balance across learning modalities in the chapters that follow.

## The Journey Ahead

As you embark on the rest of your journey through this book, I hope you notice some of the "habits for living" that the teachers spotlighted in these pages embrace. They are excellent kid watchers (Goodman, 1978). They closely observe their learners and let students' actions, words, and body language guide them as to what to teach next. As a result, they are incredibly responsive educators. They learn alongside their students and create the conditions for students to think across the school day. They recognize that learners have unique needs and they differentiate in a variety of ways to provide an equitable experience for all who walk into their classrooms.

In the chapters that follow, you'll see my thoughts in parallel to the teachers' stories. When you see this image of me, I'll offer my reflections on the piece and ideas for authentically differentiating or extending the lesson for unique learning styles.

**In some places I'll provide insight into the research behind the practice or name the instructional moves that make lessons powerful.**

In some places I'll provide insight into the research behind the practice or name the instructional moves that make lessons powerful. You'll also see anchor charts and instructional tips, how to's, and QR codes that link to additional content. You'll find moments to reflect and invitations to try or to share online.

Linda Hoyt always reminded us, "Learning is joyful." When we bring joyful learning into our classrooms and our lives, everybody wins. I hope you find joy in the stories to come.

# Putting It into *Practice*

**1. Engage in a read-aloud with a digital book.**
Refer back to the chart on page 23, then use a document camera or hold up a device to show the book and model how you:

- Pause to think about the text.
- Go back a few pages to clarify your understanding.
- Write down new information or questions on a sticky note or thinksheet so you can follow up when you're done reading.
- Take a break in your reading to turn and talk with a think partner.
- For readers new to ebooks, you can adapt the lesson to model the basics. New-to-ebook readers will need to know how to:
  » Locate the book on their device.
  » Turn the page forward and turn the page back.
  » Look up the definition of a word they do not know.
  » Hear the unknown word read to them.

**2. Read online.**
Offer students a choice between two to three websites with age-appropriate content and interest. Ask students to read online. When they are finished, ask: "What did you notice about your reading as you engaged with this website?" Chart responses. Use this as a building block for becoming aware of print and digital texts.

## 3. Plan a lesson.

Raise awareness of the similarities and differences between print and digital texts.

- Find a print text and a digital text that you can compare and contrast

    » Name of print text _____

    » Name of digital text _____

- What do you notice that is similar?




- What do you notice that is different?




- Charge your students to pay attention while reading to see what other features and structures they notice.

    Create a chart with students to name the similarities and differences between the two. See the chart on page 23 for additional ideas.

# CHAPTER 2

# Weaving Digital into the Literacy Classroom

In Brittany Bonanno's second-grade classroom in Pontiac, Michigan, the buzz of learning fills the room. A tent decorated with twinkly lights is surrounded by soft pillows. Books at a variety of reading levels are organized in bins on top of the cabinet that runs the length of the room. A colorful rug serves as a gathering place for students. An easel with chart paper is positioned near the rug, ready for the next anchor chart, as is a large touchscreen display board. Seven- and eight-year-olds work around the room during their literacy block. A schedule is projected on the board, guiding students on how to use their time. A group of five sits at a cluster of desks, and each student uses a Chromebook to work on iReady. Four students lie near the tent, working on their independent reading. Five students use their laptops to access the online library Epic! Brittany has organized a group of digital texts at their reading level, and they are working through the text set as they build reading fluency. Later in the week, they will capture a snapshot of their reading on Seesaw to track their progress as fluent readers. Five students listen to audiobooks in Spanish as they work to develop background knowledge for the next science unit. This scaffold provides access to the content in their home language and allows them time to preview, think, and prepare for interactions with their peers in English. Students enter and leave the classroom as they meet with their additional language support teachers, special educators, or counselors. In a corner near the back of the room, Brittany sits at a small table with a group of students. Using whiteboards, she introduces a new consonant-consonant-vowel-consonant (CCVC) word pattern to help students decode more words as they develop their reading skills. Chromebooks, hardcover and paperback texts, clipboards, headphones, whiteboards, and markers are all used with purpose.

Learning is layered within this classroom. Increased access offers more opportunities to personalize learning for students. Personalization leads to more reading, which enhances background knowledge and vocabulary acquisition, promotes critical thinking, and invites all students into this rich learning ecosystem.

Just like the students in Brittany's classroom utilize their tools, we intentionally plan how to organize instruction in this evolving learning environment.

## Reading Today

This is reading…

…this is reading…

…this is reading…

…this is reading…

…and this is reading.

What counts as reading? As teachers, we've expanded our definition of what it means to read as there are so many new ways for students to interact with information and to access stories. We mindfully position print and digital text alongside each other to scale access, choice, and readability. We layer options for students and teach them new strategies to access content and to comprehend diverse formats. We align new practices with familiar tenets and use research to guide our instruction.

Throughout this book, you'll hear us talk about texts and modes and use the word *multimodal* frequently. For our purposes, texts communicate a message to the audience. They are designed based on the purpose of the message to be communicated. When we speak of modes, they are the ways we access information. We read the newspaper, we watch a video on YouTube, we speak to a friend—there are a wide variety of modes in which information can be shared, including visual, auditory, print, kinesthetic, and more. When referencing multimodal learning, we're naming learning environments that include instruction and student response by integrating two or more modes.

Multimodal learning (MML) is the process of sense-making in which learners take information, process it, and make the ideas their own (Bezemer & Kress, 2016; Moreno & Mayer, 2007). MML expands the range of choices available in a learning environment so that young people can co-construct learning through their preferred mode and also explore new modes and potentially adapt and adopt new preferences (Nouri, 2019; Phuong et al., 2017). MML encourages student voice by offering multiple pathways to access information and represent understanding throughout the learning cycle.

The stories in this chapter will showcase a number of examples of multimodal learning. Like the folds of origami, notice how educators layer modalities to meet the needs of all students.

## Fostering Joy

We begin by fostering joy. We read to students. We promote books in our classrooms and in our actions. We display a variety of print genres around the room. We make space for books about animals, the solar system, and how to's. We feature series books, author studies, poetry, award-winning titles, books written by kids, and so much more. We encourage stories that bring new understanding through cultural, linguistic, geographic, socioeconomic, ability, identity, and religious diversity. We showcase stories that feature those who look like our students. We post QR codes to the wall that connect students to a digital text or to their favorite author's website. We push links to students so they have easy access to digital text. We model how to search online, and we teach a lesson to ensure every child knows the best place for students to seek online information. We showcase what reading looks like and sounds like in paper text. We model what reading looks like and sounds like in digital text. We think aloud as we navigate both and name skills and strategies for students to try.

In this chapter, you'll hear from several teachers who have woven digital texts together with print to create positive literacy experiences for their students. Each teacher's voice will tell the story of how they've made this Both/And a reality in their classroom.

To begin our teacher stories, meet Shameer Bismilla. Shameer plans for joyful reading every single day. I'm constantly inspired by his recognition of reading as a personal journey for each learner and how he empowers his students to construct their own reading pathways.

**Shameer Bismilla**
Shameer is a grade 3 teacher in Singapore and is the coauthor of the picturebooks *The Boy and the Box* and *The Girl and the Box*.

## Shameer Bismilla - Embracing the Passion for Reading: Knowing Oneself through Books

In today's fast-paced, digitized world, I've learned that fostering a passion for reading isn't about choosing between print and digital formats—it's about embracing both. By doing so, I help students build their identities, fuel their creativity, and connect with stories that inspire them. In this article, I'll share some of the strategies and experiences I've implemented in my classroom to ignite a love for reading, including innovative practices and digital tools that encourage collaboration and meaningful conversations.

### Building Reading Identities

Teaching in an international school means working with a beautifully diverse group of students from various nationalities, each with unique cultural and linguistic backgrounds. Within this vibrant environment, I encounter striving readers who are working to build their confidence with reading, and thriving readers who read fluently and eagerly. It's also common to teach students who are not native English speakers or who are still developing their English proficiency. My role as their teacher is to provide positive and meaningful reading experiences that make every student want to engage with books.

In my twenty-five years of teaching readers, I've come to understand just how personal and transformative the journey with books can be. Each student brings their own unique experiences and challenges, and I've seen firsthand the power of helping them discover their reading identities. I remember one student in particular who struggled to see herself as a reader. By introducing her to

---

Shameer helps readers discover their voices as he unites students around books and empowers them to adopt leadership roles of book curator, title sharer, celebration planner, and identity creator.

What I appreciate about Shameer's work is:
- His teaching is child-centered.
  - His constructivist approach invites students to build their reading habits and preferences.
  - Shameer uses his knowledge of students as a launchpad for developing a reading identity that lasts a lifetime.

graphic novels, wordless books, and ebooks, we found formats that truly resonated with her. These resources allowed her to engage with stories visually and at her own pace, building confidence and a genuine love for reading.

Additionally, I've found that digital tools like audiobooks and reading apps have been invaluable in supporting students at different stages of their reading journeys. Watching this student's excitement as she shared her favorite book was a humbling reminder of why fostering a love of reading is so important. In a multicultural and multilingual classroom, these tools and approaches open up new ways for students to connect with stories, build confidence, and discover their own voices.

**Figure 2.1:** Encouraging rich book discussions: These mini anchor charts guide students in meaningful conversations during read-aloud, fostering deeper comprehension and critical thinking.

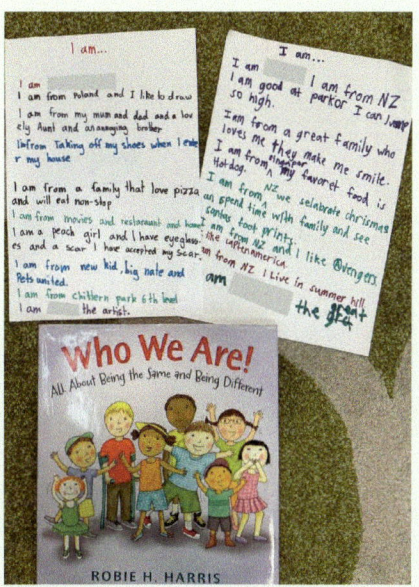

**Figure 2.2:** Using *Who We Are* as inspiration, students craft their own identity statements, celebrating their unique backgrounds, values, and experiences.

**Figure 2.3:** Excited readers! After a read-aloud session, students eagerly showcase their favorite books and are ready to share their recommendations with their peers.

WEAVING DIGITAL INTO THE LITERACY CLASSROOM

**Building a Love for Reading through Classroom Libraries**

My classroom library is both the starting point and the heart of fostering a passion for reading and helping students discover themselves through books. To create this space, I began with a parent survey to explore: *Do children from families in cities with access to public libraries still need a classroom library?* The responses reinforced the importance of having a dedicated reading space in our classroom.

I then asked students what they wanted in the library and provided sticky notes for them to share why a classroom library matters to them. Their input shaped a library filled with diverse and engaging materials tailored to their interests and needs.

**Figure 2.4:** Honoring student voices! By sharing their book preferences, students take ownership of their classroom library, fostering a love for reading through choice and engagement.

**Our Voices, Our Library: Why It Matters to Us**
My library also includes digital tools like audiobooks, ebooks, and interactive apps, making stories accessible to all students, including multilingual learners. By offering choice and accessibility, the library empowers every student to see themselves as a reader and to discover the joy of books. Additionally, creating spaces for students to discuss their reading—whether in small groups, book clubs, or digital forums—has enriched the culture of authentic literacy exchanges in my classroom, encouraging students to share, connect, and grow through stories.

**Shifting Focus: Building a System for Reading**
I focus on creating a reading system based on James Clear's Four Laws of Behavior Change:

**Law 1: Make It Obvious**
- I make reading visible with a well-stocked library and regular independent reading time.
- Books are prominently displayed, and we often discuss what we're reading.
- Collections of books from Epic! are carefully curated based on children's interest.

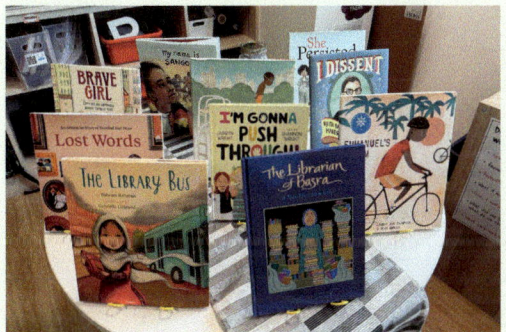

**Figure 2.5:** Books are prominently displayed to spark curiosity and engagement. Students are encouraged to revisit, discuss, and reread their favorites, fostering a lifelong love for reading.

**Figure 2.6:** Curated book collections on Epic! These selections are thoughtfully organized based on students' interests, reading abilities, and unit themes, making reading engaging and accessible for all learners.

**Law 2: Make It Attractive**
- I've worked to normalize the desired behavior of reading. In our classroom, it's not just okay to love books—it's celebrated.
- To lure students to books, I curate visually appealing displays and host events like book tastings where students can "try" different genres and authors.

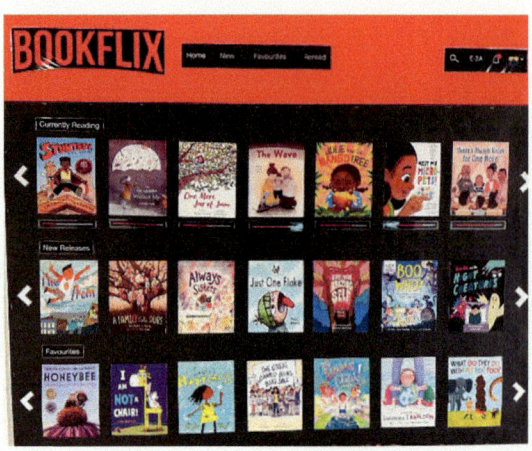

**Figure 2.7:** Making reading irresistible! Bookflix engages students by showcasing exciting reads in a visually appealing way. In our classroom, books are celebrated, and students are encouraged to explore different genres through creative displays and book tasting.

**Figure 2.8:** A feast for readers! Our book tasting event gives students the opportunity to explore new arrivals, sample different genres, and share their thoughts on exciting new reads.

**Figure 2.9:** (left) Our reading journey! This board showcases the books we've read aloud in class, motivating students to keep adding to our growing collection and sparking meaningful discussions.

**Figure 2.10:** (right) Our book door showcases the stories we've loved, fostering a culture where reading is proudly celebrated. Every book read is a step on our journey as lifelong readers!

**Law 3: Make It Easy**
- I prime the environment by keeping books organized and easy to access, ensuring that there are no barriers to picking up a book.
- Choices are optimized for each student's interests and reading level, and I incorporate digital tools like audiobooks and ebooks to meet diverse needs.
- Reading routines are automated with regular time set aside for independent reading and sharing sessions.

**Law 4: Make It Satisfying**
- To ensure habits stick, I focus on making reading rewarding. Students celebrate milestones like finishing a series or discovering a new favorite author, and we share these moments as a class.

**Figure 2.11:** Our readers proudly showcase books that spark joy and curiosity, inspiring their peers to explore new stories. Taking ownership of their learning, they initiate how they want to respond in creative and meaningful ways. Inspired by *Milo Imagines the World*, students designed glasses to see the world through Milo's perspective, discovering the power of imagination and empathy.

**Figure 2.12:** During our Reading Celebration, students stacked books they love and crafted personal reading identity statements. They selected quotes that resonated with them, reflecting on how reading shapes their lives. A powerful reminder that books are more than just pages—they're pathways to growth, imagination, and connection!

**Celebrating Our Reading Journey!**
As part of our annual Reading Celebration, I include external rewards like certificates or medals, but I use them sparingly, ensuring they complement the emphasis on intrinsic joy and personal growth. On this special day, students also get the opportunity to share their favorite authors and to reflect on their reading journey.

While I include medals and certificates, the true reward is seeing my students grow as readers, discover books they love, and share their favorite authors. This day is all about reflecting on their journey and embracing the joy of reading.

By focusing on a system rather than goals, I've seen a transformative shift in my classroom. Students aren't just meeting targets; they're discovering the joy of reading and building habits that will last a lifetime. The journey to becoming a reader is personal, and it's my privilege to guide my students as they uncover their own paths.

**Figure 2.13:** During our reading celebrations, my students proudly wore T-shirts printed with their reading identity statements and created thoughtful "I Am" pledges.

## More Books for Students

In the past decade, digital libraries have burst onto the classroom scene and increased access for readers of all ages. Now, new texts are available at the click of a button! The books that can be accessed through digital libraries offer so much opportunity. Most can be differentiated for students with ease.

**Benefits of Digital Libraries**
- Access to age-appropriate grade-level text through print, audio and visual mediums
- Text selection can be translated into multiple languages
- Diverse text selection
- Assistive technologies support students to turn pages and read text aloud
- Visual supports such as words highlighted when read
- Closed captioning for videos
- Diversified access fosters student choice and abundant reading opportunities

As we use digital libraries, we see that the approach is quite different from how we access print in our classroom or school libraries. Students need to search to locate a text they want to read. Upon locating a text, students preview the book by opening it on a device (quite different from looking at the cover and reading the book jacket!). Turning the page becomes a swipe or click. Tapping a word to hear it spoken or defined is a necessary mini-lesson in kindergarten through second grade.

When we think about student agency and autonomy, we strive for our students to gain confidence and independence as readers. We provide careful support in how to navigate the tool or platform and how to think and comprehend in digital text. We create new lessons and strategies based on our students' needs and discuss the similarities and differences between print and digital text.

Here are some mini-lessons you might want to plan for to support readers with digital text.

**Mini-Lessons for Digital Libraries**
- How to
  » turn the page
  » go back pages to reread
  » locate and think about a read-to-me book
  » access a library or book bin created by the teacher
- When to
  » use a thinksheet, notebook, or digital notes embedded in the platform to hold your thinking
  » use audio supports to scaffold your reading

Clare Landrigan was quick to notice the benefits of digital text but realized a difference between how we access print books in the classroom library and how we use digital texts in our classroom. On the pages that follow, she'll share strategies for organizing digital text to connect learners to the books they can and want to read.

**Clare Landrigan**
Clare is a preschool lead teacher, staff developer, and coauthor of *It's All about the Books: How to Create Bookrooms and Classroom Libraries That Inspire Readers.*

## Clare Landrigan – Creating a Digital Classroom Library

Classroom libraries are the heart and soul of literacy instruction. Research repeatedly demonstrates that access to an abundant supply of books in classroom libraries increases motivation, engagement, and achievement.

**Classroom libraries—physical or virtual—play a key role in providing access to books and promoting literacy; they have the potential . . . to help students become critical thinkers, analytical readers, and informed citizens. We know that no book is right for every student, and classroom libraries offer ongoing opportunities for teachers to work with students as individuals to find books that will ignite their love of learning, calm their fears, answer their questions, and improve their lives in any of the multiple ways only literature can. (NCTE 2017, p. 1)**

We know that the right text at the right time can make all the difference for our readers . . . but we need to support them in finding it! We need to organize texts so teachers can scaffold students as they browse and choose books they want to read.

While classroom library design has been my professional focus for over a decade, I never thought about organizing digital texts until March 2020. We were without our classroom, school, and even public libraries at the beginning of the pandemic. We were missing the most critical component of our literacy instruction—BOOKS. It seemed everyone jumped in to save the day by offering free access to digital versions of books. The internet was flooded with authors sharing videos of themselves reading their books aloud, publishers suspending Fair Use laws, and ebook platforms providing free access to educators and caregivers. The volume of texts was no longer a problem, but the lack of organization of these texts was limiting access.

It was late one night that I realized it was the classroom library itself that was missing. This space is where readers connect, and we connect them to books. We design this space to reflect our literacy beliefs and goals. This space is where we organize and reorganize baskets of books to reflect our students and our curriculum. It got me thinking. How could I virtually create this space? What tools and platforms could I use? How could the design allow students to browse and choose texts? How could it integrate with the physical classroom library? In *Amplify: Digital Teaching and Learning in the K–6 Classroom*, Muhtaris and Ziemke remind us, when it comes to digital teaching and learning, "to let our core beliefs and mindset guide how we use tools in the classroom—to focus on the overall goal of teaching kids how to think and then layer in purposeful tools" (2015, p.4). I outlined my priorities for a virtual classroom library. I wanted this space to provide and scaffold:

- Choice
- Agency
- Identity
- Relationships
- Engagement
- Reading Dispositions

Like the physical classroom library, the virtual one must be integral to the instructional environment. "The learning environment is 'the third teacher' that can either enhance the kind of learning that optimizes our students' potential to respond creatively and meaningfully to future challenges or detract from it" (Student Achievement Division, 2012). The virtual design needs to look familiar to students, support their continued growth in choosing books that matter to them, and work seamlessly with the digital tools used in the classroom. I use three tools or platforms for the virtual classroom libraries I design: Bitmoji to create graphics, Google Docs, and Padlet. Each of these uses digital bins to house the collections of texts in virtual baskets. These baskets contain hyperlinks to digital books, PDFs, audiobooks, videos, images, songs, maps, and other resources. The possibilities are endless once you learn how to create a digital bin.

> Clare's Free Virtual Book Room has been a gift to so many! What hits home for me in this article is that Clare organizes her ebook library just as she would her print library—by grouping titles into digital book bins and text sets.
>
> Clare offers many ideas, and what I notice is how she:
> - Prioritizes representation and inclusivity across digital bins.
> - Honors the cultural and linguistic diversity of readers from the start, not as an afterthought.
> - Uses simple tools with consistency so that students are familiar with the technology and can focus on reading.

### What Is a Digital Bin?

Dr. Sonja Cherry-Paul and Dr. Dana Johansen introduced me to the concept of a digital bin in their book, *Teaching Interpretation Using Text-Based Evidence to Construct Meaning*.

> **A digital bin is a collection of digital text sets related to a topic. Just like book bins, students and teachers can go to the bin for texts related to a specific genre, topic, or theme. We like to think of digital bins as "living folders" because they are not simply static collections but are constantly changing and growing. A digital bin contains links. These links are connected to digital texts online, such as websites, photographs, primary sources, video clips, audio, etc. Digital bins can also contain links to the classroom blog, wiki, Google Docs, etc. (Johansen, 2014)**

### How to Create a Digital Bin

Use an online, cloud-based document platform. I typically use Google Docs. Create a list of hyperlinks you want in the same digital bin on the Google Doc. It is important to decide who can access the links and edit the links. If you want your students to be able to add to the digital bin they will need access to edit.

**How to Add a Digital Bin to Your Virtual Library**

A digital bin is an online, cloud-based document. Once you create your virtual library using Padlet, Bitmoji, or Google Docs, you insert the hyperlink for each digital bin to the object, book cover, or section.

Here are some examples of virtual libraries:

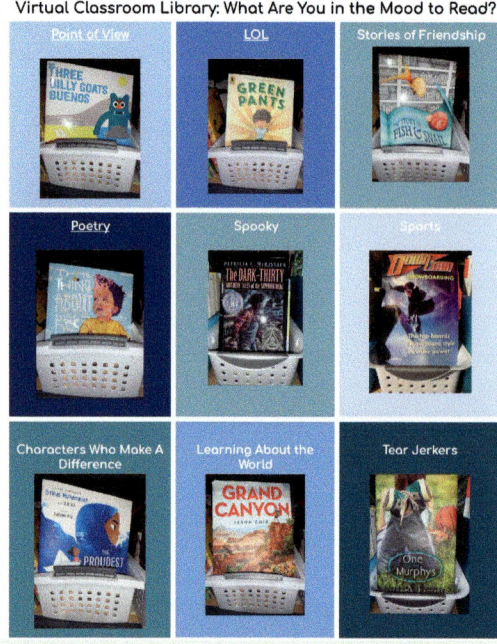

**Figure 2.14:** We survey students to find out what they are in the mood to read and organize these titles into virtual baskets using Google Docs. We love when students add to these baskets as well. Once we model how to add titles, they are off and running. It gives them so much ownership and voice in the classroom library.

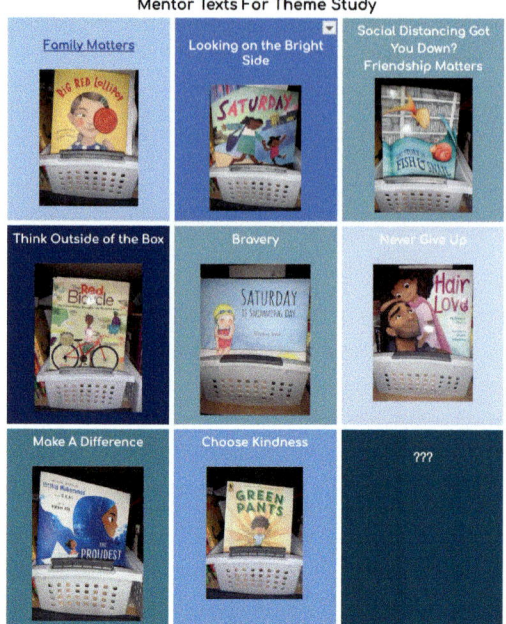

**Figure 2.15:** Elementary literacy standards focus on theme starting in first grade. It isn't about just naming a theme. Readers need to analyze what an author is saying about that theme. For example: What is the message about friendship or courage? Students choose the themes they want to explore on their own, in partnerships, or in book clubs and help us curate digital bins for each theme. It is powerful to hear their discussions and debates when some texts are placed in multiple theme baskets. This is an example of theme baskets organized using Google Docs.

Five years later, I am in awe of how young readers and educators worldwide continue to enhance this idea. Students are creating ways for kids to recommend books to each other, curate text sets for peers they may never meet in person, and design innovative ways to browse, sample, and choose books. Regardless of your design, if you want to center your students, remember the key organizational elements are using the same digital tools you use throughout your classroom and a flexible and responsive design.

I typically include the following sections in a virtual classroom library:
- Independent Reading—Topic, Interest, Mood
- Series
- Book Clubs
- Mentor Texts
- Read Aloud

- Creators
- Content Area Topics

Within each of these sections, I typically include these digital bins or "baskets":

- Class Recommendations
- #Trending
- New Titles
- Poetry
- Favorite Characters
- LOL
- Collections Curated by Kids for Kids

When curating a digital collection, it is critical to reflect on the representation and inclusivity of the texts and be "mindful of the voices and own voices being represented and how these voices are integrated rather than othered in our organization" (Tricia Ebarvia, "How Inclusive Is Your Literacy Classroom Really?" *Heinemann Blog*, 2017). These texts, including multilingual texts, are included in every digital bin. To disrupt the inequity in our publishing industry, #ownvoice texts should be prioritized in as many digital bins as possible. When using images of book covers in the virtual library, I am intentional about which text covers I choose to display to ensure creators from marginalized communities are highlighted. You can also promote cultural awareness by listing these texts first on the Google doc.

**What Do the Kids Say?**

"Books bring me places."

"I have learned to make a lot of things this year with books."

"I have learned about places I want to visit."

"I like talking with my friends about the books we are reading together."

"Whenever I feel sad, I head to the LOL basket or my favorite funny series."

"Books help me escape to places far, far away."

"Books keep me company."

"Fantasy books help me forget everything."

"Sad books help me get out my feelings."

"There is always a book ready to go so I keep reading."

"Whenever I feel overwhelmed, I find a quiet spot and a book. It helps a lot."

"I like that you can listen to books too."

"I have changed as a reader this year."

"I look forward to reading."

"It used to be something I had to do, but now it is something I love to do."

"I read more this year than I ever have before."

"I listen to podcasts when I'm cleaning my room or walking my dog."

"I read magazines— I never did that before."

I am often asked, "Now that we are back in the classroom, don't you think we should stop using these virtual libraries? Don't you think they should read 'real' books?" My answer is no! The more resources, the better. The more authentic the use of the available technology, the better. The more kids learn to use devices to build their reading lives, the better. Let's focus on how physical and virtual classroom libraries can work together so students have the agency to discover their reading identities and author their reading lives. Kids' responses make it clear why we should continue to use virtual libraries in addition to our physical classroom libraries . . . I'm sold—how about you?

**Here are some of my favorite student-created virtual library ideas:**
- Choosing Book Clubs
- Starting Inquiry Clubs
- Learning More about Content Area Topics
- Passion Projects

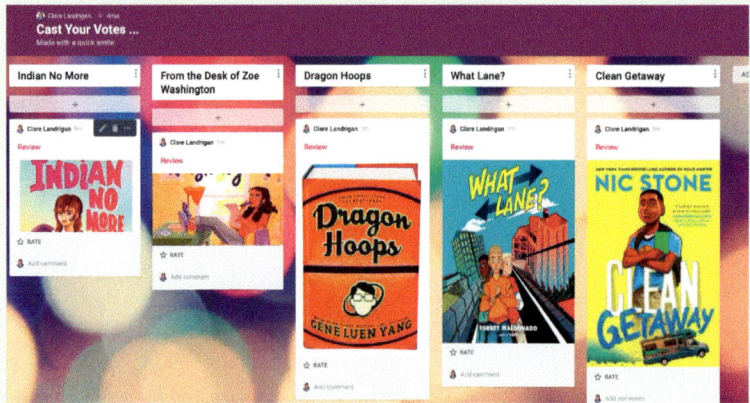

**Figure 2.16:** As we purchase texts to add to our classroom, grade level, and school libraries, we want to center our students' preferences. We use a Padlet to provide a space for students to suggest and vote on titles they want added to our collections.

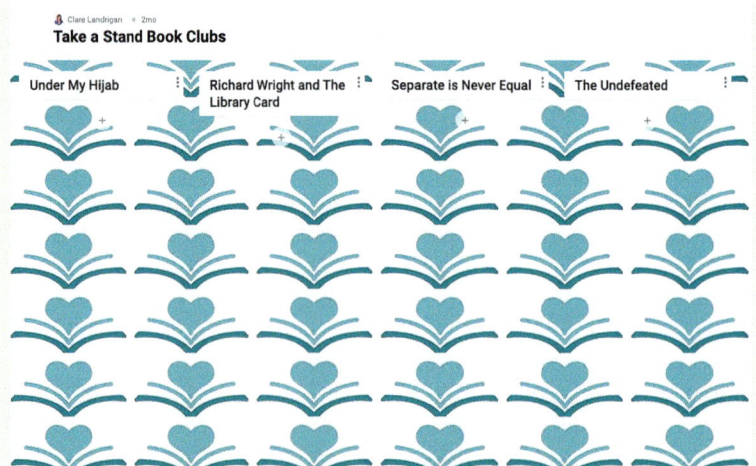

**Figure 2.17:** Students engaged in learning about themes in their reading block choose themes they want to explore in book clubs. Readers suggested books they have read for each book club. These titles were suggested for the Take a Stand Book Club. Students could sign up for any titles of interest and form book clubs.

**Here are some easy ideas to maximize access for independent reading:**
- Student's Virtual Reading Bags
- Student's Virtual Reading Baskets

**Figure 2.18:** We teach students how to browse books in the virtual classroom library and make a reading plan for school and home. Each reader has a virtual book bag and selects books to listen to, read on their own, and read with a buddy. Now books are readily available and easy to refresh when they are ready for new titles.

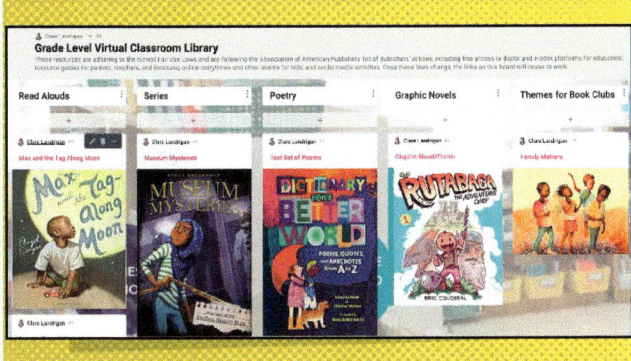

**Figure 2.19:** Here is an example of a third-grade virtual library created with Padlet. The library included sections for students to browse and choose texts for their virtual book bag. We included the types of books they requested, books we read as a class, and new text structures we wanted to introduce. We intentionally selected a range of text complexity to support the development of the readers in this classroom.

**Here are some ways to scaffold browsing and choosing texts:**
- Series Browsing
- Book Browsing
- Class Recommendations

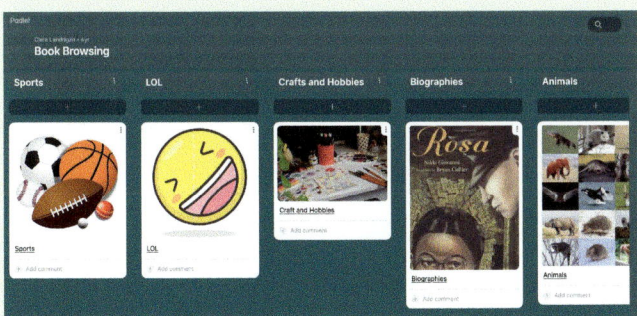

**Figure 2.20:** It is important to teach young readers how to find books that engage them. We can do this in the physical and virtual library. Students choose topics, genres, and what they are in the mood to read. We organize our virtual library baskets so they can browse to find books they want to add to their virtual reading bags. Students love that they can easily see the covers, read a description, and even scan the book to see how it is structured.

**Here are some ways to spread reading beyond your classroom library:**
- Layering Virtual Resources into Classroom Library Baskets
- Virtual Books Baskets around the Classroom
- Virtual Books Baskets around the School
- Home-School Connections with Virtual Libraries

Let your core beliefs about teaching literacy guide you, be ready to experiment to find what works for you, and let the kids' interests and sense of wonder lead the way!

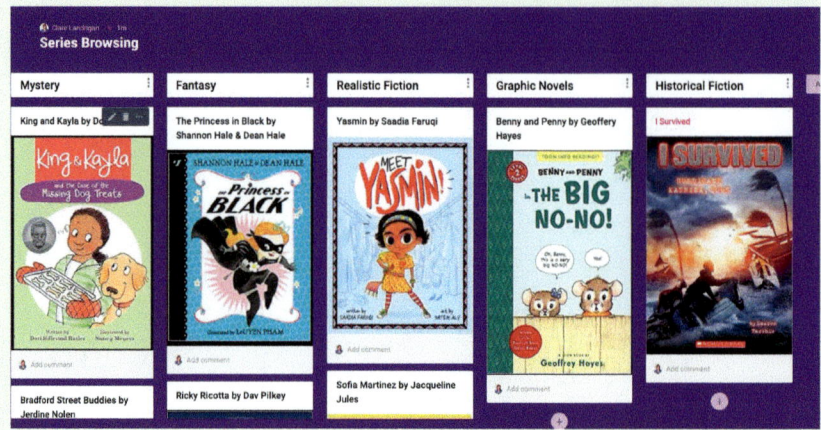

**Figure 2.21:** Research demonstrates the importance of series books in developing lifelong reading habits. We always include a series section in our virtual libraries so readers can easily browse the varied options. They can choose by genre, author, or type. Students love that they can easily see the covers, read a description and even scan the book to see how it is structured.

Here are resources to get you started on creating a virtual classroom library. 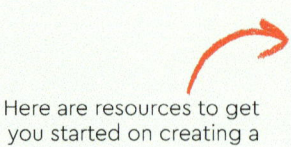  bit.ly/42SRb0k

Here is the link to the Free Virtual Bookroom I curated and continue to update with the help of educators and students worldwide. bit.ly/3ENdEnz

Here is a list of free digital texts and publishers who are currently offering free access to digital texts. 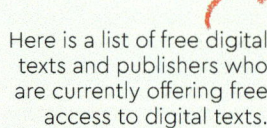  bit.ly/42Bi7Tu

Here is a list of subscription digital texts and publishers who offer digital texts for a fee.  bit.ly/4cXCqy3

## Planning for Instruction

Effectively leveraging quality print and digital texts does not occur by happenstance. As my mentor, Stephanie Harvey, always says, "Text matters!" The text and titles we place before our students need to be selected with care. We strive to know a wide range of picturebooks, novels, periodicals, websites, graphic novels, and informational texts so that we can place materials into the hands of students that will inspire them to read, ask questions, and think deeply. When we place treasured titles and texts in the hands of students we give them a purpose for reading; through this experience they learn that quality texts are exciting, teach you something new, and can transport you to another world.

Multimodal texts offer even more options for us to choose from. Content-specific videos connect students to topics they didn't even know they were curious about. Podcasts offer information and short stories. Infographics show readers math and science datasets in pictorial format. Just like with text, "Tech matters!" We guide students to only the highest quality tools, sites, and sources because we don't have any time to waste on mediocre products.

> School and local librarians can be tremendous resources for quality texts. If you don't have access to either of those, follow librarians online or in social media spaces. A few favorites include:
> - Jennifer LaGarde: **LibraryGirl.net**
> - K.C. Boyd: **KCBoyd.com**
> - Kimbra Power: **KimbraPower.com**
> - Maya Lê: **MaiStoryBook.com**

Each time we place a new text or source before students we are modeling why we read. How we design our learning experiences signals to students that we know you as a reader, we recognize how you learn, we desire for you to find joy, we respect you as a human; you matter.

For this to happen, intentional planning is key. Franki Sibberson will walk you through her planning process as she gathers materials for a multimodal unit of study. Using picturebooks, images, video, audio, and more, Franki plans with her students in mind and adjusts depending on the background knowledge her students possess. She'll share how she determines which tools to use to curate content and how to invite readers into the research experience.

### Franki Sibberson - Pairing Powerful Picturebooks with Digital Texts for Deeper Reading

**Franki Sibberson**

Franki is a former elementary teacher, literacy consultant, coauthor of *In Community With Readers*, and former President of NCTE.

I love to curate a menu of mentors when we are planning a unit of study, whether it be literacy or a science or social studies topic. I'm never sure if I'll use all of the texts but I like to have options depending on what I learn about children's background knowledge on the topic.

I'm impressed by how Franki's organization of resources helps students build background knowledge for the coming lesson or unit, introduces content or text-specific vocabulary, and hooks learners into the topic.

I value how Franki:

- Centers the power of visuals and picturebooks right from the start.
- Intentionally adds value to the reading experience by enlarging text and adding audio.
- Engages students to discuss the similarities and differences between formats.

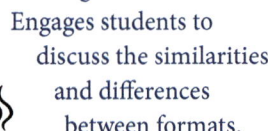

I always want to include a variety of quality children's picturebooks. Picturebooks that are well-researched and have powerful visuals are accessible to all children and having several books by different authors is important.

I also like to include digital texts. It is important for readers to learn from different media so combining picturebooks with digital texts is critical. I look for blogs, online articles, videos, podcasts, images, and infographics that are accessible to elementary readers.

I typically start with picturebooks or an image/video because I find that, no matter the unit of study, I want us to have something to look at together. Something that everyone can access.

That first piece has to share information and also give me information because until I provide the first text, I am not sure what background knowledge and understanding children already have about the topic.

Once I have the collection, I think through the best way to share the resources with the class. Sometimes I want to gather the class close and read a book aloud, and sometimes I choose to use an ebook and project it on the screen so that we can all see it. My decision is based on my goals and on the text I am sharing:

- What kind of quality is the ebook? Often, especially with picturebooks, the pages do not align and the images cannot be projected as they are meant to be read. (Note: When I talk about quality, I am thinking of the children I serve and how the specific ebook will work for their needs. Depending on the children, font size, layout, and ease of use will all play into my thinking about this.)
- Is there something we want to annotate as a class so that everyone can see the annotations?
- Can children access the text and visuals better if it is projected? Is that important for this book?

Sometimes I choose to read a text aloud and sometimes I choose to share the audiobook version. I want to make sure to include audiobooks throughout the year. Listening to a well-done audiobook is very different than listening to someone read the book to you. Some audiobooks have music, multiple narrators, and other features that make them perfect to share with young readers. I ask myself these questions:

- Does the narrator bring the book to life in a way that I can't?
- Is the audiobook done in a way that there are natural places to stop and have conversations as needed throughout?

When thinking about a third-grade science unit on animal adaptations, below is the start of the text set that I would use to build conceptual understanding of the topic:

| COVER | NOTES | LINK |
|---|---|---|
| | • Digital ebook<br>• Photographs<br>• Ebook navigation | bit.ly/3TLKFEG |
| | • *Shell, Beak, Tusk: Shared Traits and the Wonders of Adaptation* by Bridget Heos<br>• Informational picturebook | |
| | • *Two Whats?! and a Wow! Game Show*: "Adaptation"<br>• Video<br>• Not much to the video, it is mostly an audio with a few visuals | bit.ly/4cRbUGp |
| | • *Feathers: Not Just for Flying* by Melissa Stewart<br>• Informational picturebook | |
| | • Online encyclopedia entry/article<br>• Hyperlinked vocabulary<br>• Video and images embedded | bit.ly/3UmyC0J |

WEAVING DIGITAL INTO THE LITERACY CLASSROOM

| COVER | NOTES | LINK |
|---|---|---|
| | • *Butt or Face: Can You Tell Which End You're Looking At?* by Kari Lavelle<br>• Informational picturebook<br>• Q&A format<br>• There is a second volume in the series. | |
| | • *The Book of Turtles* by Sy Montgomery and Matt Patterson<br>• Informational picturebook | |
| | • *Find Out about Animal Camouflage* by Marvin Jenkins<br>• Informational picturebook | |
| | • National Geographic Kids: "Wacky Weekend: Hidden Animals"<br>• Collection of images | bit.ly/42P1tyC |

## Enhancing Learning with Audiobooks

When we think about multimodal literacy, audiobooks are another tremendous asset for literacy learning.

We know what some of you are thinking right now. Yes, listening to an audiobook is real reading. Researchers at the University of California, Berkeley (Deniz et al., 2019), analyzed the brain activity of those participating in the study as they read and listened to the same story. Their findings were published in the *Journal of Neuroscience* (September 2019) and revealed that "both reading and listening stimulated the same cognitive and emotional areas of the brain, indicating no discernible gap in comprehension between traditional reading and 'ear-reading'" (Coustillac, 2020).

It's exciting to know the brain responds to print and audio similarly, and as teachers and librarians, we observe the many benefits of audio all the time!

> **Benefits of Audiobooks**
> - Foster a love of reading
> - Offer equitable access for developing readers
> - Promote visualization
> - Build background knowledge
> - Enhance comprehension
> - Readers who can not yet decode complex text can gain new information and enrich vocabulary through audiobooks
> - Narrators pull readers into the story and develop a connection with them
> - Bring text to life!

For students who are learning to decode or still haven't cracked the code, audiobooks offer a gateway to reading joy. Even middle school students love listening to an adult read to them! We know from decades of research (Albright, 2005; Lesesne, 2006; Trelease, 2006) that read-alouds for older students are an extremely powerful way to increase vocabulary, model fluency, and deepen comprehension. A learner can fall in love with a book that is read aloud by a teacher and they can learn to fall in love with a book by listening to a recorded version. In fact, we choose to use audiobooks during our read-aloud time when it can offer a different context or perspective. Often an audiobook uses a full cast of voices or offers music in the background that sets the scene. Sometimes an audiobook is the best way to engage with a text together.

**Figure 2.22:** *Chooch Helped*, written by Andrea L. Rogers, illustrated by Rebecca Lee Kunz, and narrated by DeLanna Studi; all are members of the Cherokee Nation. Written in English and Cherokee, the audiobook version invites the reader to learn about a family's traditions as they listen to the book in two languages.

There are many ways we can use audiobooks to support our students, but it is important to note that all audiobooks are not the same. We steer students away from audiobooks that use robotic-sounding voices to read a text. The short, often staccato, reading of a text is less engaging for students and fails to produce the range of emotions needed to add depth to the text. It also doesn't model the fluency we strive for, where developing readers hear proper reading rate, changes in expression and inflection, and a voice that is natural and expresses ideas clearly. Just like developing readers who have yet to become fluent, a robotic reading voice focuses on each word, one at a time, instead of stringing words together to create meaning. As a result, the lack of fluency makes it difficult for listeners to focus on the text's meaning.

High-quality audiobooks go beyond the conversion of robotic text-to-speech and add value to the text. They are typically audio productions with actors or authors who read the book; they offer many voices, sound effects, and a high rate of expression that matches the mood and tone of the book. High-quality audiobooks pull readers into the text by stringing words into ideas and helping the reader to see, hear, and feel the story. These features help readers make connections between the text and their background knowledge as they construct meaning.

I always consult the American Library Association (ALA) Notable Children's Recordings list when looking for high-quality audiobooks. This is my first stop as I think about introducing works that are creative, match young people's interests, and respect them as learners. The list is intended for children fourteen years and younger, and it notes the title, author, reader (which not all sites recognize), offers a suggested grade range for the audiobooks, and provides a short description of the book. I also reference the ALA Youth Media Awards. Each year the association presents the Odyssey Award to the best audiobook for children and young adults. They additionally name honorable mention awards for audiobooks; the award process is robust so you can feel confident that you are placing distinguished books in the ears of children. Incidentally, the ALA Youth Media Awards also select the Newberry, Caldecott, Coretta Scott King, Pura Belpre, and Printz Awards; a visit to this site is a wonderful way to stay abreast of the current list of best books.

There is a lot of buzz right now about AI-narrated books. AI-produced narration is more natural sounding than automated speech-to-text converters. It allows for cheaper and faster narration options and the ability to translate into another language with ease, which could increase access to text for the global community of readers. AI brings with it a number of biases and sustainability concerns, and many argue that human narrators are still superior at conveying emotion and nuance, enhancing the value of the listening experience. Others fear that AI will make human narrators obsolete. One thing is certain with AI-narrated audiobooks: we can expect rapid growth in the field and continued change.

Additionally, we recognize there might be challenges to using audiobooks in the classroom. Kathleen Fox, former sixth- through eighth-grade ELA teacher and now principal of St. Ann School in Chicago, will share how she has navigated some of these challenges with her middle school students.

## Kathleen Fox - Audiobooks in the Middle School Classroom

**Kathleen Fox**
Kathleen is a middle school teacher and newly named principal at St. Ann School in Chicago, Illinois.

Getting middle schoolers to read can, at times, be a monumental task. Of the students who walked into my classroom, some always had their noses in a book, others hadn't opened a book in weeks, and still others opened a different book every day but had yet to finish one. I've had students reading at a college level and students reading at a kindergarten level all in the same class. Keeping track of the many books and reading levels of my students was often overwhelming, and I tried and failed at several systems. Eventually, I focused on finding a way to get my reluctant readers to engage and my notorious book ghosters to finish what they started.

Students, no matter their age or reading level, still love to be read to. I noticed that our class read-alouds engaged all of my readers and not just because of my outstanding narration skills. During read-alouds, some students would draw while listening, others requested their own copy of the book to follow along, some rested their heads, and others simply stared into space as the story unraveled around us; all were taking in the story in a way that worked for them. After seeing the success and engagement of read-alouds, an instructional coach of mine suggested that I invite some of my students who were struggling to use audiobooks.

I'll be honest. I was an audiobook hater to start. As a reader, I don't like listening to audiobooks because I struggle to process and follow a story auditorily. What if my students had the same struggle? What if students misused their technology? I resisted until I was shown the program LearningAlly. Through this program, students had access to many different audiobooks in Spanish and English. They had the option for audio only or audio with the text highlighted on the screen. I first tried the program with a few of my diverse learners, who were able to engage with grade-level texts when they had the texts read aloud to them. Classmates saw that students had access to more books and were jealous of the students who were using LearningAlly. Many asked if they could use it too. Unfortunately, we did not have a subscription large enough to make accounts for all my readers, only those for whom it was deemed necessary.

Kathleen wisely recognizes that all students, no matter their age, love to be read to. I love how she learns with her students and increases access to read-alouds by pairing print text with audiobooks.

I respect how Kathleen:
- Listens to her students and cocreates norms for using audiobooks.
- Uses audiobooks to support student fluency and stamina.
- Boosts reading engagement through access to audiobooks.

Then, one of my students showed me that YouTube has many audiobook videos and asked if they could use it as a tool. Again, I was worried. Could I trust middle school students to use YouTube correctly? My students continued to push to use the tool. I continued to have doubts. Then, we sat down and had a conversation. I heard my students, and they listened to my concerns. After our conversation, we made a deal. We agreed that in order to use YouTube audiobooks, they had to either find a video where the words were on the screen or have a hard copy of the book to follow along while they listened. They also agreed that when using audiobook videos, they would sit in a way in which I could always see their screens. And finally, they agreed that if they misused the technology, they lost it, no questions asked.

At last, I agreed that audiobooks could be used by whomever, as long as they also had the text in front of them or on the screen. As a result, more students were meeting their independent reading goal, learners were recommending books to each other, and student comprehension was improving.

Now, I am still not all in for audiobooks. I believe students need to read text, and they should read as much as possible on paper so that they can annotate and interact with the text. But, audiobooks have increased our classroom library, allowed English learners access to more texts, and grown student excitement about reading.

> **TIP:** Anytime we access YouTube with students it's a terrific opportunity to discuss copyright. There are many who are doing online read-alouds or taking a photo of a book cover and then reading aloud the book. During COVID-19 we saw a surge in these types of practices as many educators lacked materials to teach students remotely. Most books are protected by copyright and give the copyright holder exclusive use to "publicly perform" the book, which includes a read-aloud. Look for videos of the author reading the book, books read aloud on publisher channels, or books listed in the public domain as those uphold copyright law and are designed to use with students.

Reading and storytelling is an ever-evolving art. Before writing existed, we only knew stories as an oral tradition. Once writing was created, only certain people learned how to read and write and many continued to learn through oral tradition until the invention of the printing press. Then, our primary source of information came through reading. Now that podcasts and videos are constantly available at the tips of our fingers, students need to be able to comprehend a story that they are taking in auditorily.

Our modes of information are continuously changing and it is essential that we open all avenues to students so that when they are presented with them, they understand how to comprehend what they are learning, no matter the mode or the material. As teachers, we are not the gatekeepers of information, but the traffic directors.

## Print and Digital Working Together to Boost Independent Reading Volume

Print and digital tools are great when paired together to track student learning. When we partner books or print text with tools like Seesaw or any video or audio recording tool, we offer readers of all ages a space to reflect upon their learning. Using a multitude of tools, we teach students how to make good choices about what they read through reflection. We model how to ask "How'd it go with my learning?" and we teach strategies they can use to grow as readers. We practice reflecting on reading in conversation with others, in writing, and in multimodal means like audio or video.

| Easy Ways to Reflect on Learning | |
| --- | --- |
| Video/Audio Reflection | Learners can tell what they liked about the book and why, what they noticed about themselves as readers, and share plans for what they might read next. |
| Audio | Learners can read a book at their level and record audio of themselves as they read; when finished they can self-assess their fluency and determine what they plan to work on moving forward. |
| Conversation | Students can turn and talk, work with a small group of peers, or share in a larger setting about what they noticed about their reading. Sharing in a group allows students to hear strategies that others employ and often encourages them to attempt or apply one of the strategies shared. |
| Slides or Docs | Can be used to track a young person's reading life with photos of books, written reflections, or a five-star rating system. |
| 3-2-1 Reflection | On paper or on a digital bulletin board, students can do a 3-2-1 reflection where they share:<br>3 things they noticed about their reading<br>2 things that went well for them<br>1 thing to work on next |

**Figure 2.23:** A fourth-grade sample of #2 from a 54321 project. For this project, students describe:

- Five books they love
- Four books they want to read
- Three books they recommend
- Two books they always give five stars to
- One book they are reading right now

Here, the student shows the two books she always gives five stars to are *Mercy Watson* by Kate DiCamillo (because it was her first series book!) and *Tales of a Fourth Grade Nothing* by Judy Blume.

When we teach learners how to reflect, we help them become metacognitive. We ignite a sense of awareness that helps them to tune in to what's happening with their thinking. We guide them to pay attention to those moments when the lightbulb goes on in their brain. We name what it feels like when our eyebrows go up because we read something exciting. We model what it looks like when understanding breaks down. Questions like the ones below can scaffold student reflection as you begin this work:

- What did I notice about myself as a reader?
- How did I approach my reading today?
- Was there something I didn't understand?
- What do I need to practice?
- What do I plan to try next?

Through classroom conversations, the video and audio snapshots you listen to, and by reading student work you'll be able to see and hear your students' thinking, as well as be able to identify what strategies and supports they need next to grow as readers. Then, we teach them the strategies they need, allow them plenty of time to practice, and help them monitor their growth as readers.

It's not enough for the teacher to be the only one involved in progress monitoring. Learners need to take an active role in their growth. Students as young as first graders are capable of knowing where they are and where they need to go.

**Teacher:** Alright, so it looks like your rate was pretty good. Talk to me about your clarity and your expression.

**Hannah:** Well, it kinda like hit me, by these two , because then . . . I sounded kind of funny, and it kinda like, it kinda didn't sound like the expression that it was supposed to have.

bit.ly/4dz16gl
For a copy of this fluency check, head over to the website. (Password: **KZTandT**)

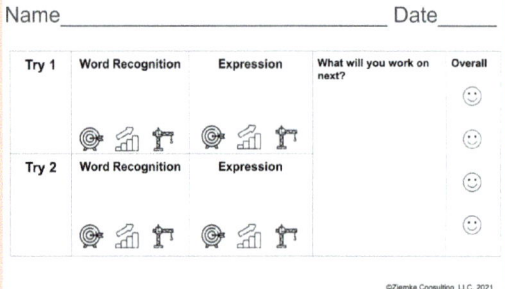

**Figure 2.24:** Students self-assess their fluency using a short fluency check to rate their word recognition, expression, and plan for what they will work on next.

**Teacher:** Okay, so you're gonna do it again now, and what are you gonna try to work on?

**Hannah:** I'm gonna try to make it better to get it all smiles.

**Teacher:** Great. Well, good luck. I can't wait to hear how it goes your second time.

When students can identify how it's going, what they're going to work on next, and how they're going to practice what they need to work on, they move from being metacognitive thinkers to being metastrategic thinkers. Metastrategic thinking is a person's ability to use their knowledge of thinking strategies to plan, monitor, and evaluate their learning (Hammond, 2024). When young people become metastrategic thinkers they become active and intentional learners and are aware of how they learn and acquire information. They possess a set of strategies that they can apply and transfer across learning contexts. They adapt and adopt strategies as new learning conditions arrive. As a result, they continuously grow.

At Edgebrook Elementary, Nessy Moos leverages technology tools to monitor and support reading development. With her teaching partner and seventh- and eighth-grade students, they set goals, track reading experiences, and reflect on student data to illuminate what students can learn about themselves as readers. Using Google tools, she guides students to monitor their reading behaviors as a catalyst for growth.

## Nessy Moos - Leveraging Technology to Monitor and Support Independent Reading

**Nessy Moos**
Nessy is a long-time special education and resource teacher. Committed to student agency and equity in education, Nessy continues to support students, families, and fellow educators in building a future where every child has the tools to thrive and be happy. She currently teaches middle school in Chicago, Illinois.

Independent reading is one of the most powerful tools for stimulating a lifelong love of learning and literacy. In today's screen-dominated world, it's easy to overlook the value of reading on one's own, yet this practice plays a critical role in refining reading skills, enhancing vocabulary, and cultivating critical thinking. When student readers choose what to read, they become more invested in their own learning, improving both their comprehension and enjoyment. Independent reading supports creativity, offering the freedom that structured, guided reading instruction does not. Making space and time in the classroom for daily independent reading can deepen the way students engage with the world, promoting both empathy and appreciation for things not yet experienced. A pragmatic purpose of independent reading is to build the stamina necessary for success in high school, college, and beyond, preparing the student for a complex academic future. This idea is well-explained in research (Allington et al., 2012; Kittle, 2012; Gallagher, 2009) and proves to be true every day in classrooms.

Even as the benefits of independent reading have been explored and explained, reading real books has become increasingly less attractive to the students I work with. Students who have always struggled to find interest in reading

I admire how Nessy recognizes that literacy is a gateway for her students. With her strong literacy foundations, she masterfully crafts experiences that are inclusive and outpace expectations.

I notice how Nessy:
- Helps students "see" their reading progress with visuals and graphs.
- Engages students to reflect on their data and to self-assess progress.
- Leverages Google tools as her go-to with students because she knows that in her district, students (and teachers!) will always have access to the Google Suite.

independently avoid those experiences with more and more vigor, while those who once may have become "lost in the story" with ease no longer routinely construct personal reading identities. In my experience, today's fifth through eighth graders struggle to identify their favorite genres, series, and authors. At home, rather than being told to turn off the flashlight that is illuminating the book under the covers well past bedtime, parents now instruct their children to shut down their perpetual social media feeds. This is our current reality, and we must meet students where they are in their development as independent readers of high-quality "just right" literature. Setting achievable reading goals and monitoring progress can make a big difference.

**Goal-Setting Is Where We Begin**

On the wall between the windows in Room 216 at Edgebrook Elementary School in Chicago, the displayed learning target for seventh- and eighth-grade independent readers is as follows: "I will increase my reading stamina by engaging with large blocks of text written at my 'just right' level, reading at least ___ pages of independently read text per week." This target is specific, measurable, achievable, relevant, and time-bound. A posted, visible goal like this can be tailored to a group's current capabilities for page volume. The expectations for weekly page volume can be increased as stamina increases, and might even be individualized so that each student can reach their goal.

In room 216, each seventh- and eighth-grade student has the opportunity to choose independent reading materials from a stocked library that includes a range of genres and titles. Students are welcomed and encouraged to read books from home or from the library. While it's true that the classroom library has a deficit of books written in all of the languages represented by multilingual students, we are working to address this. As needed, students are given support in selecting "just right" titles that are interesting to them personally. Good reading habits, such as choosing books written at a "just right" level, finishing one novel before beginning another novel, using a bookmark, and avoiding book abandonment, are

Nessy identifies "just right" text for her students and their needs, by asking:
- Does it catch the interest of the student?
- Will it serve the reading needs of the student right now? For example, is the reader hoping to continue a great series?
- Is the reader looking for a cozy comfort read (a familiar author or maybe a reread)?
- Is the reader in the mood to try something new (memoir, poetry, etc.)?
- Does the reader want to learn some new content via Informational nonfiction?

Additionally, after many years working with readers, she's adjusted her stance as an educator to be slightly less rigid about text bands and students staying within their band. All this is dynamic, based on student need, interest, and a variety of other factors.

taught and monitored. Students are afforded time to read independently during class, and are expected to read independently at home. Caregivers are educated regarding the importance of and expectations for independent reading via curriculum night presentations, report card conferences, and email messages.

**Tracking Reading Helps Students Visualize Their Progress and Stay Motivated**

It is safe to say that most reading teachers have systems for keeping track of students' independent reading. These systems might involve a paper grid kept in a folder and signed by someone at home, or even a simple digital reading log (Figure 2.25) where students type in their progress each day or

**Figure 2.25:** The student reading log tracks daily reading activity.

week. Using available technology can maximize what students can see about themselves as readers by illustrating trends, illuminating patterns, and showing progress. When students can access visual representations of what is actually happening with their independent reading, they can increase their goals, stay on track, or course-correct, which allows them to practice personal agency and autonomy. Carefully tracking and quantifying independent reading volume and quality also helps teachers to assess progress toward the stated objectives.

Using the Google tools that are available to me as a teacher, I have developed a system for independent reading documentation that depicts a student's reading life in a few different ways. This daily reading record is simple for students to use, and only calls for them to document their independent reading between five and seven days per week, which is similar

WEAVING DIGITAL INTO THE LITERACY CLASSROOM    65

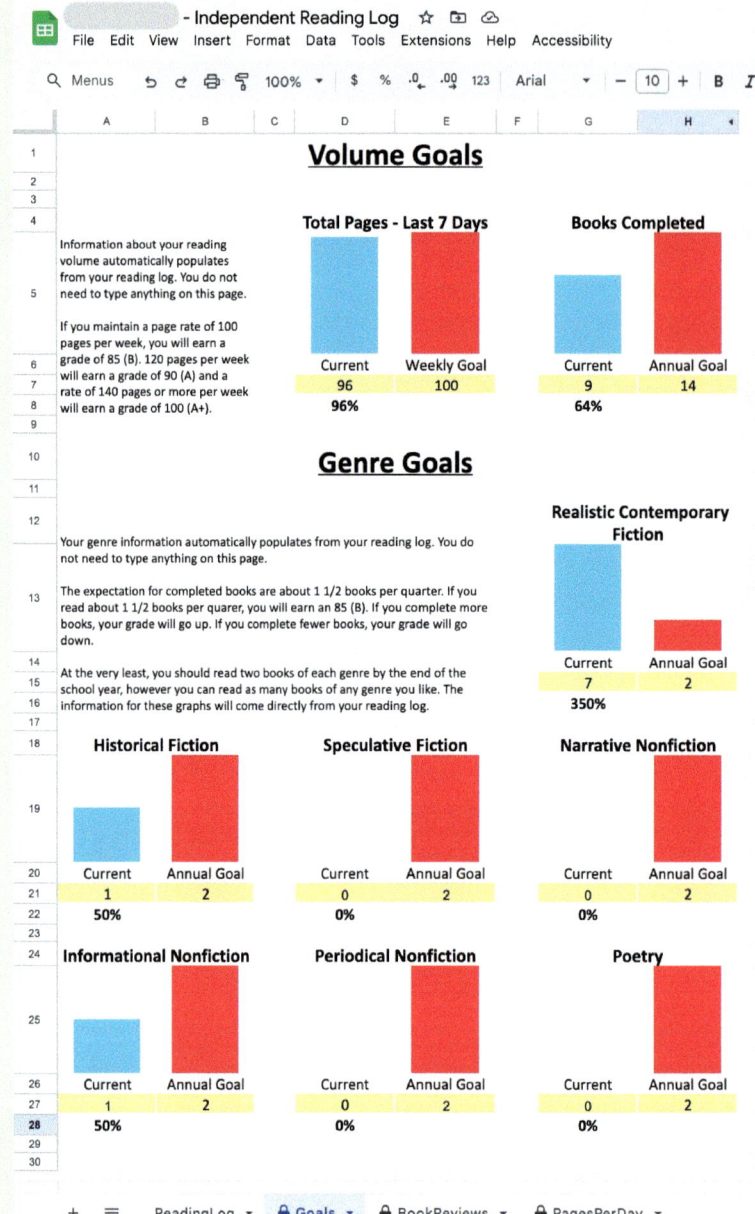

**Figure 2.26:** The goals tab is customizable and uses bar graphs to show progress.

to the demands placed on any student. The system relies on spreadsheets with simple formulas, and each student has their own copy, which is bookmarked for ease of access. Individuals' data is presented in several ways, all of which are easily comprehensible for students and their families.

The first tab in a student's independent reading log (Figure 2.25) is where they enter the date, title, genre, start page, end page, and status (ongoing, completed, abandoned). This tool is easy to use, with its efficient features and simple language. There is a checkbox for the books written in the graphic novel format. The purpose of this checkbox is to monitor, at a glance, the frequency of graphic novel reading. While graphic novels are highly engaging, we'd like the reading diet to include larger blocks of complex text. The system does the rest

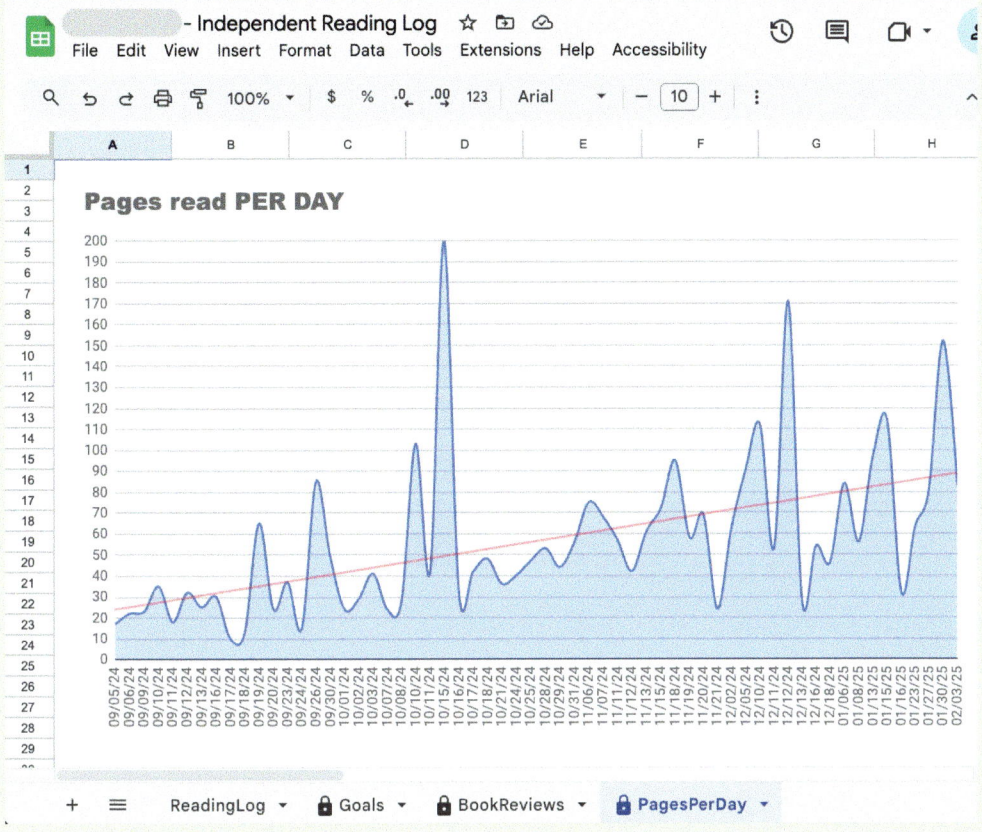

**Figure 2.27:** This graph shows reading volume per day and reading trends over time.

of the work, presenting data in a format easily understood by anyone. The data reporting system relies on simple, bright graphics that deliver real information, which students can use to self-manage and teachers can use to provide guidance.

The Goals tab (Figure 2.26) can be customized to the needs of any class, and shows progress using bright bar graphs. I created the charts and graphs using the chart option from the Insert dropdown menu in Sheets. On this tab, students can see what their page count is for the last seven days, and how many books they have completed in each genre. The PagesPerDay tab (Figure 2.27) shows readers their habits in another way. This graph depicts trends in reading volume per day, and whether daily reading is increasing or decreasing over time. All of the information shown in these charts comes directly from what students enter in their routine, simple daily documentation.

**Structured Reflection Is Essential**

Twice per quarter, a four-number summary (Figure 2.28) is generated using the Google add-on Autocrat. This is an opportunity for a reader to self-assess. Students use this document to reflect on their independent reading over the year and over the prior five weeks. My partner and I also participate in this bi-quarterly reflection, gaining insight into a student's thinking and to assign a grade. Families receive this reflection via email, along with a link to the child's independent reading record. The four number summary is used during conversations and

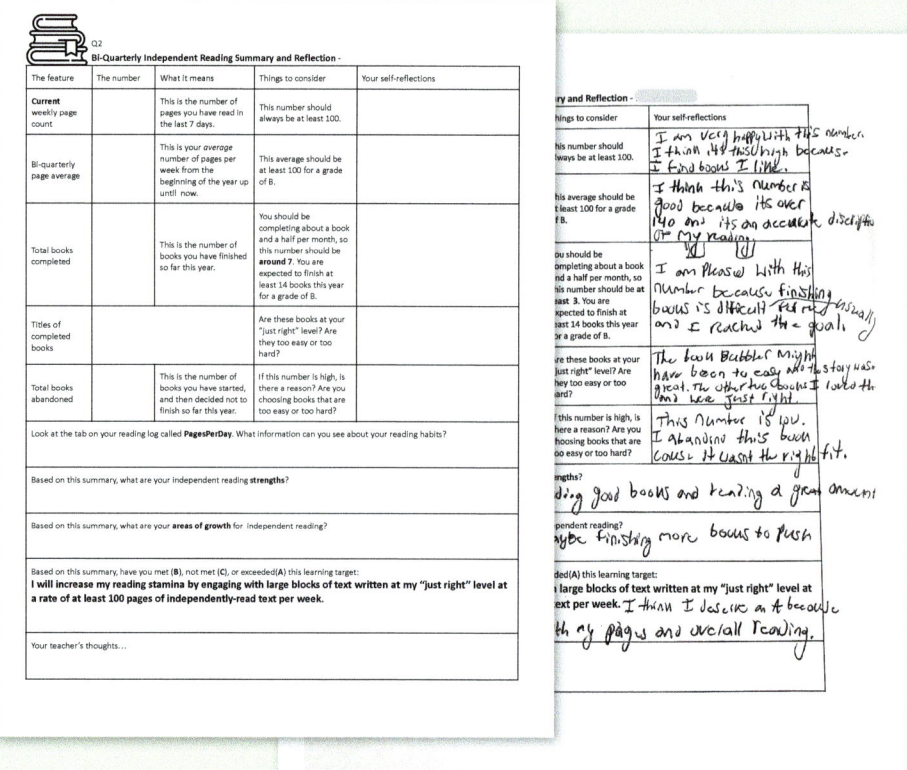

**Figure 2.28:** Students reflect upon their reading.

conferences with caregivers. The colorful graphs and charts in the digital reading log, along with the students' self-reflection, ease communication about independent reading quality and volume.

In addition to this bi-quarterly assessment, my partner and I can assess independent reading via a dashboard that presents a wide range of independent reading data for entire groups of students (Figure 2.29). The class data presented in the dash can be considered in several ways. At a glance, we can look at titles to evaluate whether the choices are at the students' "just right" levels. Another component to our evaluation of this data is observing the rate at which students are moving through texts, and tracking the number of titles that have been completed vs. abandoned. Quality readers finish books. There are a few good reasons to abandon texts as an adolescent or juvenile reader, but there are not as many good reasons as one might believe. Some students harbor bad abandonment habits, which is problematic. This can be due to general disorganization, perseverance problems, or poor reading habits. If a book is written at an inappropriate level (too easy or too hard) or is offensive, it can be abandoned, but other reasons for abandonment must be weighed carefully. Many students claim "boredom" regarding almost every book they pick up. An organized reading experience—which includes reading novels one at a time and the use of a bookmark—are essential. We also look at the seven-day page total. The seven-day page total tabulates today's pages, and the pages read during the prior six calendar days. The

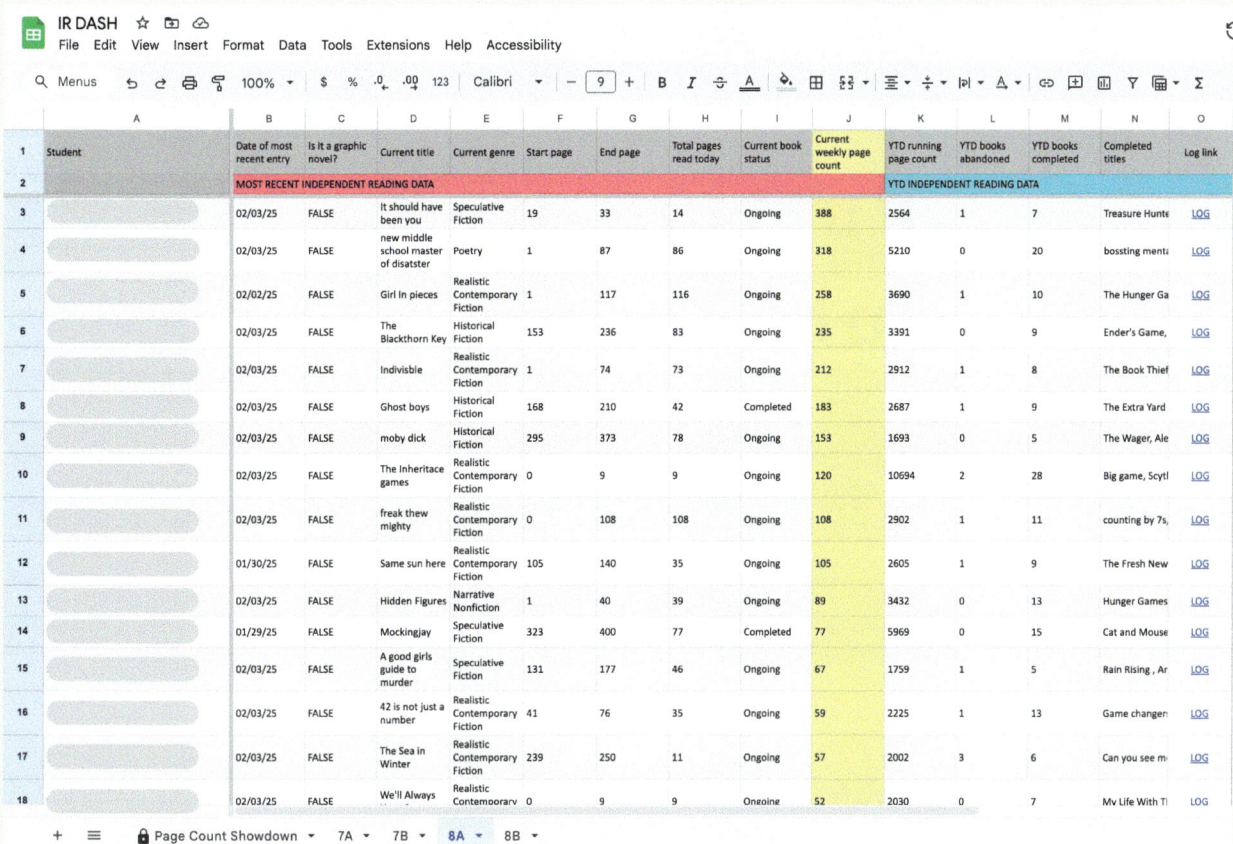

**Figure 2.29:** The teacher dashboard provides an at-a-glance view of student reading data across the class.

expectation should generally correspond to the learning target that has been established for the class or for the individual.

In conclusion, leveraging technology to track and support independent reading provides a powerful tool for teachers, students, and caregivers to enhance literacy outcomes. By setting clear, measurable goals, offering personalized reading choices, and using digital tools to monitor progress, students are more motivated to develop strong reading habits and increase their reading volume. The integration of data tracking not only helps students visualize their growth, but also assists teachers in offering targeted guidance based on students' actual reading behaviors. As we continue to address challenges such as student disengagement, it's important to meet our readers where they are, offering them the tools and support needed to move toward high-volume reading.

bit.ly/4dz16gl
Visit the website to hear Kristin share more about Chapter 2.
(Password: **KZTandT**)

Are you feeling inspired? As you see from these stories, teachers are trying new strategies with learners and you should too! Here are a few ideas for you to try right away with students.

# Putting It into *Practice*

**1. Bring it back to readers.**
Find a terrific picturebook that connects to a topic you are learning about, to your students' interest, or to a title that is purely joyful. Pair it with the audio version of that text and play it for students as you read the book aloud together.

Notice:
- Does the audio add something new?
- What makes the audio different?
- What happens to our thinking when we can see and listen to the book at the same time?

This is a great opportunity to pair digital alongside print and model for students how we use both to engage in deeper thinking.

**2. Dabble with diverse resources.**
Gather three different resources you can use to teach students later this week. Maybe you'll select a digital article, a short YouTube video, and a high-quality image. Maybe you'll use a selection from a science text, a graphic, and a video. Think about how you might layer these elements to fuel background knowledge, foster vocabulary, and introduce new content to students in a variety of modalities.

The Three Resources I Plan to Use:

1. _____

2. _____

3. _____

## 3. Ask students to reflect on their reading.

Refer back to the table, "Easy Ways to Reflect on Learning" on page 61.

- After a read-aloud, think aloud in front of students to model how to reflect on a text using one of the reflection strategies shared on the chart. Offer students a window into your thinking:
    > "One thing I noticed while reading was that I had to read this part twice before I understood it..."
    > "I got very excited at this part when..."
    > "Next time, I plan to work on..."
- The following day, remind students about how you reflected on your reading. Then, invite them to read independently, and after, have them reflect on their reading using one of the strategies shared in the chart.
- After students have reflected, jot a few notes about their reflections and use that information to plan for subsequent student reflections.

| What did students try? | What did students notice about their reading? | Plan for next time |
|---|---|---|
|  |  |  |

– CHAPTER 3 –

# Agency and Action: Tracking Thinking and Learning

In Kristina Labadie's third-grade classroom, students are active agents in their learning journey from the first week of school. Kristina quietly steps aside and invites students to teach her about their learning styles, preferences, and skills. From rearranging the furniture to meet their comfort and visual preferences, to conversations about books they love and science experiments they hope to conduct, Kristina invites students to take the lead. In doing so, she develops a learning environment that is by students for students.

Students in Kristina's classroom all have access to Chromebooks and use them as needed throughout the day. Some students prefer to get them from the cart in the morning and leave them on their table, while others like to return them to the cart when not in use. Either way, students determine how the tools and the environment should work for them.

Early in the year, Kristina watches how her students interact with their Chromebooks rather than teaching them specific lessons on using the devices. She wants them to enter the instructional experience however they are able to, promoting a sense of agency. She knows they enter third grade with a number of skills, and rather than spending time teaching tools and applications they already know, she notices what they are doing and then names the skill for the other learners in the room.

"David! Show me what you did right there."

David looks at her, then points to his Chromebook. "Well, I was trying to create a timeline of the books I read this week and last, and I wanted to do it with pictures of the book covers. I took a few photos of books in the room by holding them up to my camera. But I couldn't find The Last Stand in the classroom library, so I went to the

*Bookelicious website, searched for the book, and took a screen capture of the cover on the website."*

*"How did you know how to take a photo of the screen like that?"*

*"Oh, that's easy! We learned how to do that in second grade. You just click right here." He models the process. "And there you get your photo!"*

*Kristina uses this conversation as a teachable moment for students. "Room 5, take thirty seconds and listen to what David did . . ." She invites David to quickly share how he used the Bookelicious site to find a book cover that he wanted to photograph and how he used his device to capture the image for his timeline.*

*"Thank you, David. Room 5, if you need to find a book, I invite you to go to the Bookelicious website, too. And if you need to capture a photo off your screen, ask David for help."*

*Throughout the early weeks of the school year, she names the strategies students use to track thinking as they read and how they use their devices to hold their learning. Then she invites others to have a go and try the skill or tool as well. Rather than modeling and practicing one strategy at a time, she meets students where they are. Then she observes their actions to determine what skills and strategies they need next. As a responsive educator, Kristina crafts the just-in-time instruction that her students need to grow. Across the school year, students use technology to track their thinking and to make plans for future learning. This intentional work early in the year sets students up to be powerful learners, learners who are able to use the tools available to them throughout the school day.*

## Developing Agentive Learners

Throughout this book, you see a common thread across the classrooms featured: teachers who believe that students are competent, capable learners and engage them as partners in planning, collaborators in the learning process, archivists of documentation, and co-teachers on their learning journey. Teachers who create the conditions for and support student agency.

bit.ly/4lQP59R
Link to Learning Compass 2030

The Organisation for Economic Co-operation and Development (OECD) Learning Compass 2030 defines student agency as "the capacity to set a goal, reflect and act responsibly to effect change. It is about acting rather than being acted upon; shaping rather than being shaped; and making responsible decisions and choices rather than accepting those determined by others."

Ferguson et al. (2015) name student agency as the capacity and propensity to take purposeful initiative. It emphasizes students' voice, choice, and ownership in their learning, leading to greater engagement, motivation, and equity among learners. Educators can enable learners to be agentive by inviting them to take a proactive role in setting and working toward learning goals, in actively pursuing learning opportunities, and in shaping the contexts of their learning (Grotzer et al., 2021).

For me, student agency is so much more than voice and choice. It's a mindset and a habit for living. It extends across contexts. It's the respect we give young people. Peter Johnston's work is foundational to how I think about agency and in his book *Choice Words*, he writes, "Having a sense of agency, is fundamental. Our well-being depends on it . . . . Teachers' conversations with children help the children build the bridges between action and consequence that develop their sense of agency" (Johnston, 2004, p. 30). Student agency is malleable and learnable. Classrooms that embrace student agency strive toward their goals and use all tools to support thinking along the way.

*Children should leave school with a sense that if they act,*
*and act strategically, they can accomplish their goals.*
*I call this feeling a sense of agency.*

— *Peter Johnston,* Choice Words *(2004)* —

## Making Thinking Visible through Documentation

We value the work that students produce in our classroom, but more than evaluating the final product, we celebrate the process and seek to learn from how students interact with information and transform it into knowledge. Documentation is the practice of observing, recording, interpreting (either on one's own or, ideally, in a group), and sharing through different media the processes and products of learning in order to deepen learning (Krechevsky, 2021). When students document their learning, their thinking becomes visible as it presents itself on paper, in art form, through conversation, and as a process to be reflected upon. Documentation grounds reflections on learning in concrete artifacts and invites educators and students to understand a child's needs and plan for next steps.

Documentation is a core principle of a number of educational approaches. In the Reggio Emilia approach to learning, educators believe that children have a "Hundred Languages" to express their ideas and learn (Edwards et al., 1998). "Languages" is used as a metaphor for how young people interact and learn from the world, through painting, dramatic play, storytelling, conversations, making, and more. Today, technology extends those languages and offers even more ways to track thinking and document learning. Video and audio recordings add new lenses to our understanding as they capture the process. Digital drawings and writing tools offer new modes for archiving ideas. Digital work products are easy to save and share; as a result, students can curate their own digital portfolios to communicate their process and current understanding to peers and caregivers. Digital documentation captures a more complete version of a child's learning journey. From early ideas to synthesized understandings, technology offers a unique opportunity for us to know students even better.

Chrissy Moore creates an environment for her first graders that is rooted in student agency. She helps students gain confidence as learners and organizes her instruction using a blend of print and digital text and tools to support individual student needs. Chrissy identifies a few core tenets that promote agency, result in positive reading identities, and yield curious, independent thinkers across the curriculum.

**Chrissy Moore**
Chrissy is a first-grade teacher at St. Ann School in Chicago and recently completed her reading specialist endorsement. She creates a safe, nurturing, and inclusive classroom where all students feel valued and empowered to reach their full potential.

## Chrissy Moore – Structuring for Student Agency

"Ms. Moore, Ms. Moore! I finished the book!"

These words make me smile many times each day in my first-grade classroom in Chicago's Pilsen community. I spend my days with eighteen excitable learners who enter our school building with unique stories and backgrounds. We build community through shared text, conversations, experiences, and living and learning together.

I've been teaching for seven years, and as I reflect on my career, I recognize that there have been many changes to how we teach and how students learn. New standards and curriculum require teachers to learn and adjust. At my school, we use a combination of packaged curriculum materials and curricula that we have authored to address the unique needs of learners in our community. I intentionally weave what I know to be good instruction into and around the packaged curricular materials we use.

Standardized assessments monitor student progress. I pair data from standardized assessments with classroom observations and student work to develop a more robust understanding of what my students know and are able to do. Mobile devices and technology offer new access to information, assessment tools, and authentic learning opportunities; it also augments how we interact with traditional learning materials and each other. Change can be challenging but also exciting at the same time!

I recognize that curriculum and technology tools will continue to evolve, but one aspect of learning that I can control

**Figure 3.1:** Chrissy positions herself at student level as she leans in to confer with a reader; in doing so, she centers the student.

is my belief and trust in students. I believe all learners are capable intellectuals. With a bit of support, they can and will take ownership of their learning journey. Developing readers and writers are powerful thinkers regardless of their Lexile level or ability to express themselves in writing. They have tremendous capacity for new information, and I can leverage their ability to think to further their reading and writing development. By creating a classroom environment that is designed for reflective learning and structured for independence, student agency thrives as learners are motivated by their ability to seek and figure out more.

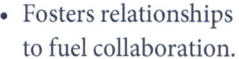

**Figure 3.2:** A chart hangs in the classroom, naming students' expertise and celebrating that they are all smart, capable learners. By recognizing all students' assets, each learner knows they can teach others and that they play an important role in the classroom community.

I value the intentionality that goes into the organization of Chrissy's space. She creates a classroom ecosystem that enhances reflective learning and promotes student agency. She guides students to discover their interests and passions and makes space for them to explore and grow.

I appreciate how Chrissy:
- Promotes student independence through personalized learning.
- Helps developing readers track their learning and reflect upon where they are and where they want to go.
- Fosters relationships to fuel collaboration.

I track student conversations, work samples, initiative, and stamina as I look for evidence of agentive learning. I look at the number of books students have read online, how much time they have spent reading, how they use time with digital and print text, and how they reflect upon their learning using Seesaw. I observe how students move around the room, use materials, and interact with others. All of this informs how I personalize learning for students so they develop a strong literacy foundation and are on track to become lifelong learners.

When structuring for student agency, I center students and strive to create a space where curiosity and capability meet. I balance traditional and digital tools so students have even more options for access and increased opportunities to capture their thinking and learning. Here are a few elements that support literacy development and student agency in our classroom:

**Figure 3.3:** A comfortable and cozy library space invites readers to snuggle up with a favorite book. Personalized book boxes with titles matched to students form the perimeter of the library. A string of lights and a lamp soften the space. Above the lounge chair, photos of the books they've read this year are displayed.

**Figure 3.4:** The classroom has a large gathering area where students come together for a mini-lesson, to practice phonics and word work, or to read aloud.

**Physical environment:** Around my classroom, I have many different types of learning, reading, and collaboration spaces available to students. Soft seating, cozy chairs, spaces to spread out, and tables and chairs for students to work together all serve different purposes. When I work with a small group, I want students to be close to me and their peers so they can feel the support of our learning community as we work on a new reading or spelling strategy. I want to quickly pull together a group and work efficiently, so I have areas with tables and chairs, clipboards and markers, and mobile devices all at the ready. There are many spaces for personal and individualized learning, as some students need quiet and seclusion to focus on their reading. Pillows, swivel chairs, desks, and cozy nooks invite readers to find a quiet space that works for them. The room is dotted with soft light, as I want students to feel calm and inspired to spend more time with text. Supplies can be found on tables, in bins, and on shelves around the room so that students always have access to the materials they need. The learning environment provides choice in how and where students learn. It signals to students that the work they do is so important that I want them to feel comfortable and inspired in our space and make choices that work for them throughout our learning day.

**Meeting area:** We gather in the meeting area to build shared knowledge every single day. Learning is proximal, and when we're close together, we engage in deeper conversation and collaborate to learn even more. When teaching a new strategy, I want students to be next to the book I'm reading or the projector that I'm sharing on so they can engage fully with the lesson. I want them close to a partner so they can turn and talk and process new learning. I want to be able to quickly see what they're drawing and jotting so I can correct any misconceptions or use their annotations to extend an instructional point. With devices on their laps, I want to be able to see where they have success and where they might struggle so I can follow up with instruction if needed.

**Independent reading:** Regardless of whatever else is going on at school, I know my students need time to self-select text and time to practice reading. Religiously, we engage in independent reading and safeguard this time above all else. Kids have the right to read, whether accessing titles on their iPads or spending time with books from our classroom library or their book boxes. I confer with readers regularly, and students track their reading on charts and by viewing the number of books they have read on Accelerated Reader, Raz Kids, or Epic! When my students can see that they have read sixty-seven books on Epic! they are joyful and proud. Students who don't have access to reading materials at home demonstrate an exceptional level of personal satisfaction and pride, as classroom reading time offers a path to leading a literate life. For developing readers, the number of books read is the documentation of an accomplishment: I read books. I finish books. I am a reader!

**Figure 3.5:** Students share the reading experience as they read books they've self-selected. Regardless of their reading levels, reading together is what matters.

**Figure 3.6:** During independent reading, students have books they've selected and books to practice. They transition between print and digital reading materials, depending upon their reading purpose.

**Personalized reading materials:** Each child has a box of reading materials that is created with their reading interest and level in mind. I want to ensure that all students have books they can and want to read, as well as titles that push them at a level that will result in their growth. Similarly, I create book bins for students online in Epic! and RAZ Kids that match the same criteria. My students need access to lots of reading materials each week, and I want to provide them with a springboard of titles they can dive right into.

 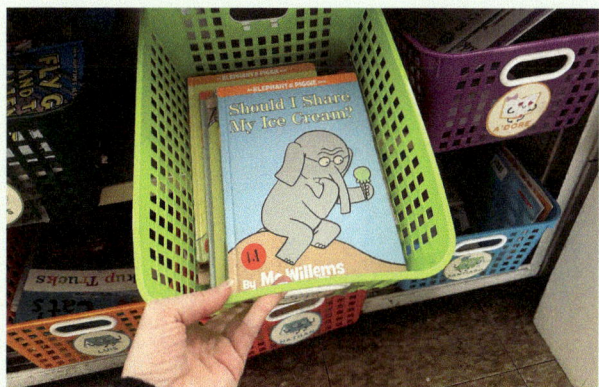

**Figure 3.7:** Each student has a personalized book bin filled with titles they can and want to read.

**Figure 3.8:** One student is currently reading Mo Willems's Elephant & Piggie series and has a bin filled with his favorite titles.

**Learning is social:** I provide ample time for students to share the reading experience with others. Students regularly partner with a buddy to read various types of text. Together, learners collaboratively figure out the words and the meaning as they go. You'll see partners or small groups with the same copy of the Elephant & Piggie titles reading aloud together, taking turns from page to page, or listening to a student reader. Similarly, readers will access the same text on RAZ Kids or share a device while using the read-to-me feature on Epic! Weekly, students lead discussions of books they have read and enjoyed. They recommend books to each other, share books from home, and discuss books they wish to read next. My students often ask about my own reading and book clubs. They see that learning and reading is lifelong. Reading is fun. They even begin to refer to some of their time together as book clubs. Their love of reading is shared and celebrated!

**Digital conversation and response:** The ability to respond to reading and have a conversation about a text builds background knowledge, promotes expressive language skills, fuels comprehension, and solidifies new learning so that students can remember and reuse what they have learned. We use conversation, paper and pencil, and digital platforms to discuss our thinking and respond to text and each other. Easy-to-use tools like Seesaw encourage students to record their ideas in drawing, writing, audio, or video and quickly share the responses with the group. When students can hear and learn from the ideas of their peers, they experience the joy that goes hand-in-hand with learning.

**Figure 3.9:** Students select the titles they want to read and who they want to read with. Here, two students read digital texts together on their iPads.

**Relationships:** The relationships we form in our classroom have a significant impact on learning. When we can openly ask questions, take risks, make mistakes, and celebrate our successes, we are able to grow together. Learners run to show me the silly thing Gerald and Piggie did or tell me a Dog Man joke. They see older students coming into the classroom to book shop and share their reading. It is important that students feel a sense of belonging and know that their ideas and suggestions benefit the group. When we can establish a sense of collective ownership over our learning, we inspire each other with our thinking and actions.

These structures allow me to step out of the way and invite even more agency into our space as students pursue knowledge. I hope that a robust literacy foundation paired with a strong sense of self and understanding that they are capable beings who can ask, seek, and guide their learning journey will provide the skills they need to adapt and adjust to whatever lies ahead of them.

**Figure 3.10:** Students care about reading and care about each other. Their passion for books is a shared classroom value, as they read together whenever they are able.

Chrissy shares a few elements of her classroom design and practice. Across schools and states, I've seen many of these same elements present in classrooms that support student agency. Agency is not something you teach once to students and cross off the list. It's a stance, an approach, a mindset, and a habit for living.

## Amplifying Active Literacy

David Pearson's work on active literacy (Duke & Pearson, 2002) taught us that adding modes for students to interact with text resulted in students who accessed, remembered, and reused information more effectively than those who interacted with text alone. We build upon his work and continue to enrich the learning experience by making it multisensory, layered, and personalized. We invite students to enter the learning where they are able and to create learning spaces that value markers and chart paper, sticky notes and student thinksheets, photos and digital drawings, reflection videos and small-group collaboration, clipboards and online publications, and more. We teach students to show what they know in traditional and digital contexts and celebrate that we have many more ways to capture student thinking.

**Active Literacy**
Read
Write
Talk
Draw
View
Listen
Investigate
Share

Today, the possibility for response is infinite as we add new digital tools that invite students to communicate across modalities in order to amplify their thinking. In offering diverse formats for interaction, we welcome and celebrate each child's unique learning preferences and invite students to show what they know in a manner that works for them. Learners use a combination of traditional and multimedia options as they construct knowledge across the instructional day. Frequently, we employ the language of "make something" to invite students to document their current understanding. And when students are invited to "make something," it is the best assessment of what they know and are able to do today. The teacher can use these work products to monitor progress and plan for follow-up instruction and next steps in the student's learning progression. Throughout the school year, we introduce students to new tools as well as invite them to layer traditional and digital tools together to create something new.

As students gain more ways to show their thinking, we help them think through why they selected a particular mode or medium. Reflecting upon the tools they use, students can learn to identify which tool is best for them to communicate understanding in relation to the task at hand. This knowledge helps students make effective choices when selecting tools and ensures that time is spent thinking and learning, not on navigating the tool.

In addition to offering students more choice over their learning process, new technologies offer affordances that make tracking thinking and learning easier than ever before. Digital work products are often easily saved to a student's device or account. When student work is easy to save, we can curate a more complete continuum of learning over time. The ease of saving allows both students and teachers the opportunity to look back at work, assess growth, and make plans for future learning. Because the work products are archived on a device or within each student's account, it is easy to search for specific work samples, gather artifacts by date, or pull examples to share with caregivers or school support staff. By default, these digital work products become a living, breathing digital portfolio for students.

Not only is saving work easy to do, it's also easy for students to share work with others! Adding a classmate to a document or presentation, posting content to Google Classroom or Seesaw, or adding an artifact to a digital bulletin board expands access for learners in the room. The ease of sharing invites conversation and collaboration, as students can see the work of their peers. Being able to see how others are thinking and creating often inspires new questions and ideas as kids construct knowledge together. I've been in many classrooms where students are viewing the annotations posted by their peers, and someone suddenly exclaims, "Oh, Jacob! I didn't think of it like that! Great idea!" Collaborative digital spaces invite students to interact with new information and each other.

Another benefit of digital work products and digital collaboration spaces is that they extend learning, as students can access information online beyond the school day. Just because the bell rings at three doesn't mean that the thinking and learning has to stop. With digital learning spaces, students can keep thinking and collaborate as needed.

**Figure 3.11:** Students share work to a digital bulletin board so they can learn from each other's annotations and thinking.

## Annotating as a Means to Understanding

As long as I've been an educator, we've taught students how to annotate text. From sticky notes posted on the pages of a book to notes in the margin of an article, we guide students to leave tracks of their thinking. These annotations serve as a window to a child's brain and as a physical extension of their cognition. We instruct students how to monitor their comprehension and document new learning and questions they have about a text. We coach them to document key details and changes in their thinking. We show them how to identify topics for further research and how to use their annotations to summarize a text. Over time, we've used sticky notes, two and three-column thinksheets, chart paper, markers, and organizers to capture student thinking. As our learning environments have embraced multimedia, we move beyond the pages of a text to annotate images, primary source artifacts, graphics, and realia. With the influx of digital content, we've expanded our annotations to include video, websites, ebooks, podcasts and audiobooks, memes, virtual and augmented reality, and more.

**Figure 3.13:** First-grade students use sticky notes and markers to collaboratively annotate an image launching a unit on Ancient China. Students write in different color markers so that the teacher can track each child's contributions and thinking.

**Figure 3.12:** A student annotates a video using a six-box thinksheet and markers.

With simple tools like Seesaw or Slides, we can interact with text and tech by taking a photo of the page of a book or an article and dropping it into a digital annotation tool. Now, students can add their thinking and annotate nearly any content source. With the affordances of the device, students can draw and sketch, type or use speech-to-text, add an audio recording of themselves thinking about the artifact, or even insert a short video clip talking through their process. The benefits of digital invite readers to have even more transactions with the text (Rosenblatt, 1978). As we layer opportunities for interacting with text, students build background knowledge and vocabulary, employ critical thinking skills, gain perspective, and foster agency. Most significantly, once students learn to annotate images, videos, and the text that others produce, they can adapt the practice and annotate their own work as a way to reflect upon their process.

In Lynsey Burkins's classroom, students use annotation to understand themselves, others, and the world. By turning annotation into a community process, Lynsey invites her learners to grow their understanding and build knowledge together. Read about how her students use paper, markers, highlighters, Slides, digital stickies, and digital bulletin boards not only as tools for thinking but as a means to liberation.

**Lynsey Burkins**

Lynsey Burkins has worked for children for more than twenty years. Lynsey works with young people to create antiracist spaces where children feel free, have agency, and know they are loved. She is the coauthor of *Classroom Design for Student Agency* and *In Community With Readers: Transforming Reading Instruction with Read-Alouds and Minilessons*.

## Lynsey Burkins – Annotation as a Liberatory Experience

Early in my graduate work at The Ohio State University, I took my first course with Dr. Brian Edmiston, focusing on teaching and learning through drama. At the time, I was teaching third grade in a suburban school district outside Columbus, Ohio. This course changed the way I approached teaching, sparking a fascination with how my students came to know and understand a text. While many call this process comprehension, I began to see it as something much deeper: a social and liberatory act. As educators, we often overlook how social differences shape the reading experience. Inspired by the work of Louise Rosenblatt and Brian Street, I began to see reading as a dynamic and socially constructed practice, one that could empower students to critically engage with their world.

According to Rosenblatt's transactional theory (1978), the act of reading involves a transaction between the reader and the text. Each reading experience is unique, with meaning constructed as the reader and text continuously interact. Brian Street's (2003) argument that literacy is a social practice, shaped by power dynamics and multiple literacies, further deepened my understanding of reading as a communal and liberatory process. These ideas, combined with Edmiston's work on dramatic inquiry and a collaborative and imaginative approach to exploring texts, led me to reimagine how I taught reading in my classroom.

I realized that creating a liberatory space for meaning-making required not only discussion but also a tangible method for students to capture their thoughts. Annotation became that method. By annotating, students could independently engage with texts and then bring their insights to a collective space for deeper exploration. This practice transformed the reading experience from an individual task to a communal journey, fostering critical thinking, agency, and a shared understanding of the world.

### Annotation as a Vehicle for Critical Comprehension

In my classroom, annotation is more than a tool for comprehension; it is a practice of liberation. It allows students to interrogate texts, reflect on their own identities, and explore power dynamics. Annotation begins with students reading a text independently and marking their thoughts using symbols, colors, or notes. This initial engagement is crucial because it captures their authentic reactions and personal connections to the text. By annotating, students take ownership of their learning, grounding their interpretations in their lived experiences.

After this independent work, we transition to whole-group discussions. Here, students share their annotations and collectively annotate a shared version of the text. This process, which I call co-annotation, is where the magic happens. It is a dynamic, collaborative exploration of the text, enriched by the diverse perspectives of the reading community. Students see how their peers interpret the same text differently, broadening their understanding and challenging their assumptions. Co-annotation is charted visibly on a whiteboard, chart paper, or a digital platform, creating a communal artifact of our collective thinking.

The final step is reflection. Students compare their initial annotations with the group's co-annotations and consider how their understanding has evolved. This reflective process helps them see reading as a journey, one that incorporates their own voices, the voices of their peers, and the broader context of power, identity, and lived experience. Annotation, in this sense, becomes a road map for critical comprehension, allowing students to move from personal insight to collective understanding and, ultimately, to liberation.

### Tools for Annotation

In our classroom, we use a variety of tools for annotation, both paper and digital. Each method offers unique benefits, allowing students to engage with texts in ways that suit their learning styles and needs.

### Annotating on Paper

When we annotate on paper, we use highlighters, markers, washi tape, sticky notes, and other materials to make our thinking visible. Paper annotation offers a tactile experience that many students find engaging. It allows them to physically manipulate the text, circling words, drawing arrows, and adding layers of meaning with colors and symbols. This method is particularly effective for younger students, who benefit from the sensory engagement and the opportunity to express their ideas visually.

---

Lynsey recognizes that literacy is not a neutral set of transferable skills but a highly personal experience that is colored by the reader's background, social context, and cultural norms.

I value how Lynsey:

- Supports students as they move seamlessly between paper, sticky notes, and digital tools as they track their thinking and build knowledge together.
- Uses collective annotations as a pathway to construct meaning through multiple interactions with the text and multiple interactions with each other.
- Leverages reflection to help students synthesize thinking as they organize their new learning and think about their positionality in response to what they've learned.

**Annotating Digitally**
Digital annotation tools like Padlet, Google Slides, and Kindle Web provide flexibility and accessibility. With these tools, students can easily edit, reorganize, and share their annotations. Digital platforms also enable collaboration in real time, allowing students to annotate texts together even when they are not in the same physical space. This method is especially powerful for integrating multimedia elements, such as videos, images, and hyperlinks, which can deepen students' understanding of the text and its broader context.

**Theoretical Work I Stand On**
The practice of annotation is deeply rooted in critical pedagogy and the work of scholars like Paulo Freire, Vivian Vasquez, and Brian Edmiston. Freire's emphasis on dialogue and critical consciousness underscores the importance of annotation as a tool for liberation. Through annotation, students engage in a dialogic process with the text, asking questions, challenging assumptions, and uncovering hidden power dynamics. This practice helps them develop the critical awareness needed to navigate and transform their world.

Vivian Vasquez's work on critical literacy further informs my approach. Vasquez (2004) argues that literacy is not just about decoding words but about understanding and challenging the social and cultural contexts in which those words exist. Annotation supports this work by giving students a concrete way to examine texts critically, connecting them to broader social issues and their own lived experiences.

Finally, Edmiston's concept of dramatic inquiry highlights the role of imagination in meaning-making. By approaching annotation as a form of inquiry, students can explore texts as if they were participants in the story, cocreating meaning and connecting it to their own lives. This imaginative and collaborative process makes annotation not just an academic exercise but a liberatory act.

**Takeaways for Teachers**
Teachers looking to implement annotation as a liberatory practice can start with these steps:
1. **Create a Culture of Inquiry:** Foster a classroom environment where students feel safe to share their thoughts and question texts. Encourage them to see annotation as a tool for exploration, not just a requirement.
2. **Use Multiple Tools:** Provide a variety of annotation tools, both analog and digital, to meet the diverse needs of your students. Let them experiment with different methods to find what works best for them.
3. **Model the Process:** Demonstrate how to annotate a text, showing students how to mark their thoughts, ask questions, and make connections. Share your own annotations to model critical thinking.
4. **Emphasize Reflection:** Build time for students to revisit their annotations, compare them with their peers', and reflect on how their understanding has changed. This step is crucial for developing critical consciousness.

5. **Connect to the Real World:** Choose texts that resonate with your students' lives and experiences. I choose texts that connect to topics I've heard them share about, wonder about, and/or engage in. Use annotation to help them see how the themes and issues in the text relate to the world around them.

Annotation is more than a strategy for understanding texts; it is a practice of liberation. By engaging in annotation, students become active participants in their learning, using texts as tools to understand and challenge their world. Whether through colorful notes on paper or collaborative digital platforms, annotation fosters critical thinking, agency, and a sense of community. It allows students to see reading not just as a solitary act but as a shared journey, one that empowers them to make meaning, embrace their identities, and imagine a more just world. In the words of Paulo Freire, "Reading is not walking on the words; it's grasping the soul of them" (1985, p. 19). Through annotation, we help our students grasp not only the soul of the text but also the soul of their own power as thinkers and changemakers.

## Capturing Conversation, Conferring Moments, and Student Thinking with Audio and Video

In their book *Strategies That Work* (2000), Stephanie Harvey and Anne Goudvis write about the power of analyzing student work to assess a child's learning. Both discuss reviewing sticky notes, thinksheets, and margin annotations for information about a child's process. Over the years, Harvey and Goudvis's work has taught teachers to find evidence of how a young person builds understanding by monitoring changes in thinking, exclamations of new learning, the ability to ask questions within a text, and how to react or respond to new information. By looking at student work samples, we gain a window into a child's thinking. Even though student work gives us a tremendous amount of insight, Harvey has always advocated that when we pair student work samples with a conversation, we get infinitely more information about a child's thinking. Anyone who has conferred with students can agree; the conversation provides deep insight into a child's understanding.

Video and audio offer significant affordances in the classroom, as they have the power to capture learning in the moment. Now, we can gain access to those conversations and add a young person's voice to any work sample. When we can see a child in action, when we can hear them think through a process, and when we can look at a physical artifact that they've created, we understand infinitely more about what a child knows and is able to do. When used thoughtfully, these tools make learning more visible, inclusive, and collaborative.

**Figure 3.14:** A student annotates his new learning while reading an ebook about bugs. Notice how he reads the bugs on the screen in order to accurately represent them on his thinksheet. He labels his bugs with beginning sounds and notes that bugs have stripes and circle or triangle shapes on their body. Bugs have six legs. Bugs have two antennae. Moths are bugs. He draws a stick bug. He then shares his learning by creating a video using Seesaw. In the video, he holds up his clipboard and offers a detailed explanation of what each drawing represents. Sometimes we look at student work and think, "Oh, that's cute!" Instead, we need to look and listen to what they're really telling us and shift our thinking to "Oh, that's so SMART!"

Video has the power to extend our time with students, as we can watch students learn asynchronously while they are at recess, while attending a special class, even when they are at home. The ability to "check in" with learning can be viewed as a one-directional conferring moment. When we watch video, we have time to identify a personalized instructional point and circle back with the child the following day to continue the conversation.

One beautiful thing about video is that the use of it is not conditional upon a child's reading level, their home language, or their grade level. All learners can access video, and thus it becomes a powerful tool to promote student agency and reflect upon learning. When we can access video work samples across time, we can document student growth for learners. The concrete nature of video reflection allows students to see, hear, view progress, and benchmark growth. We say, "Watch this video of yourself reading in October. What do you notice? Now, watch this video of you reading in January. What do you notice about yourself as a reader now?" Because the documentation of learning is tangible, it invites students to make plans for future learning, as they can see how far they've come and can recognize that they might continue to advance their skills. Students develop a sense of agency and are empowered

**Figure 3.15:** A kindergartner tracks his new learning about weather. He draws his thinking using the tools on Seesaw and takes a photo of the book he read for the teacher's reference. He adds an audio recording of himself talking about his learning.

Transcript of recording: "The rainclouds come in handy, so they evaporated into a cloud. Condensation, and when they fall, it's called precipitation. So, when it happens, that means it's working to make it rain. And the rain would reverse back up into the sun again to go back down."

At first glance, we may think that this student drew a nice picture of a raincloud and a rainbow. But when we listen to the audio clip of his thinking, we grasp the depth of knowledge he has built. Content-specific vocabulary like evaporated, condensation, and precipitation and the application of the language in a real-world situation signal that he owns the thinking. When he explains "the rain reversing back up into the sun again," he uses his own vocabulary to explain the process of the water cycle. This is evidence of deep comprehension from a six-year-old.

to strive for growth. They see that they are the active agent who can make gains, grow, and guide their learning.

For multilingual learners, video invites students to speak in their preferred language or a combination of the languages they can access. When we create space for translanguaging in our classrooms, we invite students to use their complete repertoire of language skills to communicate and learn. Multilingual learners possess a powerful linguistic skill set; when they use all their assets to interact with new information, ask questions,

**TIP:** As with most things, if we want students to create quality classroom videos, we must show them how. As teachers, we need to use video regularly in front of our students and be the mentor they need to see. Our modeling shows how to use the technology, but more importantly, it shows how to talk about thinking. At first, you may feel uncomfortable recording a video in front of students, but after a few times, you'll see how powerful it is for students to have this mentor tech model.

synthesize and share their learning, they comprehend deeply across diverse contexts. By leveraging all languages, we validate a child's unique ability to construct knowledge and express themselves.

Most important, learning is joyful, and when we learn something new and exciting, we want to share that with others! Video allows young people to experience the reinforcement of that joy quickly. In a sixty-second video recording, students can tell what they've learned and post the video to the classroom learning management system or website. Through these platforms, students gain authentic audiences for their learning, as the video can be viewed by peers, other classrooms, caregivers, or the public. In the classroom, students can talk about the videos they create and build upon the ideas of others. Online viewers can add comments, provide feedback, or ask follow-up questions, inspiring students to keep thinking. Learning is social. And when students experience the joy of teaching others, they want to do it again and again. As a result, the cycle of learning and sharing never stops.

**Figure 3.16:** A student creates a video book review for the book *Home in a Lunchbox*.

bit.ly/4dz16gl
Check in with Kristin on the website to learn more about the power of video. (Password: **KZTandT**)

> **Easy Ways to Use Video in the Classroom**
> - Teach students how to talk about their work by holding up a drawing, piece of writing, or thinksheet in front of the video camera to record their thinking.
> - Record a child reading a book at their level and use that video sample to do a running record or words per minute fluency assessment.
> - Have a child hold up their right-now book and create a book review or book talk.
> - Use video as a tool for prewriting! Have a child record their story idea in a video. This video serves as a planning tool, and students can access it frequently to revisit the plan and add detail.
> - After viewing a young person explain something on video, create a feedback video to respond to that student. Video allows teachers to provide quick, detailed feedback that a child can watch and rewatch as they work to apply the instruction.
> - Create a short teaching video for students. Video invites students to access the content as many times as needed in order to understand the concept. Instructional videos also allow students to progress at their own pace, as the video provides just-in-time teaching as needed.

In Sophia Garcia-Smith's second-grade classroom, students use the power of video and audio recording tools to share more about their learning. Across the curriculum, they use Seesaw to capture their brilliant ideas and to track progress over time.

## Sophia Garcia-Smith – A Look into Student Learning

**Sophia Garcia-Smith**
Sophia is a library media specialist who loves to create, collaborate, and share her love of teaching and technology with the world. She uses digital tools to connect her students to classrooms, experts, and authors online to offer her students authentic audiences for their work.

I have been using audio and video tools for the past ten years, and these tools have proven to be an invaluable platform for enabling students to demonstrate their thinking and learning. I use Seesaw, which has these tools as part of the larger program. Seesaw offers flexibility, allowing me to tailor and personalize my instruction while providing resources and feedback to support students' progress. Seesaw empowers students by giving them a voice and choice in expressing their understanding. Its multimodal tools and intuitive interface ensure that learners of all ages can engage with the program effectively. Although I am talking about Seesaw, any audio and video recording tools will work to support student learning in this way.

**Access**

A few years ago I had a multilingual student with a speech IEP. He did not speak in class very often, and when he did, it was in Spanish to his Spanish-speaking peers. I struggled with how to connect with this student. I had begun to use Seesaw that school year and was still getting a feel for how this tool would fit into my instruction. I let students take some ownership of how they showed what they had learned in that day's small-group reading lesson. I had students take a picture of their favorite part of the story, and they could record a video, record just their voice, or draw a picture. This student decided to record his voice. At the time, I had created a "recording studio" in my classroom—it was copy paper boxes that I had decorated with duct tape and added a tap light on top of the box to indicate that someone was recording. This student took his iPad and entered the recording studio. When the lesson was over, I asked the students to submit their work. As most days went, I did not listen or look at that assignment until later in the evening. I can remember where I was when I heard him speak English for the first time. In a timid voice, he shared everything he learned. That's when I realized the power of giving students a choice in how to show their learning.

I really respect how Sophia believes that young people can create, that their work is worthy of living in the world, and that they can teach others.

What stands out about Sophia's article is how she:
- Teaches students to capture fluency snapshots to safeguard time to confer with students.
- Multiplies herself using video to differentiate for student needs.
- Uses video and audio to capture the conversation that tells us so much more about a child's learning.

AGENCY AND ACTION: TRACKING THINKING AND LEARNING

**Figure 3.17:** A student records their thinking in a cardboard "recording studio." A recording studio enhances the quality of the audio captured when recording in a classroom where others are also recording. When working in a setting in which students share devices, a studio becomes a shared space where kids archive their ideas.

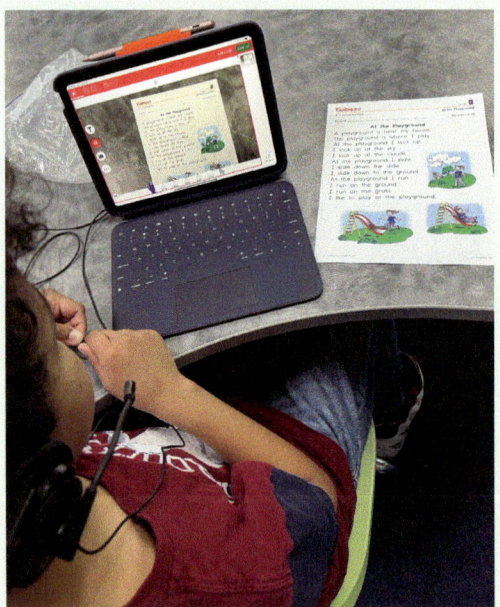

**Figure 3.18:** Sophia's student captures a fluency recording using Seesaw. Sophia can listen to the recording and assess the student's reading fluency at a later time.

### Data Collection

As a classroom teacher, I find that my time is often limited, and video and audio recording tools help alleviate this challenge by enabling me to "clone" myself. Students can work independently, fostering a more efficient and productive learning environment. Every teacher feels the time crunch when it comes to weekly running records. The data we collect is crucial to our instruction, but instruction time suffers when we take extended time to assess. I knew that putting procedures in place and practicing those procedures is essential when working with primary students. For weeks, we practiced how students would record a running record during centers. We used Reading A–Z fluency passages and I made copies of the passages and placed them in a binder. When my students had that center, they would take their iPads, take a picture of the fluency passage they were assigned, and record their reading. This process became a huge timesaver for me. I was able to spend more face-to-face time with students who needed direct instruction while having other students become more independent. I was able to listen, score, and give feedback to students in the comment section to let them know how they did. The best part about this center was that parents were getting a recording of their child's reading progress instead of just a paper that went home to show them their child moved from level G to level H. I had parents attend conferences with a better understanding of their child's accomplishments and growth each week. With the success of this procedure, I began to use it in other subject areas.

### Differentiation with Video

In math centers, I began to record videos to demonstrate how to play a math game in a center or reteach a skill that other students were struggling with. I could then push those videos out with a QR code or send them directly to a group of students. I could differentiate the videos for each group to ensure they were receiving personalized instruction. The benefit for me was that I had fewer students approaching me during small-group work. They were able to stay focused and engaged in their centers when they knew where to look for additional support.

### Recordings for Understanding

Using an audio recording tool allows me to "see student thinking" in a way that traditional methods cannot. For example, students can create a simple drawing and add a recorded explanation to clarify their understanding of the task. This multimedia approach provides much deeper insight into their thought processes than a drawing on paper alone. For years, I taught whole-group lessons, sent students back to their seats, and had them practice the skill or standard and then recite the information back to me in a pre-made assessment. I had no problem showing growth, but I struggled when they could not carry over the concept to another subject. I began to question if they were learning or if they were like me as a child—I was very good at memorization and could relay the information back when needed. I knew there had to be a better way to see what they were truly learning. I remember sitting with a student who was struggling with basic math foundational skills. This student could show me with manipulatives how to add up to 10, but for anything beyond that, the answers never matched up. As teachers of primary students, we become masters of decoding what students are writing, thinking, and processing. However, with this student, I just couldn't understand the struggle.

**Figure 3.19:** Sophia records an instructional video for students. In doing so, she multiplies herself by being able to meet with a group in class while others learn from her on video.

One day, I saw their answer to a daily math word problem. I was again confused by their answer, so I asked them to record themselves explaining their answer. Now, I am going to give you a little backstory on something I said while teaching multiples of 10: I told students that once we get to 10, it's very simple because we would have a transition word like 20, 30, 40, but we would always repeat the ones place with 1–9. Now back to what I heard when I listened to that recording. The question was 7 + 18; the student's answer was 10. He explained that 7 + 18 was 25 and then, because there were two 10s, you had to repeat the ones place. This student was adding the 5 in the ones places twice—because there were two 10s. I can honestly say that my mind was blown by the confidence in his voice as he explained this answer. I wondered for a moment how he had learned this process, and then I remembered my words, and it all made sense. I was able to identify the cause of his confusion, reteach the skill, and watch him grow. I know that I could possibly have come to the same conclusion through just a conversation with the student, but in a classroom of twenty-eight students, sometimes there is just not enough time to have those conversations. Seesaw was a tool that helped me see and hear the student's thinking, change my instructions, and individualize my student's learning.

The video and audio recording tools in Seesaw changed the way I teach. I was giving students a choice in how they shared their learning. I was giving them the freedom to share with not only me but with their families and beyond. The pride and confidence that we built in my classroom was an amazing thing to witness. The students showed me what it was like to go beyond surface learning and how to become a better facilitator of their learning.

> **Differentiation TIP:** Like Sophia, I always think: *How can I multiply myself as the teacher?* Frequently, I use video to record myself teaching a mini-lesson, showing students how to interact with a new learning center, or using it as a tool to differentiate instruction. It's incredibly easy to be in multiple places at once with video! And one of the best aspects about video is that the recordings we create endure.

If I'm creating a mini-lesson for students about how to document thinking in a podcast, I can share that video with students on a classroom website or in a learning management system, and students can access it whenever they need it. We all have learners who need the mini-lesson multiple times. For students who may be absent, they can return to class and watch the short mini-lesson video. Think about how powerful it is to invite students into the learning by saying, "Watch the ninety-second video and then come to the meeting area and we'll pick up where we left off." And for caregivers, how would at-home support change if they could watch a video on a classroom website and understand what was taught? On-demand learning through video offers young people instruction as they need it, offering equitable access to information.

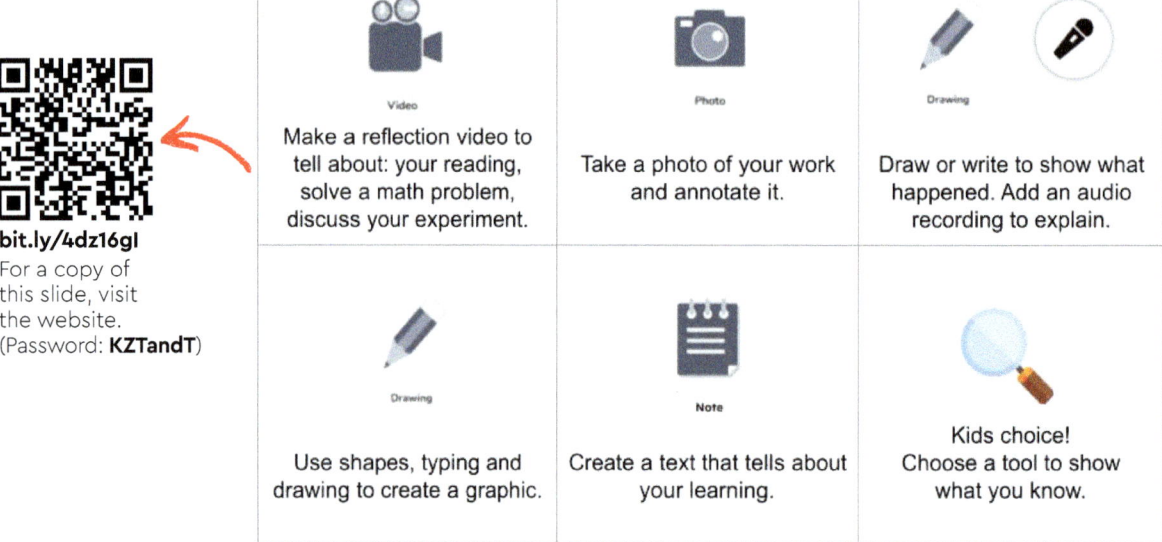

**bit.ly/4dz16gl**
For a copy of this slide, visit the website. (Password: **KZTandT**)

**Figure 3.20:** This digital response choice board offers students a menu of options to choose from when reflecting upon their learning. Students can select any mode to document their learning.

## The Active Body's Role in Cognition

There are many ways to track thinking with digital tools, but often, paper and markers are effective tools of technology as well. When we think about using laptops or tablets to gain access to digital content, and as we've observed students' attempts to navigate multiple tabs, we recognize that using digital for everything is rarely the best option. When we ask students to access information on a device, we often invite them to hold their thinking on a physical tool like a notebook or a thinksheet.

Looking back to the 4 E's of Cognition framework mentioned in Chapter 1 (p. 20), we now know that reading and comprehending is not only the result of what happens in our brain but the result of what occurs across multisensory inputs. When reading, we use our hands, fingers, arms, eyes, and head in a sophisticated fashion to interact with text. The physicality of reading requires sensorimotor interaction and cognitive skills. Think about a young person reading to gather new information: The student has text, a pen, and a notebook in front of them where they're documenting what they've read. They're sitting on a chair at a table and leaning into the text. Possibly they're interacting with multiple texts, or print texts and devices, as they highlight information and think through new ideas. A significant portion of the body is active in the reading process, illustrating the concept of embodied reading. With the notebook and the pencil, the reader is enacting with text as they write in the margins, highlight new information, or summarize an idea. The active engagement with the physical text is a way to slow down the pace of reading, to make space for reflection and inference, and to allow the reader time to think beyond the text to make meaning (Baron et al., 2017; Hillesund, 2010). Reading is a joint activity of the body and the brain (Mangen, 2016). From an extended cognition point of view, "the active body, the pencil, the text, and the device are all parts of the extended cognitive process" (Malafouris, 2013).

**Figure 3.21:** The active body in action. Headphones off to the side, this student reads a read-to-me ebook on Epic! As he reads, he taps the pause button to document his learning and questions on a thinksheet. He manipulates multiple pens and leaves his wobble stool to physically lean into the reading experience. This is cognition! To once again quote Malafouris, "the active body, the pencil, the text and the device are all parts of the extended cognitive process."

The 4 E's of Cognition framework helps us understand how our brains, bodies, environment, and tools work together to help us learn. We use this information to create learning conditions in which we apply the tenets of active literacy, multimodal, and multisensory learning to ensure that our students have all the opportunities to think deeply. As with many aspects of digital learning, it's about layering additional resources onto our robust repertoire of strategies to activate, extend, and capture student thinking.

## Doodles and Sketchnoting to Track Thinking

Many times, when we ask young people to read, listen, or view using a device, we also ask them to hold their thinking on paper. The paper is the physical space where learners can slow down their thinking. With labels, written text, and sketches, students can merge their reading with their thinking to capture new learning, reactions, and responses to the text.

In Carrie Baughcum's classroom, students are taught visual literacy lessons right from the start. Carrie recognizes how powerful thinking occurs when young people are afforded creative choice in how they demonstrate their understanding. Each year, she teaches her students how to sketchnote, a method of visual notetaking that uses hand-drawn doodles, captions, labels, symbols, and more to represent their learning. Not only does she leverage drawing and doodling, she establishes thinking routines that students can apply across the curriculum.

**Carrie Baughcum**

Carrie is an extended resource teacher, learning enthusiast and, most of all, a passionate believer that all children can learn; we just need to find out how. She infuses her classroom practice with creative thinking, boundless joy, and endless doodling. She is the author of *My Pencil Made Me Do It: A Guide to Sketchnoting* and *Stanley and the Very Messy Desk: An Adventure in Sketchnoting*.

## Carrie Baughcum - One of My Favorite Days of the Year: Introducing Sketchnoting

It's time to switch from math to social studies. I look at Tess and ask her to get our container of sticky notes. Then I look at Tom. "Take the table caddy and put it on another table please." I smile, make eye contact with Will, ask him to get the markers and notecards from the cabinet, and then I tell Jose to grab our Sketchnote Charter[1] from my desk. Today is one of my favorite days of the school year: the day we start our first sketchnote.

The rest of the students check the projected class agenda and join us in the front of the classroom with their pencils at the big table with the green butcher paper spread out on it. Tess hands the container of sticky notes to me, Will puts the container of markers and stack of notecards on the table, and then Jose hands me the copy of the Sketchnote Charter. We start by reviewing our Sketchnote Charter.

Each year for the last eight years, I spend time teaching students how to take in information with their eyes and ears, connect with the information by thinking about what is new, interesting, or makes them feel something and is on topic, and then write it in words, imagine it, and add a doodle to it.[2] I teach them how to sketchnote.

After eight years of intentionally teaching sketchnoting, each year how I teach it changes just a little.

---

1 According to the RULER Approach, a charter is a document that establishes common goals and a shared vision for a classroom or family community. The charter is created by the community, and everyone should be involved in the process. Students identify the feelings they want to experience and create action items to help uphold those feelings.

2 Kevin Thorn (*Nuggethead*) defined sketchnoting as "A form of Visual Writing by expressing ideas, concepts, and important thoughts in a meaningful flow by listening, processing, and transferring what you hear by sketching either by analog or digital."

Mike Rohde, author of *The Sketchnote Handbook: The Illustrated Guide to Visual Note Taking*, said, "Sketchnotes are rich visual notes created from a mix of handwriting, drawings, hand drawn typography, shapes and visual elements like arrows, boxes and lines."

Doug Neill of the Verbal to Visual website (https://verbaltovisual.com/) stated, "Sketchnoting is a form of note-taking, hence the 'noting' part of it, but as you might guess it involves bringing more visuals into the process compared to typical note-taking, hence the 'sketch' part. . . . The whole idea behind adding sketches to your notes is that it taps into parts of your brain that would lie dormant if you only use words to explore ideas. It's the combination of the two that's most powerful—using both words and visuals while taking notes."

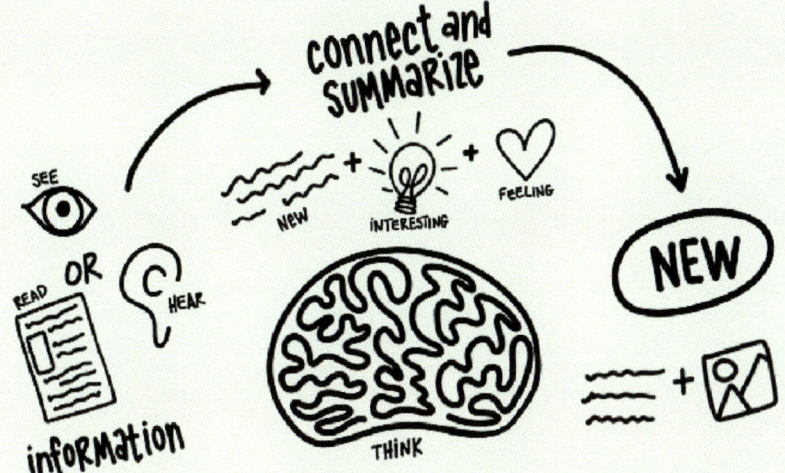

In the early years, I taught sketchnoting as an individual task, each student learning to sketchnote in their own space. We would each fearlessly dive into the process together (even if students would resist or I needed to adapt for students who were really nervous to draw). After we read, listened to, and looked at the information together, students would work to connect with the information, write it down on their paper, and then add doodles. Other times, we might spend time cutting up our notes, organizing facts, gluing and pasting them on the paper, and then adding doodles to the facts. And sometimes, students would write all the facts they'd connected with clumped up in one section of their paper and then add their doodles.

Today, we start our sketchnoting experience together. We sit at a large table, elbow to elbow. We openly prepare for and talk about our worries about drawing, and we share the learning and doodling experience together.

We read, hear, and see the same information, connect with it, then talk about it in what I call "family style" conversations (because we talk like we are sitting at the dinner table together. No raising your hand to talk; instead you wait your turn and then jump in). We share our connections and "ahas" openly, think about our thinking out loud. We collaborate, compromise, and have conversations about the topic and how we think we should build the sketchnote. Then we all doodle and chat together to finish it.

What hasn't changed after eight years—after all that time filled with new curriculums, administration changes, new students, district initiatives, world changes, different types of learners, and hours and hours spent learning and doodling together—are the timeless benefits and impact the sketchnoting process has on learning and teaching.

- Students learn how to intentionally connect with information, slow down, think about their thinking, and make connections that make their learning stronger and more solidified.

I think it's brilliant how Carrie introduces sketchnoting and launches it through collaborative annotation around a common text. This move is incredibly responsive to middle school students' insecurities as readers and artists. Carrie meets students where they are and supports their next steps.

It's important how Carrie:
- Plans before they start to sketchnote to allow students time to think about the topic and mentally plan for their visual representation.
- Encourages risk taking and ownership.
- Builds thinking routines and habits that students can come back to time and time again as they interact with content across the curriculum.

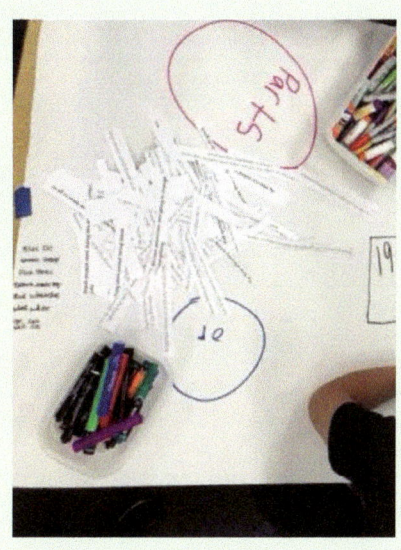

AGENCY AND ACTION: TRACKING THINKING AND LEARNING

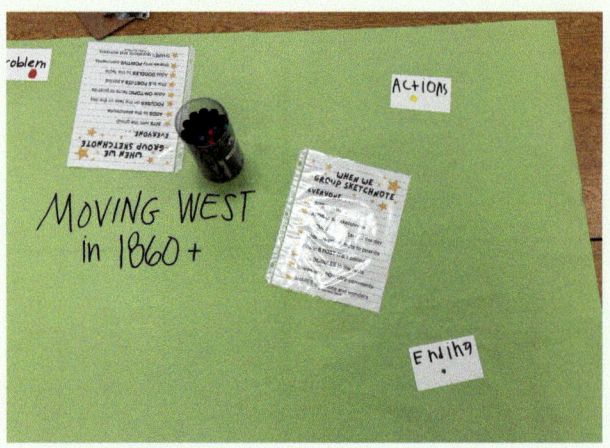

*During a lesson consider how you can teach, build, and practice thinking routines:*

*As you and students read or listen to information about a topic, routinely pause and ask, "What was new, interesting, or made you feel something (a strong emotion or an aha)?" Then write it down.*

*As you and students read or listen to information about a topic, routinely pause and ask questions that force students to visualize the information: what they wonder about the information, what connections this information has to them and their lives, what comments they have about the information.*

- Students learn to visualize their learning with doodles, which improves their comprehension and provides languageless support that enhances their memory and recall of information.

  *During a lesson, consider how you can teach, build, and practice visualizing and doodling routines. As you and students read or listen to information about a topic, routinely pause, ask, and doodle:*

  *"What do you imagine when I read that? What movie is playing in your head? Doodle that." (Students doodle.)*

  *"What do you imagine when I read that? What movie is playing in your head?" (Teacher doodles.)*

  *"What do you imagine when I read that? What movie is playing in your head?" (Doodle on sticky notes, notecards, in the margin of a paper, in between the lines of a paragraph, on the board.)*

*How can you use the doodles connected to learning to support students' conversations, recall, comprehension, idea production, writing process?*

- Students are empowered to try something new and different that gives them experiences and moments together and that helps create a space encouraging the freedom to take more risks.

    *Before a lesson, consider how you can create spaces and have conversations with your students that support visualizing and doodling routines, and then when you start sketchnoting with your students, sit down with them and join them in the experience.*

- Students learn how putting pencil to paper centers us, improves self-regulation, and increases our focus.

    *The singular act of pairing doodling with learning calms us, causes us to increase our focus, forces both sides of our brain to work together, brings motor planning and movement into the learning, and improves our overall feeling of happiness.*

    *Where else can you infuse the benefits of doodling into your classroom? Besides learning, where else can choices be given to allow its impact on regulation, calming, and improving focus to be used in your classroom?*

As I pass out sticky notes to each student, read the sketchnoting charter, and review our focus for today, I smile to myself thinking of the new additions I've made to our sketchnoting process. I hope they allow students to connect with the process even more. I press play on the video we are sketchnoting about, and with pencils in one hand and their sticky notes resting next to their other hand, my students look forward—because what hasn't changed is that we still get out our pencil and paper, we chat, we imagine the learning, we smile, we write, we doodle, and we sketchnote together every day.

AGENCY AND ACTION: TRACKING THINKING AND LEARNING   99

## Digital Sketchnotes

Many teachers also use sketchnoting as a means to capture ideas digitally. Using a simple drawing tool on a laptop or tablet, students can create sketchnotes in response to a video, podcast, or print or digital text. With a quick mini-lesson, students can use shapes, drawing, and short bits of text to capture new information.

| What Can You Sketch? | |
|---|---|
| Circle | A moon, a clock, a tire, an orange, a portal, a baseball, the sun, a planet, a pool float, a sign, a target |
| Square | A present, a pack of crayons, a car, an iPad, a laptop, a book, a cake, a pillow, a wallet |
| Squiggle | A road, a river, a path, waves, bushes, mountains, birds flying, footprints in the snow, a map |

### Sketchnoting in Response to a Video

I regularly use sketching as a means for students to hold their thinking when accessing a video to learn. When using a video with the whole class, it's a perfect opportunity to sketchnote digitally, as I can show the video on the projector and students can use their devices to capture their learning and questions. Video can transmit a significant amount of information in just a few short minutes, so when viewing to learn, we often watch a video more than one time. On the first viewing, students use a tool that allows them to sketch and type their new learning and questions. When we go back and reread the video a second time, I ask students to sketch in a different color than their first view. This helps me see where their thinking has changed with multiple exposures to the video text. The second viewing helps students build upon their thinking and often provides answers to some of the questions they had during the first viewing.

> We use a similar strategy when students are sketchnoting or annotating on paper. Whenever possible, we use markers or pens to archive thinking. Because they cannot be erased, markers give us more opportunity to see errors and changes in thinking. Something that a student crosses out signals, "I used to think___, but now I think___." Changes in thinking offer powerful insight into a student's process.

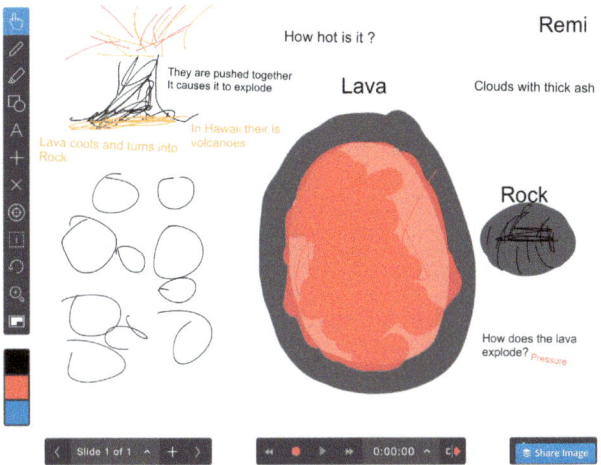

**Figure 3.22:** In this sketchnote, a student documents their initial viewing by drawing and typing in black. On the second viewing, the student uses red and orange text to document the additions to their thinking. Notice how the student asked, "How does the lava explode?" in the first viewing and found the answer to that question when interacting with the content a second time: "Pressure."

**Figure 3.23:** In Damani McClellan's sixth-grade classroom, students watch a video about Canadian Inuit dogs and document their understanding with sketches and text in Seesaw.

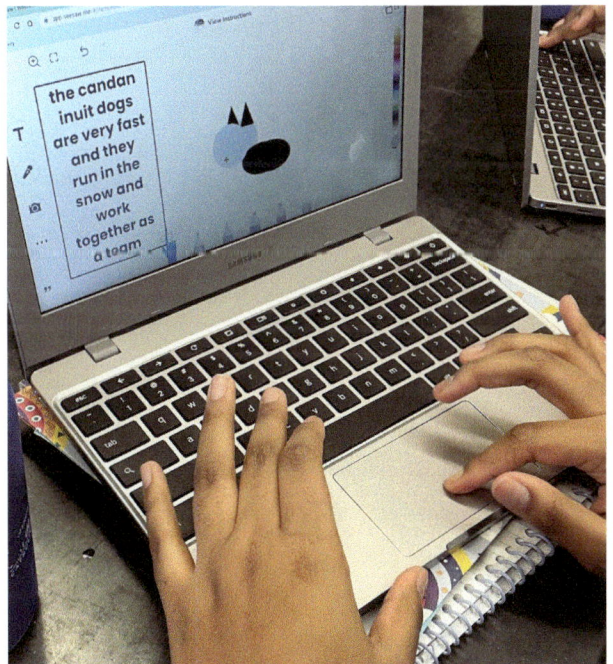

**Figure 3.24:** A student uses a series of shapes to sketch the Canadian Inuit dog. They summarize what they've learned using the text feature on the drawing tool.

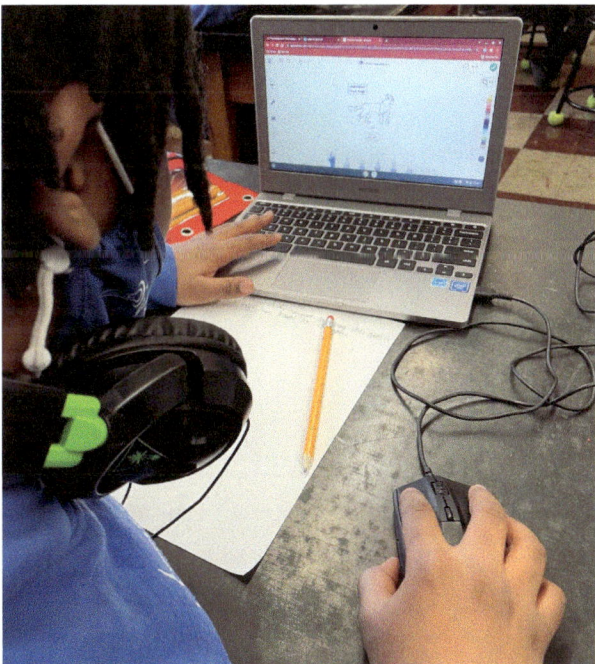

**Figure 3.25:** This student uses the drawing tools to create a detailed sketch of the Canadian Inuit dog. He uses labels to add detail to his drawing, pulling his thoughts from the notes he captured on paper while viewing the video—a perfect example of a young person using all the tools available to further understanding.

### Sketchnoting in Response to a Podcast

We're also doing a lot of sketchnotes in response to podcasts (Ziemke & Muhtaris, 2020). When listening to a podcast with headphones, students can sketch on their device, making the listening experience more active. We also listen to podcasts and sketch on paper, as it's important for students to know how to use all tools available to them.

**Shared sketchnotes:** Sketchnoting on a device increases the shareability of the note. When students post to a digital bulletin board space or a learning management system, they can view what and how their peers documented their understanding and learn from each other. These spaces also give authentic audience to their work.

**Figure 3.26:** Kindergarten students use Google's AutoDraw to represent the lifecycle of a butterfly. Working with a buddy, they used the digital markers and text, and a few figured out how to use the AutoDraw images in their work. With proper scaffolding and intentional partnerships, they were able to do this on their first day using a Chromebook!

The interactive nature of sketchnoting promotes active listening as young people tune in to new information, read with intent, and translate ideas into a tangible, visible artifact. When creating a sketchnote, students layer together visuals, texts, and concepts, requiring more cognitive lift than text alone, thus deepening interaction with the content (Pillars, 2015). Accessing auditory, visual, and kinesthetic processes, sketchnoting requires dual hemispherical thinking, resulting in increased blood flow to the brain and increased neurological synapses. As a result, students are able to learn, remember, and reuse information more effectively than accessing text alone.

**Try It!**

I invite you to take a moment and try your first sketchnote right now! It's important for us to learn alongside our students and to take risks, experience discomfort, and make plans for continued learning. Happy doodling!

Draw your sketchnote here.

## Power to the Little People

Technology in classrooms changes the conditions for all learners, but it might have the biggest impact on developing readers and writers. For students who are learning letters and sounds, decoding, and writing, technology provides a new modality for capturing and honoring their powerful thinking and learning. Whether a child is retelling a story with toys or building with blocks to create a city, we can capture the learning with a photo that signals to students that the learning they do in the classroom is valued and worthy of archiving.

The ease of use of a camera invites students to document learning in the moment and affords the students and the teacher a space to revisit the learning at a later time. The ability to look at an image and use it to remind a child of their learning promotes conversation and offers an opportunity to reflect on learning. We can enlarge the photo so that all students in the room can see another child's work. When we share a photo of a child's work, we can engage in conversation about the image, the materials, and the thinking behind the artifact. In doing so, we promote language acquisition and expression, build background knowledge, and expose learners to new vocabulary.

Photos in the classroom can also capture students collaborating, inquiring, and solving problems. The photos of students in the room build a sense of community, as young learners can see themselves and their peers working and learning together. As educators, we can leverage these photos as a means to have kids teach each other. When we ask "What can you learn from Davieon's photo?", we position students as the teacher and model for how we can learn from each other. This shared learning stance scaffolds and supports students, as young learners can build upon another's idea or attempt to craft a learning moment in the style of a peer: "I'm going to make a book like Davieon did!"

Photos become an easy tool we can use to document learning over time. A snapshot of a child writing their name or a drawing that shows a stick figure with body parts can be used to monitor progress. We can use photos as self-assessment tools, as they are concrete in nature and root a child's thinking in a tangible artifact they can react and respond to. And because photos are easy to share, we send them to caregivers and invite them to reflect upon a child's development.

Katie Keier engages her kindergarten students to document their learning across the curriculum. Early in the year, she teaches them how to use an iPad to take a photo and record a video and then entrusts them to capture, tell, and share their own learning journey.

**Katie Keier**
Katie has been a public school educator in grades preK–8 for over thirty years. She is passionate about play, equity, and access for all learners. She is the coauthor of *Catching Readers before They Fall*.

## Katie Keier - Turning Documentation Over to the Children

*We cannot see what is "out there" merely by looking around. Everything depends on the lenses through which we view the world. By putting on new lenses, we can see things that would otherwise remain invisible.*

— *Parker Palmer,* The Courage to Teach: Exploring the Inner Landscape of a Teacher's Life —

As a kindergarten teacher, I have multiple lenses through which to see myself, my children, their work, and our community. I also believe that children have multiple lenses through which they see themselves, each other, their work, and their community.

Every day, these brilliant five- and six-year-olds engage in story making during our Writers Playshop and math exploration during our Mathematicians Playshop. I spend much of my time observing, engaging in conversations, and playing alongside these learners as they make sense of their world. I take many photos, videos, and notes as I document their learning. But I also provide many opportunities and much encouragement for children to document their own learning. I start by taking photos and videos as children share their stories and their thinking, but I quickly turn it over to them. They learn how to use the iPad to document their own stories through video and photographs. They choose which images are shown on the projector as they tell their stories and share with an audience. Their voices and how they capture their learning give me a new look at how they are growing as readers, writers, and mathematicians.

By turning the documentation over to the children, we get a chance to see the world through their eyes. We see their interpretation—unclouded by our lenses—as they capture the moment, tell the story, and share it with their peers. All voices are heard and elevated, growing confidence with our multilingual learners, developing oral language and communication skills and honoring their voices and thoughts. This is possible through trusting children, honoring them, and believing that they are capable—not only with the tools but with sharing the brilliance of their thinking and learning.

> I appreciate how Katie is an expert kid-watcher and carefully observes students to know where they are developmentally, academically, and socially. Using photos, video, and audio recordings, she documents students' growth and experiences.
>
> What resonated in Katie's article is how she:
> - Creates space for playful learning across the day.
> - Supports learners to independently and collectively build knowledge.
> - Empowers students to curate their learning journey.

**Figure 3.27:** Children often collaborate on a story together, using loose parts to create a story. When they finish their story, they can get their iPad and take photos or a video narrating their story. This is then shared out during our sharing time at the end of Writers Playshop. When children have ownership over their documentation, it allows us to see deeply into what they are thinking without our adult interpretation getting in the way.

**Figure 3.28:** The children use the photos they take to share their stories as they are projected onto our SMART Board. This can be done in addition to a paper book they have written or as a standalone story. They use the images as the "illustrations" for their stories. The children own the story, the documentation, and the sharing and have a strong sense of agency throughout the process.

**Figure 3.29:** Children have access to a large variety of "loose parts"—materials that can be moved, repurposed, redesigned, transformed, and imagined as endless items. They use their imagination along with these loose parts to create stories with characters, settings, problems, solutions, and all the other elements of stories. Each object serves a purpose in the stories, and children joyfully tell their stories with the loose parts serving as an incredibly detailed "illustration" and window into their thinking.

**Figure 3.30:** Teachers also take photos or videos as we observe children and listen to their thinking. This documentation is then shared out to the whole group, and the author invited to describe, storytell, or elaborate on an idea. The rest of the class serves as the audience, asking questions and giving compliments—similar to a traditional sharing time at the end of Writers Playshop.

**Figure 3.31:** Children are trusted to use their devices as they see fit to document their learning and their stories. They decide if photos or videos are best, and they practice making their documentation look how they would like for it to look. Giving them the responsibility for documenting and believing they are capable of capturing their thinking allows for us to truly see the world through their eyes.

**Figure 3.32:** Children writing nonfiction, or "learn about the world" texts, can use videos to learn more about their topic. These videos inspire them to play the story out with loose parts, act it out with their bodies, and then write what they learn in their books.

**Figure 3.33:** We use many "languages" to tell stories in our classroom, and the light table is another space to create a story. Using texts, loose parts, and our imagination, many stories are made, played out, and then put into a book.

Photos and documentation are not only for developing readers and writers! Photos can be used across the curriculum to benchmark growth, as a tool to promote collaboration, or as a means to document a process. Using a device, the overwritability on an image means that now we can annotate anything we snap a photo of! We can annotate text, a classroom project, the cover of a book, a graphic, and much more. Here are a few easy ways to use photos with older students:

- Take a photo of your right-now book and post to a digital bulletin board. Share a bit about the book.
- Take a snapshot of a piece of text or an anchor chart in the classroom. Add your annotations to show your understanding.
- Document the weather each day by snapping a picture out the window. Annotate it as part of your morning calendar routine.
- Take a photo of a frequently used website and have kids annotate the digital features. What is the purpose of a hyperlink? How do we interact with the text below an image? Students need to understand digital features and their purposes in order to effectively use and comprehend web content.
- Drop a photo into a tool like Seesaw. Annotate the image and add an audio clip to further explain your thinking.

## The One Hundred Languages of Children

We recognize that learners have many ways to express their brilliance. As educators, we meet them where they are and invite them to be active agents in their learning journey. We honor student choice and seek additional opportunities for learners to interact with the world. Classrooms that support student agency leverage all tools available and marry traditional and digital tools to gain robust insight into a young person's thinking and learning.

Using tech to track thinking and learning helps us document a child's lineage of thought. The emergence, development, and evolution of ideas, concepts, and skills can be traced back to their origins through multimodal artifacts. We can identify how text, multimedia, experiences, and even peers influence one's journey and how ideas are transformed, adapted, and refined over time. Learning is not a linear process but a messy one. Photos, annotations, sketches, student writing, video, and audio samples are all authentic, student-created tracks of thinking. They serve as puzzle pieces we can put together to understand the whole child. They may not be a perfect expression of a concept or idea, but they are powerful snapshots of a young person's thinking. We value powerful learning over perfect learning.

**Share what you tried!**

Have you implemented a lesson or idea from the book? If so, head to the community space on the website and share what you tried. We'd love to hear about what worked for you.

bit.ly/4dz16gl
(Password: **KZTandT**)

**bit.ly/4dz16gl**
Visit the website to hear Kristin share more about Chapter 3.
(Password: **KZTandT**)

# Putting It into *Practice*

### 1. Collaboratively annotate a text digitally.
- Using Slides, take a photo of a text or infographic and insert it on a Slide.
- Share the Slide deck with students. Quickly model how they can use the text box to add their thinking to the Slide deck. Show how to adjust the size of the text and change the color.
- Copy the Slide if needed so that all students have enough space to add their thinking.
- When done annotating, reflect! Discuss the text, student thinking, and how ideas may have changed as they processed information together.

### 2. Model a video reflection for students.
- Using the built-in camera on a laptop or tablet, create a video that you can use with students as a mentor model for reflecting upon learning. You may want to model something that you will do regularly with students like a book talk, sharing new learning or questions, or holding up a thinksheet and talking about it.
- Keep your video between 30–60 seconds, as videos this length are easy to upload and easy to review when submitted by students.
- Review the video with students and analyze what you did to craft a quality video. Chart student responses for them to reference when creating their videos.

### 3. Teach a lesson on sketchnoting.
- On chart paper or on a digital drawing platform that is projected for students to see, begin by drawing simple shapes and asking students to brainstorm what you could make with that shape. Thinking about how shapes can represent objects offers an entry point to sketching.
- Model how you might use labels or thought bubbles to add words to your drawings.
- Ask students for additional ideas as they come up with the best suggestions!
- Find a high-quality informational picturebook or a short video from The Kid Should See This and have students view the text and respond with a sketchnote.

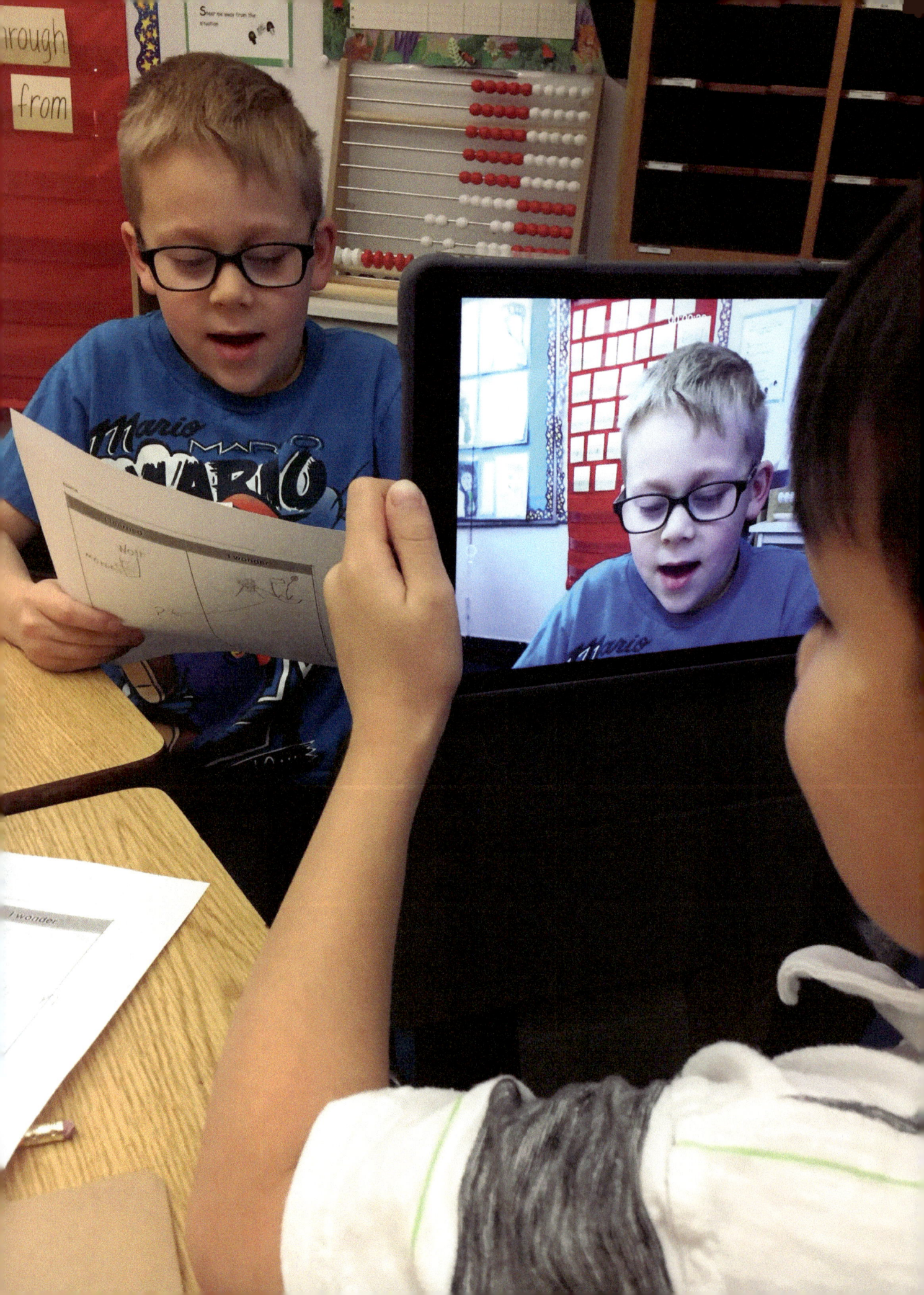

# — CHAPTER 4 —
# Embedding Digital Tools to Enhance Conversation, Collaboration, and Comprehension

*"I remember when we went to the zoo on a field trip at my other school, and all us kids were being so loud! I think we were excited or something, but I didn't think about how we were disturbing the animals."*

*Fifth grader Roberto shares with his small group after reading an article in opposition to Hong Kong's Ocean Park extending the visiting hours for their newly born resident panda twins. Roberto and his inquiry group are reading about baby animals who have reached internet fame as a result of their zookeepers and social media.*

*"Yeah, I saw where Albert wrote, 'If they're in a zoo, they can't have peace, and they can't have privacy,'" Stephanie comments. "I think all the people might scare them."*

*Using a digital bulletin board, fifth-grade students in Bernado Wilson's classroom access a variety of media posted to a digital bulletin board. Photos, newspaper articles, video clips, and live cams all help students build background knowledge of the power of social media, the challenges to zoos today, and how animals frequently fall victim to human interest and profits.*

*After viewing the multimedia sources, students reacted and responded in writing to what they learned. By typing on a digital bulletin board, students could interact with the information and each other at a pace that met their needs. Instead of immediately launching into a spoken conversation, the written conversation afforded students time to think. Working and writing collaboratively around the classroom, students could share their thinking in real time, read the reactions others had to the text and media, and revise or refine their thinking as they learned more. Contrary to what typically happens in small-group work, where one or two students do most of the talking and, as a result, most of the thinking, the independence afforded by this online conversation ensured that every member of the group had purpose and was reading, writing, interacting, and thinking.*

> **TIP:** You can also have a written conversation on chart paper or copy paper! Written conversation was originally designed for paper-based response, and it's a highly effective strategy for slowing down and organizing thinking prior to a verbal discussion. I originally learned about this strategy from Harvey "Smokey" Daniels. Check out his book *The Curious Classroom* (2017) for more on this concept.

**Figure 4.1:** A student accesses images, video, and text and adds their thinking to a digital bulletin board.

*Early on in their collaborative conversation, students shared what they liked about the animals or questions they had. "Why are they so wet? And why is he so loud?"*

*As they read more and learned more, the tenor of their conversation deepened. Questions like "Do the animals want to live there? How do they feel?" were shared with the group.*

*After reading about the pros and cons of zoos and an op-ed written by a sixth grader on why zoos should be shut down, students began to advocate for action in support of the animals.*

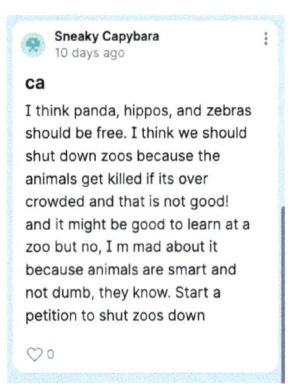

Sneaky Capybara
10 days ago

**ca**

I think panda, hippos, and zebras should be free. I think we should shut down zoos because the animals get killed if its over crowded and that is not good! and it might be good to learn at a zoo but no, I m mad about it because animals are smart and not dumb, they know. Start a petition to shut zoos down

♡ 0

Thoughtful Kangaroo
10 days ago

**sh**

I hate zoos! Now I know they are bad. I can't believe they would kill the living curters and not return them to nature. I will take actshon on this.

♡ 0

Thoughtful Kangaroo
10 days ago

**sh**

I'm mad about it and I never new about it! I'm so upset and I will do somethig.

♡ 0

I think zoos are bad because they kill the animals after there are adults. They use them for entertainment only. many people believe zoos are unethical since animals have suffering in captivity. They have a bad habitat, which causes them stress. They also can't run far

♡ 1

*When they finally gathered to discuss their research face-to-face, the inquiry group had a lot to say.*

*"I used to think that it was cool to see posts about little animals online. They're cute and stuff, but when I read that zoos only post about them so people will visit and buy merch and give money to the zoo, that changed my mind," remarked Albert.*

*"Yeah!" agreed Stephanie. "It's so wrong! Like, we know dolphins are really smart and can communicate and all sorts of things. Other animals are probably really smart, too.... They have to know that people are looking at them all the time, and they have to feel something about that."*

*"I used to think zoos were cool, but now I don't. It's sad how they get rid of animals if they don't have space for them anymore," added Roberto.*

*"People, we have to do something!" Cherie chimed in.*

Through written and in-person collaboration, students constructed knowledge together. Through a layered approach of digital text, images, and video, students gained access to a topic they never knew about. With time to read, process, and respond independently, then time to build additional thinking collaboratively as a group, students challenged each other to engage with the topic and take action.

## Benefits of Written Conversation

- Students have time to interact with and respond to information.
- Each student is engaged! No longer is the child who raises their hand quickly the only one who gets to share; instead, everyone is responding and, as a result, thinking at the same time.
- Written conversation provides an archive of the thinking and learning that takes place, and it is easy to go back to at a later time.
- It increases writing production as students respond without even realizing they're writing a whole sentence, phrase, or idea.
- It helps students build upon the ideas of others. When a child can read what another has written and say, "Kristin said it's hard to decide because you have to consider both sides, but I disagree because . . ." then they have ideas to build upon, furthering agency, understanding, and collaboration. The time to reflect allows the student to construct knowledge and own the thinking.

> **TIP:** When I do written conversation on paper with students, I have each student write in a different color marker. This helps me to track who wrote what during the conversation. I use markers because I don't want students to erase their ideas; I want to see how and when they change their thinking. Instead, I teach students to draw a line through their previous idea, noting the change so that we can see the evolution of their thinking. Learning is dynamic, and we acknowledge and embrace that.

When we present information through multimedia sources, provide different viewpoints on an issue, and afford students time to interact with the media, the ideas, and each other, students are able to process the information to build new understanding. Oftentimes, it leads to a change in thinking as students revise their ideas based on their new learning. Changes in thinking lead to powerful conversations as students share: "I used to think _____, but now I think _____." Helping students identify and name how their thinking has changed engages them in metacognitive thinking, guiding them to understand their process, monitor comprehension, and gain independence for future learning.

## Not What You Know, but How You Interact

bit.ly/4jO7d2q
The World Economic Forum (WEF)

In the white paper *Defining Education 4.0: A Taxonomy for the Future of Learning*, the World Economic Forum (WEF) identifies a comprehensive set of skills, attitudes, and values to prepare young learners for well-being in the economies of the future (2023). In their report, they identify the abilities and skills most sought after by employers as communication, creativity, collaboration, creative problem-solving, and critical thinking. As tech takes over more and more manual tasks, the human role shifts to focus on interactions with people, strategic problem-solving, and creating new value for society. To support these changes, the Organisation for Economic Co-operation and Development (OECD) challenges schools to be hubs for collaboration, continually contributing to and being influenced by the wider ecosystem. When innovating for the future, our schools need to focus less on one's ability to remember knowledge and information and more on one's agency, well-being, and interactions. By laying a strong foundation for communication and collaboration, young people will have the interpersonal skills needed to adapt to the dynamic learning and working conditions ahead. The future will be defined by one's ability to harness technology and each other to communicate and collaborate.

> **Did You Know?** The Foundation for Young Australians predicts that young people will have seventeen jobs over five different careers in their lifetimes! (Foundation for Young Australians, 2017)

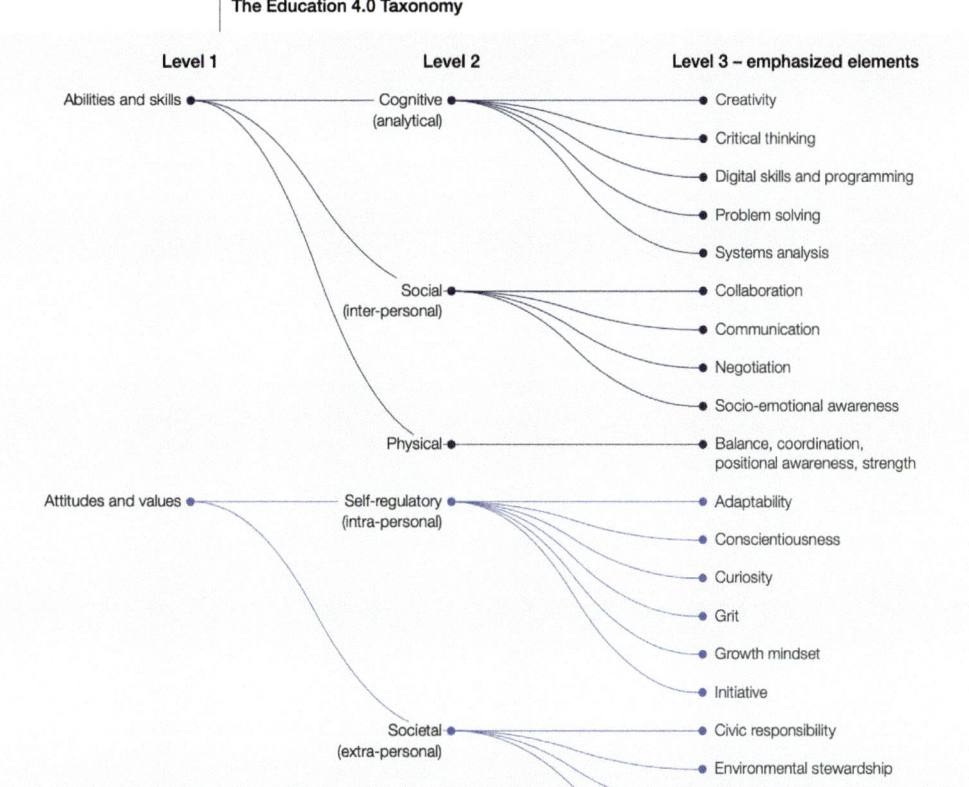

**Figure 4.2:** The World Economic Forum's Education 4.0 Taxonomy: The three groups of aptitudes identified are abilities and skills, attitudes and values, and knowledge and information. Moving left to right, the aptitudes are broken down into more specific indicators. The global community of employers, futurists, and experts identify abilities and skills, and attitudes and values aptitudes, as those that will have the most importance moving forward. In the far right column, you can see the behaviors that yield high value in the future.

The knowledge and information aptitude at the bottom suggests that new technologies have changed how people interact with information. The emphasis shifts away from what people know and instead focuses on how they access and use information and interact with others moving forward.

Digital tools in the classroom offer a multilateral approach to communication and collaboration. We can use technology to inspire writing, analyze text more intimately, and archive ideas and conversations. We expand our written conversations as we "talk" with chatbots or write prompts in AI. We collaborate in virtual spaces through typing or speech-to-text, in comments, and via video messages. We interact in side-by-side settings in the classroom as well as in online spaces after the bell rings. Today's learning ecosystem allows us to listen, share, create, collaborate, and communicate beyond the school day.

The students who Stella Villalba works with know that the way she listens to them is an act of love. Stella leans into every conversation she has with students and honors their lived experience and their current identities. Her respect for students' stories is unparalleled; Stella carefully gleans student stories for nuggets she can use to match them to texts, to inspire them as writers, and to support their humanity.

**Stella Villalba**

Stella respects each learner as the brilliant humans they are. She believes that being multilingual is a tremendous gift, and it's through those lenses that she teaches, listens, writes, and leads every day. She collaborated with Katie Wood Ray on the 2025 edition of *Wondrous Words* and is the author of the forthcoming book *Tell Me More: Conferring with Artists, Writers, and Storytellers* (2025).

I respect how Stella intentionally slows down to know learners and makes space for their struggles, joys, and the stories of their hearts.

What stood out in her article was how she:
- Plants the seeds for stories.
- Expands the definition of mentor text to include any written form of text, image, or video.
- Uses personal artifacts to connect readers and writers to their lived experiences and to inspire their next story.

## Stella Villalba - Using Photos as a Bridge

Trey enters the classroom with a photo album under his arms and a big smile on his face. As he crosses the classroom door, he simply cannot wait to tell me about the photos he has. I understand the magnitude of this simple moment because when children feel they can bring parts of home to school, it's because they feel safe, seen, and valued. These feelings grow from the intentional seeds planted in the classroom community—listening when students share, slowing down to respond in affirming ways, following up with students. When students share their stories, it is crucial that as educators and as part of that classroom community, we receive them with the care and respect that were given to us. When Trey brings photos from home, he is giving me a peek into his world. Little by little, he shares stories—with caution yet with care and hope.

We live in a world where stories are valued more than ever. And yet I must also acknowledge how listening to students' stories is a privilege. Students do not owe me any stories. I feel incredibly honored with every narrative they want to share with me. I'm certainly reminded of this as I am learning how important Trey's dogs are in his life. He feels joyful in their company. He feels rewarded by their love. How do I know this? By the photos he shares and the ways his face lights up when he talks about his dogs. Just a couple of days ago, I didn't know much about him, his life, about what brings him joy. Thanks to Trey, I can extend these connections in many different directions.

One way I can extend and connect these conversations with Trey is while conferring during Reading Workshop. Every encounter with a child brings me closer to their humanity, their lived experiences. I protect these *conversaciones del corazón* because it is through these dialogues that I understand the reader in front of me. Conferring with Trey, getting to know him first as a child, provides the foundation from which I can build. At the beginning of the year, I had yet to earn Trey's trust. Yet. It all changed when he showed up at school with a maroon photo album. Out of this precious album of memorias y recuerdos, Trey pulls two photos. I sit next to Trey, and like I do with every conferring, I get out of the way and he leads the discussion. Trey talks about his best friend, Tiko. Tiko is his dog and loyal friend who "keeps him company" in the afternoon, especially after school. "Tiko is smart. Tiko understands everything around him." He pauses and I get to ask him, "What makes you happy, Trey?" Trey is quiet for a moment and then responds, "Tiko makes me happy." He points at the photo and adds, "He does. He makes me happy because he plays with me. I am not alone. He plays with me. Every afternoon."

Trey reminded me of the natural order of learning and life. We read and write from our experiences with the world:
- What makes me cry?
- What brings me joy?
- What memories do I want to tell aloud?
- Are there books on this topic that I can explore?
- Are there other readers in the classroom I can connect with on this topic?

Personal photos are such a beautiful invitation to confer with students on. From this precise conference with Trey, a series of fortunate literate events followed. Before this moment, it was a challenge for me to connect Trey with books and authors. Now that I understood more about him first as a human being, I was able to support him better as a reader.

I needed to remind myself of the powerful influence of visual literacies in reading workshops. An image, whether digital or printed, can become a catalyst for deeper conversations. I am now able to nudge Trey with book choices and reading partnerships. Some of the book recommendations include:
- Diary of a Pug series by Kyla May
- Henry and Mudge series by Cynthia Rylant
- Stick Dog series by Tom Watson

Following my conversation with Trey, I write in my journal the following:
- Spend time while conferring learning about students' lived experiences and how they shaped their becoming a reader.
- Understanding what makes a student soar with joy is crucial to foster caring relationships.

**Figure 4.3:** Visual literacies play a significant role in connecting with readers in the learning community.

**Figure 4.4:** Learning about Trey first as a person helps us connect with him as a reader.

Trey reminds me of the power of visual literacies and its influence in the becoming of readers and writers. He reminds me that if I am going to read books as mentor texts, I should explore what pulls at a child's heart. Trey also reminds me that mentor texts include not only books and any text in the written form, but it also includes photos, pictures, images, and videos. Trey teaches me that when I cultivate and nourish learning spaces where a child knows he would be heard, then maybe he would share more parts of his identities with me next time, one moment, one photo, and one conversation at a time.

There are many ways we can approach students' stories with the same care and attention that Stella approached Trey's. Try this when looking to uplift your students' stories:

- Slow down in order to hear students' stories.
- Listen with a loving heart.
- Respect what each learner brings to the table.
- Make time to follow up. A face-to-face conversation is most impactful, but you can also use a video message or digital conversation to circle back with students.

## Knowing More about Students through Written Conversations

Years ago, Smokey Daniels (2017) taught me that you have to know your students in order to teach them. Knowing students provides insight into who they are as learners and as humans. When we know their interests, personal stories, details about their home life, sports teams, favorite books, hobbies, and fears, we demonstrate our respect and lay the stepping stones to developing a relationship with students. We have to have a relationship with them before they can truly care about what we're trying to teach them.

A few years ago, I took a mid-year position to support young people in an English language arts sixth-eighth split-grade classroom. Due to unfortunate circumstances, the students had already had three previous teachers that year. When I entered the picture, they were certain that I would only be there for a short time, too. The first few days were challenging. They were frustrated by another interruption to their learning. They didn't want another set of new rules, routines, or assignments. I understood their reaction toward me and knew it would be important to hear from them and respond to their needs.

I started each day by asking a question as part of their morning soft start. Using Google Forms, I posted a question and asked them for feedback. Day one, I asked, "What's your favorite book?" Day two, "What are two things you want to learn this year?" I started with relatively simple questions for two reasons:

**bit.ly/4dz16gl**
A link to this form is available in the Chapter 4 resources.
(Password: **KZTandT**)

1. I wanted them to learn how to use Forms. Forms is a versatile tool teachers and librarians can use to gather information and feedback from students. From morning social-emotional learning check-ins to reading logs, this tool is easy to use and efficient. Each day I added a new form to Google Classroom so they could become fluent with the tool.

2. I wanted students to know that I valued their ideas and feedback. Rather than being a teacher who told them what to do and what to learn, I wanted them to give guidance as to where they thought we should go with our learning. Daily feedback from students would become a part of our routine.

> **TIP:** Google, Microsoft, and Canva all have free forms tools for you to create surveys or gain feedback from students.

bit.ly/4dz16gl
A link to the "10 Things Your Teachers Should Know about You" form is available in the Chapter 4 resources on the website. (Password: **KZTandT**)

The following week, students knew how to navigate the form and started to provide more information in their responses. Toward the end of the week, I shared a form, "10 Things Your Teachers Should Know about You." The form offered ten short-answer response boxes for students to share their thinking. Students typed a variety of responses that you might expect to receive from middle schoolers:

> "I like to sleep."
> "I love Greek Mythology!"
> "I just turned 12."
> "I'm on the basketball team."

They also shared details that provided a new lens for me to look through and helped me to understand them in and beyond the classroom.

> "I use both of my hands to draw and write."
> "I'm an aunt."
> "I can't see, and I need glasses!"
> "I'm always hungry."

Several students revealed significant information about themselves and their relationship with school.

> "ELA is my least favorite subject."
> "I might present as a happy student because I'm well behaved, but inside, I'm bored to death."
> "And also, to all the teachers, no one cares how much you know until they know how much you care."

When we ask students and when we show that we are truly listening to who they are and what they need, young people are incredibly candid in what they share.

There was one student, an eighth-grade boy, who gave me pushback the first few days we were together. When I asked him to find a place to sit, he muttered responses under his breath that made the other kids giggle. When I asked him what he wanted to read, he replied, "Nothing." When we walked through the hall to lunch, he walked thirty paces behind the class, forcing the group to wait for him. I knew there was more to his story, but I didn't know what it was, and I struggled to connect with him.

It was the weekend before I had time to review students' responses to the "10 Things Your Teachers Should Know about You." I read in wonderment as I learned all sorts of new information about students that helped me to put together the pieces of their puzzle. And when I read what the student who was challenging me wrote, I learned so much. His first response was "That I love my family," followed by "I like basketball." What he wrote next made my heart hit the floor.

"I wanna be loved."

"I wanna be something in life."

IM GOING TO DISNEYWORLD in 2 days
I love Musical Theatre
I like playing fighting games
I just turned 12
I have two siblings.
Im on the basketball team
That i like getting As
I am 5'6 and 1/2 inch tall
That i love my family
my top three favorite rapper's are lil darkie, freddie dredd, and licu4
That i love WATER
I have 4 siblings encluding my 3 Godsisters
I love Dolphins and other animal's

My birthday is a day after cinco de mayo
I have a sister, as well as a half-sister
I different kinds of noodles/pasta
I have 4 siblings
I have a kitten.
I love deep dish pizza
That King Von is my favorite rapper
My Grandmother on my mom's side actually met Muhammad
i wanna be loved
i like to rap
I only have 3 favorite teachers
I'm the youngest sibling
I like writing book's because it's very fun and helpful

im 12 1/2!!
I love Greek Mythology
I like transformers
I have a dog
I love jewelry.
I like video games
That i like basketball
I use both of my hands to draw and write.
I like basketball
that i like to play with beyblades
I DON'T EAT CHICKEN
I love dogs
I have one brother

I have a bakers dozen friends c:
I an aunt
my favorite type of food is hibachi
My favorite color is purple
I'm a September Virgo.
I like gizzard
That i love my family
I am turning 13 in 6 days
I wanna be something in life
i like to watch cartoons
I only have 10 friends and 3 best friends
I have too many kid friends..
I love the 90's even though I wasn't born in it

These two short phrases said so much. Here, a fourteen-year-old boy is telling the stories of his heart. How he's seeking love and striving for more. The false front that he displays before his peers is a mask for his true feelings and insecurities. His words showed me that he was seeking belonging, meaningful relationships, and security. The following morning, I went to the principal and asked for insight on this child. I learned that his grandfather, who was his primary caregiver, passed away the previous year from COVID-19. The information the principal provided and what the student wrote—what he wanted his teachers to know—guided me to see that he needed a much different approach. I acted responsively, and together, the student and I worked to identify and support his physical, emotional, and academic needs. All because he was able to tell his teachers what he truly needed.

When we ask students, when we make space for spoken and written conversations, and when we listen to the stories they have to share, we learn more about who they are as people, what their identities are, and we can respond to their dynamic needs. Beyond what they need to learn, we can learn what they need to exist and thrive.

When we listen to student needs and preferences, we hear their human story. We can adjust our curriculum and make it about them. We can use their feedback to support the whole child and to match them to books, articles, websites, and multimedia that inspire them to read, research, and think even more.

## Enhancing Conversation and Collaboration around Books

We often overlook that books are amazing tools of technology. Books are the original game-changer, the OG of technology tools, that changed the conditions for learning. We continue to elevate the prominence of books in our classroom by pairing them with devices that yield a value-add to how we read, think, and interact around texts.

With a few simple adjustments, such as enhancing the size of a book with a document camera or using an ebook during a read-aloud so that everyone can see and interact with the text, we create a read-aloud experience that is more collaborative, inclusive, interactive, and thought-provoking as all students can view, listen to, and converse about the text. As a result, students engage in a deeper reading experience and build understanding through the shared process of meaning-making.

In Ann Marie Corgill's fifth-grade classroom, students build knowledge collectively through interactive read-alouds. When readers can investigate different styles of texts and genres together, rich conversation ensues.

**Ann Marie Corgill**
Ann Marie currently teachers fifth-grade students in Alabama. She has worked in education for the past thirty years and supports numerous initiatives to enrich teacher learning through NCTE. She is the author of *Of Primary Importance: What's Essential in Teaching Young Writers*.

### Ann Marie Corgill - Enhancing Read-Alouds with Digital Tools

Digital tools allow us to explore different text types and genre characteristics while at the same time providing opportunities for rich conversation and an enhanced interaction with a text. Almost every day for the past thirty years in the classroom, I've witnessed the power of reading aloud to students. Cheers erupt when it's time to gather together, listen, and have a conversation about the latest book or award-winning title by a brand-new or longtime favorite author. What I hadn't explored until recently was how to enhance conversation and comprehension around a text by simply putting a book under the document camera or sharing an ebook version on the board, projecting the pages for the class to focus on and study together as we read.

Projecting the pages of a book gives students an up-close look at the words and pictures and gives me the opportunity as their teacher to focus my teaching on one particular aspect of the text.

For example, while reading aloud Jerry Craft's *New Kid*, I was able to support students in their understanding of how to navigate the frames

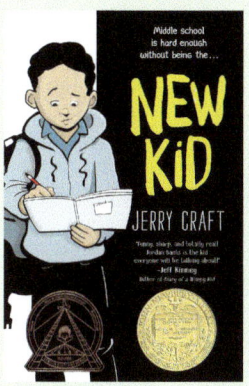

in a graphic novel. Where do your eyes go first? How do I read across the page or over a two-page spread to make sense of the events and actions of the characters throughout the story? How do the illustrations match or enhance the words in the talk bubbles? Is there a separate storyline in the pictures that's not directly stated in the text? Questions like these foster more conversation with the text digitally projected, and students can easily see what they might otherwise miss if I just read the book aloud without the "up-close" digital text image.

Ann Marie offers a simple way for all to read deeper: enhancing the size of a text. This easy adjustment yields opportunities to extend conversations about books and to gain new insight into an author or illustrator's perspective and intention.

I love how Ann Marie focuses on conversation as she:

- Uses enlarged illustrations to promote collaborative conversation with students.
- Crafts questions to guide new perspectives and enhance comprehension.
- Engages readers to collectively annotate a selection of text.

When I read *Odder*, a novel in verse by Katherine Applegate, I also gathered students together around the document camera and Promethean Board. Students were able to follow along and see how my voice, intonation, and intentional pauses matched the poetic structure on the page. We were able to explore the format and differences in how readers comprehend a novel in verse compared to a narrative text. Projecting the pages of the text also allowed us to easily annotate and highlight unfamiliar or interesting words. The time we took to stop, highlight, and talk about these interesting (or confusing) words and phrases ensured all students were comprehending both challenging and interesting vocabulary while making meaning as we read together.

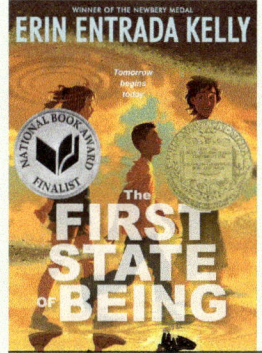

While reading, *First State of Being*, the Newbery Award-winning title by Erin Entrada Kelly, the kids wanted to know before we even opened the book, why this book was chosen for the 2025 Newbery Medal. What did Erin Entrada Kelly do as an author to draw so many readers in and get the vote of so many librarians on that Newbery committee? My students couldn't wait to dive into the text and find out for themselves what made this book THE book to read this year! From the first page, we were intentional about examining why this book won the Newbery Medal. Over the course of the novel, the children became fascinated by the inserts, written in different fonts and seemingly separate from the narrative chapters. However, upon closer examination, we recognized after projecting these "different additions" that each insert prepared us to understand the next chapter or chapters more deeply than would have otherwise been possible if the insert hadn't been there. If I had just kept reading and didn't call the kids attention to these "inserts," we might have missed the rich conversation and annotation of the text that organically began to happen. Kids could have been easily confused by my reading because these parts were definite departures from the regular narration, and the visual projection called our attention to this pattern Erin Entrada Kelly so intentionally placed before and after many of the chapters throughout the book.

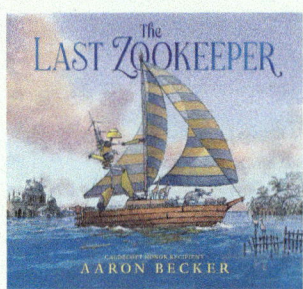

One more way I've found to use digital projection to enhance understanding is by projecting wordless picturebooks for class conversation and study. We recently spent several days "reading the illustrations" in Aaron Becker's wordless picturebook, *The Last Zookeeper*. Zooming in with the document camera is also a wonderful way to call students' attention to the details of art, photography, and illustration techniques. Rich discussion ensues and new ideas emerge every time we look closely together.

Studying text up close and annotating our questions, noticings, and meaning-making is a valuable skill that students can transfer to their own independent reading and reflection.

Ann Marie uses digital tools to enlarge text as a means to read closely with students. This shared reading experience slows down the reading process by directing students to spend time in the details. Specifically, with poetry and graphic novels, the reader needs to linger in the drawings, line breaks, layout, and word choice to understand all the aspects that influence the meaning of the text. With careful questioning, Ann Marie guides readers to unpack the text and learn from each other.

The questions she asks promote conversation as students notice drawings, speech bubbles, and foreshadowing frames because the text is more visible. If this is new to you and your students, start discussing the text with planned conversation breaks through turn-and-talks. As students become more familiar with the close viewing of text as a routine, the conversation will flow more naturally. When we ground conversation in a tangible text, students' initial conversations and interactions are rooted in the text. Language like "I see" or "It says" directly pulls from evidence within the text. As the conversation progresses, students make inferences and predictions, ask questions, and insert their thinking about the text. Comprehension deepens on the coattails of collective conversation as students build upon the ideas of others, clarify understanding, and think beyond the text. Discussion that includes language like "This reminds me of" or "Where else might we see this?" are all ideas crafted in student experience to think beyond the text.

It isn't only read-alouds that are powerful when projected on a screen; we use this with infographics as well. I love to increase the size of infographics when teaching students how to analyze these often complex data representations. With a document camera or by projecting a digital graphic on screen, we can zoom in on a chart or diagram to get a close-up look at the information or data set. Just as Ann Marie did with the frames of a graphic novel, we can help students navigate directionality and how to read a graphic by collaboratively thinking through and discussing the text.

Ann Marie celebrates reading through daily read-alouds and by fueling a book buzz among students. By elevating the reading experience with high-quality texts, she helps students see books as a source of excitement, joy, and endless discovery. When we build a book buzz, we create excitement that is palpable and contagious.

We build a book buzz by . . .
- Staying informed of new texts that appeal to the age of the readers we work with.
- Offering a preview of a book through a book talk. Regular book talks by teachers inspire students to try out a new title.
- Reading published book reviews and rankings with students. *The New York Times*, *School Library Journal*, and *The Horn Book Magazine* all publish reviews that can be shared with students. Knowing how to use a published book review as a tool for finding a new book is incredibly helpful.
- Sharing book trailers of soon-to-be-released titles. Young people love a preview, and the gratification delay that comes with waiting for the publication date of the book will have them counting the days until its release. Readers can also make their own book trailers and share their favorite texts with an audience of their peers or schoolwide.

**TIP:** When to project a book using an ebook or document camera to further collective conversations:
- When you want to closely read illustrations and collaboratively analyze the setting, examine characters' facial expressions, look for clues, or note foreshadowing.
- To illuminate how line breaks and punctuation influence the expression and tone of a poem or verse.
- To analyze text features such as captions, diagrams, maps, and graphics in informational text.
- In wordless picturebooks, photo anthologies, and graphic novels, images and illustrations tell much, if not all, of the story.
- To afford students a view the text while listening to the read-aloud.
- To promote conversation and discussion among students about, within, and beyond the text.
- To annotate a text collectively as a class or small group while students question, respond, and build upon each other's thinking in a projected piece of text.

**Did you know?**
69 percent of infrequent readers report that parents, caregivers and teachers underestimate how hard it is for them to find books to read. (Scholastic, 2025)

**bit.ly/3RFmR4k**
View the book trailer for *Below the Ice*.

**Figure 4.5:** Amanda Berger shares the book trailer for *Below the Ice* by Michaël Escoffier (illustrated by Ella Charbon) with her kindergarten students. She builds excitement for the book prior to the read-aloud, and her students carry that energy forward as they interact with the text through drawing and conversation.

Teachers like Ann Marie and Amanda, who demonstrate enthusiasm for books, shape positive reading habits and cultivate a vibrant reading culture that learners want to be part of!

Shameer Bismilla, a teacher you met in Chapter 2, is one of those teachers who leverages his passion for reading to motivate his students. Each year, he celebrates books and brings new ideas into his classroom to instill a love of reading in his students. With purposeful engagement across powerful texts and planned student-to-student collaboration, young people in Shameer's classroom learn more about themselves, each other, and local and global issues to better understand the human story. Through digital discussion, conversations with authors, and collaborative meaning-making, students develop rich comprehension strategies that support them to keep thinking.

# Shameer Bismilla - Digital Tools for Comprehension

**Shameer Bismilla**
Shameer is a grade 3 teacher in Singapore and is the coauthor of the picturebooks *The Boy and the Box* and *The Girl and the Box*.

Comprehension in our classroom is never just about answering questions at the end of a chapter—it's about sparking curiosity, making connections, and engaging in conversations that bring learning to life. I've found that when students have the opportunity to collaborate, share their thinking, and build on each other's ideas, their understanding deepens in ways that no worksheet ever could.

Over the years, I've watched how discussions—whether in small groups, on digital platforms like Padlet, or even through creative projects—turn reading into a shared experience. I've seen students light up when they discover a book that reflects their own experiences or when a classmate's insight shifts their perspective. I've also seen how technology can open new doors for collaboration, giving every student—whether the quiet thinker or the outspoken sharer—a voice in the conversation.

Below, I'll share some of the ways I've fostered comprehension through collaboration—how book talks, digital tools, and interactive reading experiences have helped my students engage more deeply with texts. My hope is that these ideas inspire new ways to make reading meaningful, relevant, and, most of all, a joy filled journey for your students.

> Shameer expertly balances text and tech. He recognizes the importance of multimodal learning and guides students through the delicate dance of consuming and creating to learn even more.
>
> In this article, I notice how Shameer:
> - Supports students with a scaffold for interaction as they learn to offer feedback.
> - Uses digital written conversation to discuss texts, test new ideas, and construct meaning before students' in-person conversations.
> - Lowers the walls of his classroom by inviting authors and caregivers to share in the reading experience.

## Book Talk and Connections

For a unit on heat, students explored nonfiction texts using digital tools like Padlet and ebooks. They crafted thin and thick questions, collaborated on ideas, and created posters to visualize their understanding.

Padlet became an essential tool for collaboration. Students used it to share their questions, post drafts of their posters, and provide feedback to their peers. Through the BAG feedback framework—**B**egin with a positive comment, **A**sk a question, and **G**ive a suggestion—students engaged in meaningful discussions. The asynchronous nature of Padlet allowed them to reflect thoughtfully before responding, ensuring feedback was constructive and encouraging.

The use of digital tools like Padlet and ebooks not only enhanced collaboration but also made nonfiction reading more engaging. Ebooks allowed students to explore topics independently, while Padlet gave them a platform to connect, share, and learn from one another. This integration of technology motivated students to approach nonfiction with curiosity and enthusiasm, transforming it into a dynamic and purposeful part of their reading journey.

**Virtual Author Connections**

One of my favorite activities has been connecting students with authors online. Hearing an author's perspective often deepens students' understanding and appreciation for the text. When we connected with a local author last year, the students were thrilled to hear about her writing process and ask their questions directly.

**Digital Tools for Conversation**

I've used platforms like Padlet and the Sketchy School app to empower my students to create their own anchor charts and discuss texts asynchronously, fostering a sense of community and engagement. After reading, my students shared their reflections on how their books acted as windows, mirrors, and sliding doors in their lives (Bishop, 1990).

One of my favorite responses came from a student who chose the book *They Call Me Teacher*. He described it as a "window" because it allowed him to learn about the historical injustices faced by people of color and reflect on his gratitude for living in a more inclusive and equitable society. This thoughtful reflection not only sparked a rich discussion around inclusivity and kindness but also inspired his peers to think more deeply about how literature can open their minds to new perspectives.

Through these digital tools, students were able to interact and exchange ideas in a way that made their learning visible and collaborative. By connecting their personal experiences with the stories they read, they deepened their understanding of themselves and the world around them while learning the power of literature to foster empathy and community.

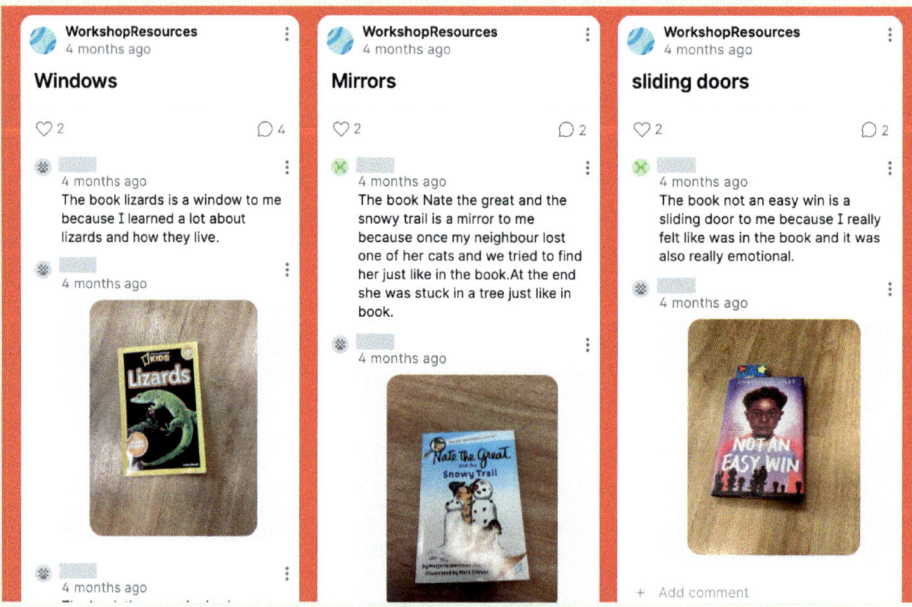

**Figure 4.6:** Using Padlet, students collaborate and share their favorite books, offering recommendations to their peers. Through their reflections, they make connections—seeing books as mirrors, windows, and sliding doors to new experiences. A wonderful way to build a community of readers who inspire each other!

### Reading across Content Areas

Using digital tools like Epic! and Newsela has transformed how I introduce age-appropriate science articles to my students. Topics like heat became more engaging as students connected their reading to real-world issues. Inspired by the articles, my students showcased their learning by creating vibrant posters that
demonstrated their understanding of heat. These activities not only deepened their comprehension but also sparked creativity and excitement for both reading and science.

### Fueling Joy in Reading

Our poetry celebration was a heartwarming journey into creativity and connection! Students crafted beautiful ode poems dedicated to their parents, placed them in jars as keepsakes, and shared their heartfelt words during a special reading. Using tools like Book Creator, they e-published their poems, allowing parents to explore both physical bound copies and digital versions. These moments capture our ultimate goal: making reading and writing personal, joyful, and deeply meaningful for every student.

In my classroom, fostering a love for reading goes beyond assigning books; it's about creating experiences that ignite curiosity, self-reflection, and joy. By engaging my students in interactive activities and crafting displays that inspire, we've transformed reading into a meaningful journey.

Each of these activities nurtures a space where students see themselves reflected in stories while discovering the stories of others. It's about connecting, learning, and growing as lifelong readers and thinkers.

**Figure 4.7:** Students use large format documentation as they create a poster to represent their learning. Students use all tools available: an iPad, markers, poster paper, and pencils to gain new knowledge and keep thinking.

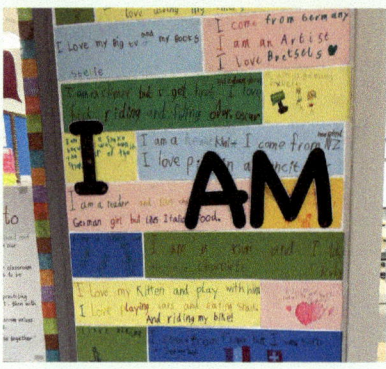

**Figure 4.8:** The "I Am" wall is a collective declaration of who we are, inspired by books that encourage self-awareness and self-love.

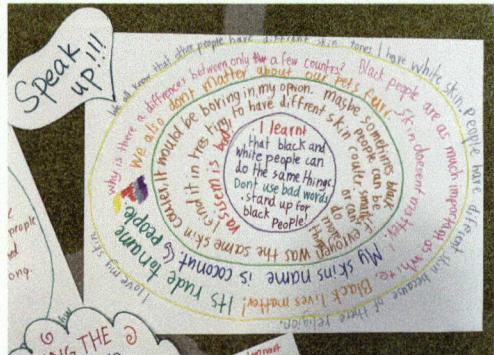

**Figure 4.9:** Diving into *Our Skin* by Megan Madison and Jessica Ralli, students collaborated in discussion circles to express their thoughts on race, acceptance, and equality.

Shameer offers terrific ideas for promoting conversation, collaboration, and comprehension around texts. It's as if he says, "Here are a few things that work for me; maybe they'll work for you too!" As he does with his students, he invites us to give it a try.

You've read ideas from Shameer, Ann Marie, Stella, and Kristin thus far in this chapter. Take a moment to reflect on your reading. What might you try with students?

## Play for Powerful Production

Play versus learning is a false dichotomy in education. Similar to how text and tech have been wrongly positioned in opposition, play and learning go hand in hand. In fact, play is learning, and it may be the most powerful tool we have to think critically and gain new understandings. When young children experience playful learning, they benefit from enhanced problem-solving, communication, decision-making, and creative skills (Neuman & Freschi, 2023). Play leads to complex interactions with others, helping learners build relationships while also building their brains (Harvard, 2019). In middle school, play-based learning can help students remember new material and transfer their learning from one context to another. Play empowers young people to guide their own learning, understand their emotions and the emotions of others, and embrace a culture of collaborative learning (Ross, 2023).

When teachers connect learning goals to play, students flourish. Providing all learners time to discover, iterate, think critically, and interact, especially when doing so with others, personalizes the experience for individuals and results in curious, engaged learning.

By maximizing children's choice, promoting wonder and enthusiasm for learning, and leveraging joy, playful learning pedagogies support development across domains and content areas and increase learning relative to more didactic methods. (Zosh et al., 2022)

In his grade 2 classroom, Gary R. Gray Jr. couples rich curriculum with playful pedagogy to help his students discover the magic of words. Through interactive stations that appeal to a range of modalities, students explore the elements of poetry. Gary's hands-on, collaborative learning approach helps students learn by doing and from each other.

**Gary R. Gray Jr.**
Gary is a grade 2 teacher from Canada currently working in Singapore. He supports students to use story as a vehicle for understanding oneself and promoting belonging. He is the author of the picturebook *I'm From* and the forthcoming *Spendin' Time* (2026).

## Gary R. Gray Jr. - Beyond the Rhyme: Teaching Poetry for Liberation

What's good, y'all?

If you know me, you know I'm all about words. I love playing with them, moving them, twisting them, and letting them flow. Growing up, I was told to write like a robot: perfect grammar, boring sentences, and "academic."

That wasn't me,
I talked like my grandma,
Uncle Hank,
Aunt Marlene,
which was perfect enough for me.

This year, I'm back in grade 2 (after eight years), and my first thought was how do I help these kids discover the magic of words? To me, poetry is like a playground for your mind. It's a place to be free, to express yourself, and to see the world in a whole new way.

Poetry can do so much more than just rhyme. It offers us a channel to:

- Express our emotions: Whether we're feeling happy, sad, angry, or confused, poetry allows us to give voice to our feelings in a creative and meaningful way.
- Open our eyes: Poetry can help us to see the world differently, challenging our perspectives and inspiring us to think outside the box.

I appreciate how Gary intentionally plans for multimodal learning that affords all students access to the unit. He leans into what young learners can do today as he plans for what they might be able to do next.

In his article, I respect how Gary:
- Identifies writing as a powerful act.
- Encourages student writing in all shapes and formats.
- Values writing production over spelling and grammar accuracy.

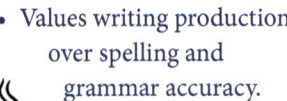

- Build connections: Poetry can help us to understand and empathize with the experiences of others, fostering a sense of community and belonging.
- Sharpen our minds: Poetry can challenge us to think critically, analyze complex ideas and text, and consider different perspectives.
- Strengthen communication: Poetry can help us to develop clarity, conciseness, and effective use of language.

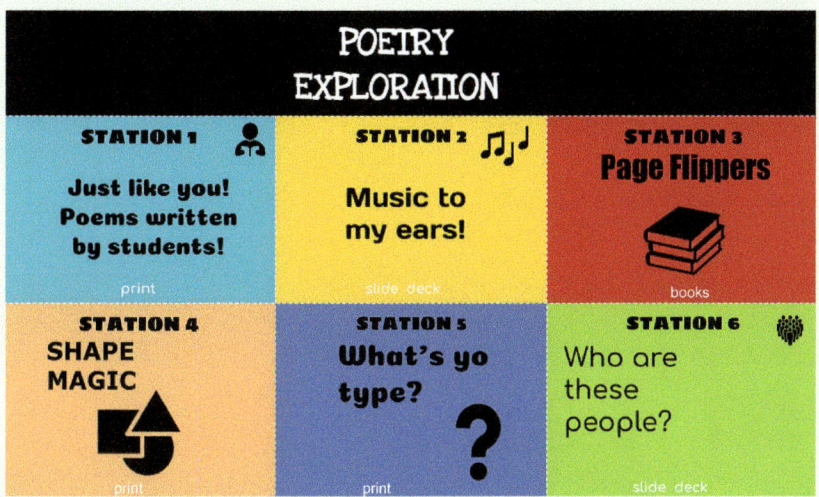

**Figure 4.10:** Stations students explored during exploration.

To help my students explore the world of poetry, I created a series of engaging stations.

- **Just like you!** Poems written by students! Read poems written by students from past years and watch slam poetry performances.
- **Music to my ears!** Listen to songs by Katy Perry, Bruno Mars, and K'naan and analyze their poetic elements.
- **Page flippers.** Read books like *Love* by Matt de la Peña and *The Day You Begin* by Jacqueline Woodson.
- **Shape magic.** Explore poems that are shaped a little different.
- **What's yo type?** Explore shape poems, haiku, list poems, and more.
- **Who are these people?** Learn about Langston Hughes, Xu Zhimo, and Ho Xuan Huong, and read their poems.

Each station was designed to spark curiosity and encourage exploration. Students worked together in groups, sharing their thoughts and ideas on anchor charts. They focused on three specific questions throughout:

- What makes this poetry?
- What is interesting about this piece?
- What emotions or feelings do you experience?

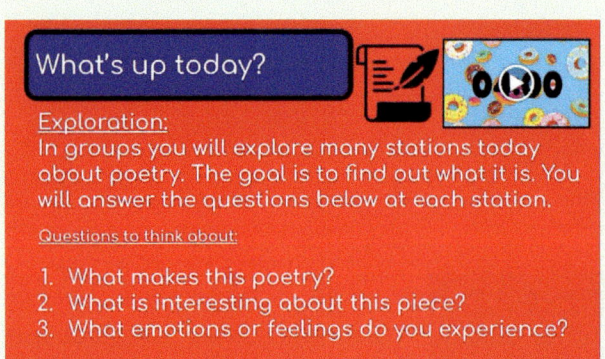

**Figure 4.11:** Slide that shares what students will do at each station.

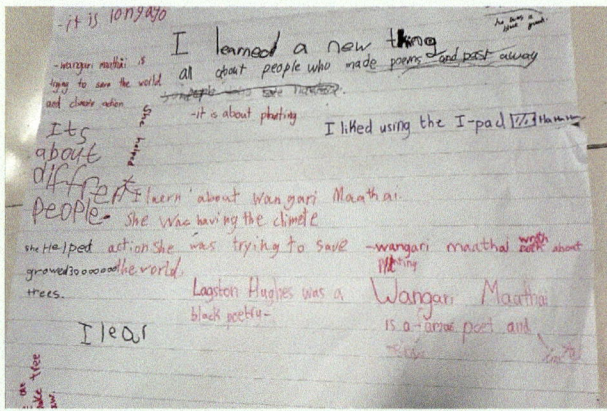

**Figure 4.12:** Student response to Station 6.

After completing the stations, we had a class discussion in which students shared their observations and insights. We realized that poetry is more than just rhyme, a riddle, or a cute phrase. It's a way to express yourself, to have fun, and to see the world in a new light.

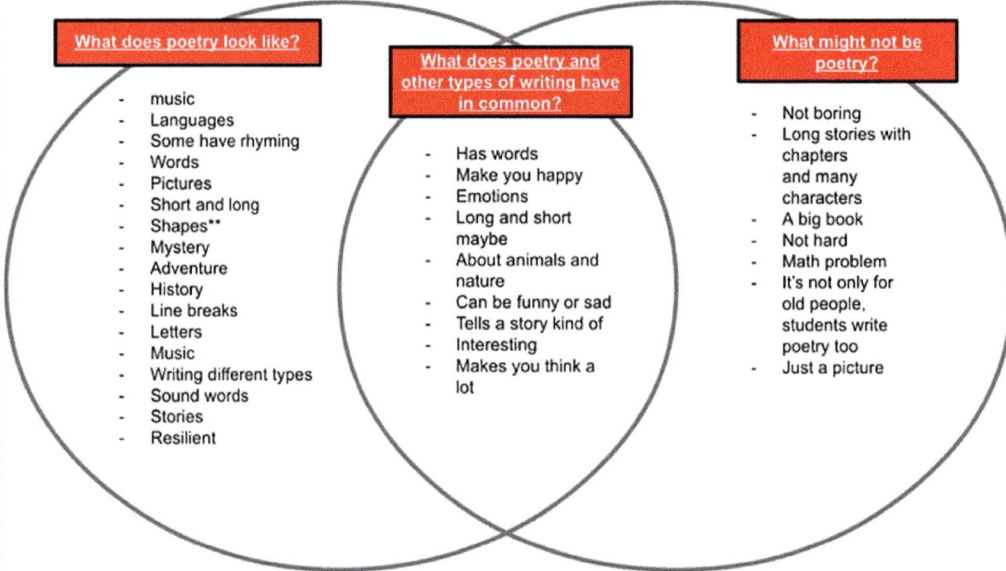

**Figure 4.13:** Venn diagram of class discussion after poetry exploration.

One of my students asked, "Gary, I thought poetry was just rhyme? It's also about song and shapes?" And I was like, "Exactly, my dude! Poetry is about expressing yourself in many ways, and being you on the page, and having fun, and seeing the world in many ways. Forget about the spelling (for now); just get your thoughts out the way you want to."

I was excited to see these kids discovering the power of words early on in their writing journey, which was unlike my own journey when I was their age. This discovery helps you connect with yourself and others, tell stories, and make the world a better place.

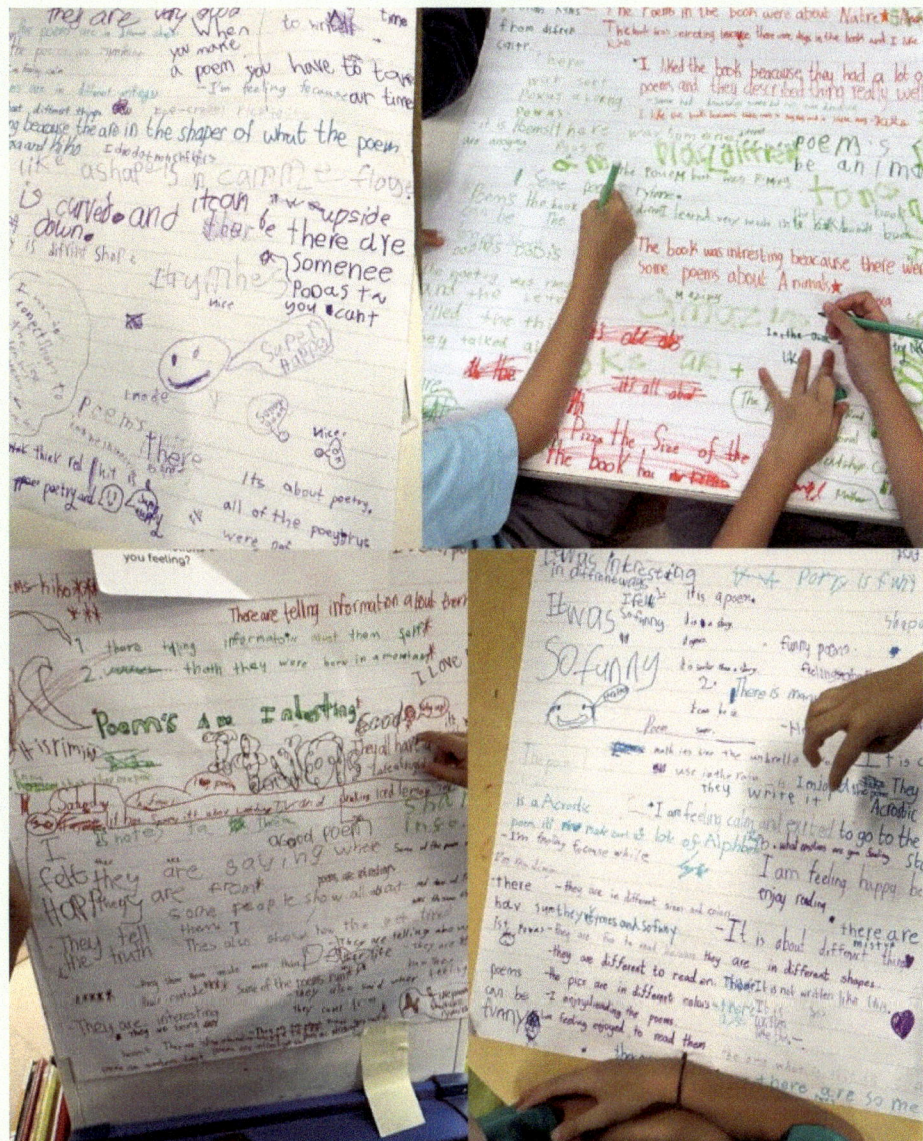

**Figure 4.14:** Student responses to exploration stations.

Poetry is a gateway to liberation. When we allow students to "write" the way they want to, it can transform their mindset. They begin to see themselves as writers and young authors, and they become capable of expressing their thoughts and feelings in meaningful ways. This confidence can have a major impact on their overall self-esteem and relationship with words.

I strongly believe that spelling and grammar are important, but first, build a love for the pen to the page and self-expression. It will give them the freedom to try new things, play with words, and empower them to become lifelong writers.

Poetry is personal growth, self-discovery, and social change.

Poetry is everything.

Let's let the kids play with words.

Our kids need poetry and play more than ever. With increased stresses on community, school, and family systems, there is less time and fewer resources to support play and creativity. While children are born with an abundance of creativity and are always willing to learn, unlearn, and relearn, school often reinforces compliance and rewards students for reproducing the established wisdom of our times (Vincent-Lancrin et al., 2019). Emphasis on high-stakes testing in the last few decades have resulted in a push for increased academics at a younger age, threatening children's right to play, particularly for young people in under-resourced communities. All children should be afforded opportunities to play, regardless of their racial group, socioeconomic class, or disability, if they have been diagnosed with one (Zosh et al., 2022). Dr. Peter Gray advocates that play is a natural, essential process for children to learn and thrive, leading to happier, more resilient, and creative individuals (TEDx Talks, 2014). Alero Akuya of the LEGO Group argues, "Play is more than just fun; it's the key to unlocking essential life skills and fostering a more inclusive, joyful world" (2024).

> **Did you know?**
> Two in five families lack access to adequate play environments or safe spaces for playful activities. (LEGO Group, 2024)

Play promotes student-to-student collaboration. Play is a platform for conversation. Play promotes questioning and enhances comprehension. Reflecting upon the research behind play, what we know about developmental appropriateness, and Gary's article, let's work to allocate more time to support and extend play.

## Teaching Collaboration and Conversation

In a perfect world, students would enter our classrooms with effective collaboration and conversation skills. Learners would know how to work with a partner or in a small group, share materials, and equally support the workload. Kids would communicate effectively and with kindness. Students would listen, offer feedback, and build upon the ideas of each other. They'd have the skills to disagree agreeably and come to shared understanding. These types of interactions are certainly possible, but they often require us to explicitly teach our students how to converse and collaborate effectively.

Lessons in conversation and collaboration need to be taught every year. Even if young people had lessons on interaction in third grade, they need to be taught again and have time to practice the skills in fourth grade. As students grow, their needs change. They advance intellectually. Their bodies and hormones develop. They may experience a shift in caregiver support, living situation, or job security. As they get older, the complexity of the tasks and interactions require greater cognitive lift. As a result, students' brains are occupied with the content and the task at hand and less with how they communicate and collaborate. All of these factors influence a young person's ability to interact with their peers; therefore, we need to teach and support these skills year to year.

Angelique Trevino develops lessons and designates time to teach her students how to converse and collaborate in face-to-face and online settings. In doing so, she safeguards instructional time, ensuring that students' interactions are meaningful and supportive throughout the year.

## Angelique Trevino - Conversations with Care: Guidance for Online Interaction

**Angelique Trevino**
Angelique is a third-grade ESL educator in Austin, Texas. She is an educational technology specialist and is passionate about teaching students to navigate the world on- and offline. She loves to share her interests and curiosity with students as she learns about them.

Third-grade students are always eager to learn. Whether researching extreme weather or posting about the book they are reading, they dive into learning with all they've got. Every day, they bring passion and energy to our classroom environment. We regularly share, reflect, and make plans for future learning together. It is important that all students learn how to interact with each other in multiple contexts and across diverse learning spaces. We discuss regularly how we treat each other both online and offline, focusing on the differences and similarities between them. These discussions often take place during morning meeting or class meetings, if we need to have extra time.

In class, we treat each other a certain way, especially when it comes to sharing our ideas and work, but students spend such a substantial amount of their time in virtual spaces that it's important to have conversations to address how we treat each other in online spaces.

For this lesson, I start with a question like, "How do we treat each other in the classroom?" Or "How do we expect to be treated in the classroom?" We create an anchor chart together with their ideas; these often read very much like our classroom rules from the beginning of the school year. Students come up with their answers for this pretty quickly and freely—they have made "class rules" so many times by this point in their third-grade lives that they know exactly what to say.

I admire how Angelique centers her students by responding to their needs in class and in online contexts. Even when students are not in school, she wants them to interact safely and communicate effectively.

In her article, I notice how Angelique:
- Shares personal experiences of communicating in online spaces.
- Uses anchor charts to scaffold virtual and face-to-face conversation.
- Names the similarities and differences between the two.

> **How do we treat each other in the classroom?**
> - Keep hands to self (even at recess)
> - Be kind/nice (includes teacher)
> - Be safe
> - Help new students
> - Ignore when necessary
> - Stand up for each other
> - Help others
> - Don't take things w/out permission
> - No trash talk
> - Include each other
>
> **Why do we treat each other well?**
> - It's the rules
> - It keeps us safe
> - So we can be friends
> - To avoid hurting each other's feelings
> - Stronger friendships ↳ TRUST
> - So we can learn
> - So we can be in the same space
> - Kindness

**Figure 4.15:** How do we treat each other in the classroom and why?

At the bottom of the anchor chart (or on a new chart if I need more space), I ask them, "Why do we treat each other that way?" My students usually have a variety of answers:

"Because it's the rules!"
"Because I want to be nice!"
"Because my mom told me I can't be mean!"

But the next question is a little more complicated for them: "Why exactly do we have the rules we do? Why do we have to be respectful to each other and take turns?"

We make a new anchor chart for a new conversation: "What are the rules for texting, group chats, and gaming?" I know for a fact that most of the students in my class are gaming online at home, and many of them have cell phones with group chats and messages from classmates and other friends. At times, in the past, conversations from their group chats have filtered into the classroom and can be a source of friction between students. While I have no say in what they chat about outside of school, I really want students to think about why those spaces have rules, too.

To illustrate this, I often share that I play video games, so they are aware that I have some experience with online gaming, and this encourages them to open up and really talk through what they perceive are the "rules" for this online space. I also like for them to think on the questions, "Who made these 'rules'? How do you know the 'rules'?" Then, like the previous chart, I also ask, "Why do we have these rules?" and I write down students' responses.

When we have finished, we look at the two charts side by side. I ask students, "What do you notice?" They point out the items that both lists have in common: being kind, being respectful, etc. We talk about how these rules affect our classroom community: When we share our ideas and our creations, how does the language we use affect our classmates' willingness to be open with us? Can we learn the same in a space where we don't feel safe to share? We discuss how the things we learn in class—and how we expect to treat each other and

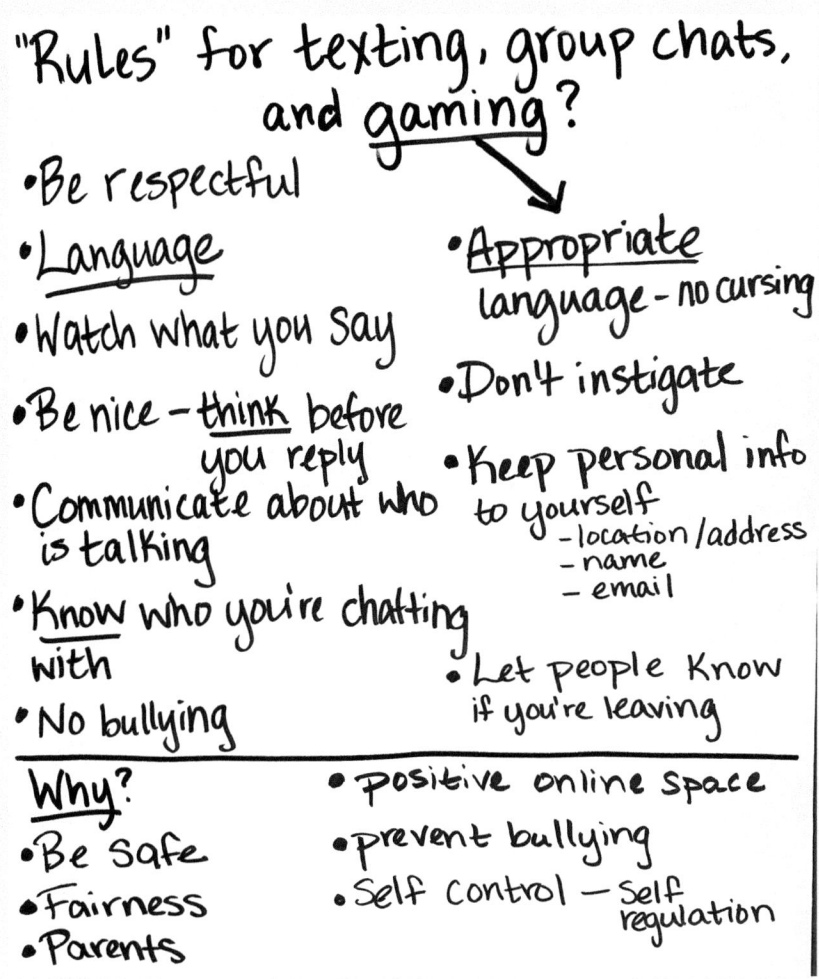

**Figure 4.16:** How do we treat each other online?

expect to be treated—can also apply in some way to their personal online lives. You want to be respectful both in person and online if you expect others to be cordial with you. If you want someone to be friends with you, speaking to them kindly will be more effective than yelling and being mean to them. If you want someone to play with you, you have to take turns and be fair (i.e., when it comes to a soccer ball or some in-game loot).

Once students see the connection, they may start to apply some of what they learned to their online spaces. In class, we sometimes use discussion boards, and that is a great place for them to practice their digital citizenship skills. They're pretty silly with it at first, but they enjoy being able to communicate with each other and read each other's writing. They can also create posters to share their new knowledge, putting a physical marker to the previously unwritten rules of their online spaces.

Angelique's students gain scaffolds and strategies for in-person and online conversations, supporting their digital citizenship skills and ability to communicate effectively. By cocreating norms for interaction, Angelique uses conversation and collaboration to honor students' ideas and implement an agreed-upon standard for interaction.

## Conclusion

The skills we previously referred to as "soft" have now become the desired aptitudes and attributes we need in order to sustain our ability to create, communicate, think critically, and interact as citizens of the world. *Forbes* magazine writes "soft skills are the most important and hardest skills to build" (Wells, 2024). Rebranded as "power skills" in the 2022 Udemy Workplace Learning Trends Report, these skills will support young people as they encounter new technologies in the future. It's not so much what they know but how they can communicate ideas, receive information and feedback, and share as a collaborative member of the community.

bit.ly/4dz16gl
View the "Then They Came for Me" Padlet on the website.
(Password: **KZTandT**)

# Putting It into Practice

1. **Engage your students in a written conversation using a piece of chart paper.**
   - Position four students around the paper, giving each a side of the paper to write on.
   - Using a picturebook, article, or piece of multimedia, provide a shared text for them to respond to.
   - Engage students to write for a few minutes. Then, instruct them to turn the page a quarter-turn so that another student's response is now in front of them. First, have them read what their classmate wrote. Then, have them respond in writing.
   - Continue to do this until the paper has rotated around to all members of the group. Once students have read and responded to all members, invite students to engage in a verbal discussion about the text and their thinking.
   - After students have engaged in verbal discussion for a few minutes, invite them to go back to the chart and add any final thoughts to their written conversation.

   *You can also do this with a piece of copy paper by having two students work together on the same paper.*

2. **Ask students to share the ten things they want you to know about them.**
   - Create a form or make a copy of the form shared on the website.
   - Share the form with students and ask them to respond.
   - Set aside time to review their responses.
     Note: For younger students, have them record a video that tells you 3–5 things they want you to know about them. Regardless of age or ability, it's important to ask students what they want you to know.

   *If a form is not an option for your students, create a handout on which they can write the ten things they want to share with you.*

3. **Live large with a read-aloud!**
   - Identify a picturebook or ebook where the reading experience would be enhanced by increasing the size of the text.
   - Project the book on a screen and engage students to closely read the text. Questions about the illustrations, facial expressions, movement lines, graphic novel frames, and speech bubbles all become entry points for examining a text when it is enlarged.

# – CHAPTER 5 –

## Reading across Content

*To build background knowledge for the NGSS science unit, "Biological Evolution: Unity and Diversity," third-grade students launched their learning with a reading frenzy on animal adaptations. As students began their investigation, they use books from National Geographic, sticky notes, clipboards, markers, articles I wrote for them on the topic, and a two-column thinksheet to track their new learning and wonders.*

*After a few minutes of research, students start conversing.*

*"Hey guys, what's mimi-cry?" asks Kaya.*

*"Do you mean 'mimicry'? It says right here." Derek points to the last sentence of the paragraph where the word is defined in the text.*

*"Oh! Thanks! I thought it was talking about a person or something," Kaya responds.*

*Kids continue to read and document their new learning and wonders.*

*"Did you see the Arctic fox's fur? The fur is so important! It keeps the fox warm and the color helps it blend into the snow so predators can't see it," exclaims Derek.*

*"The fur helps it survive!" says Kaya.*

*"Yeah. But what are the Arctic fox's predators?" asks Adalai.*

*"Ohhh, good question. It doesn't say. I'll write that on the wonder side and see if I can look it up later." Derek then writes, "What are the Arctic fox's predators?" on his two-column chart.*

*"Hey! I'm reading about the octopus, and it says that if it loses an arm, it can grow it back to stay safe," states Adalai.*

> A reading frenzy (Harvey & Daniels, 2016) sparks engagement and is used to build background knowledge rapidly. Books, articles, poems, realia, and digital content introduce students to a topic through a variety of mediums. Often used to preview upcoming content, learners are briefly introduced to a wide variety of ideas that pique their curiosity; later in the unit, they will be given more time to research specific ideas in depth.

*"Wait. Where do you see that?"* Railyn asks.

*After a few more minutes of research, I invite students to pause and debrief. In their small groups, I have them share what they've learned and what they've wondered thus far. As they wrap up their conversations, I ask students to identify one wonder they'd like to research.*

*Once they identify a question on the wonder side of their two-column thinksheet, students use the website The Kid Should See This to try and find more information. Since we are reading and learning about animal adaptations, I know The Kid Should See This will have a number of videos that will support and extend student thinking.*

*I step behind Railyn as she uses her Chromebook to type "mimicry." She searches it on the website and six videos pop up with topics that relate to mimicry. A smile spreads across her face.*

*"Railyn, tell me what you're researching,"* I ask.

*"Well, at first I didn't know about mimicry, but then I learned what it was—when an animal can look like another animal for protection. But the article only talked about insects and chameleons being able to do that, so I wanted to see if there are other animals that can change what they look like."*

*"Do you think you'll be able to find out more right now?"* I question.

*"Yes! Look here—I'm going to learn about this one right now!" She points to a video about the tawny frogmouth then clicks to start viewing.*

*As I glance around the room, there is an excited buzz as students view videos to research a question they had while reading. Markers and clipboards in hand, they continue to write and add to their new learning and wonders. Students gesture to each other to explain their learning and go back to the text to show a friend where they read something interesting. With a mix of print books, paper articles, and thinksheets, and a terrific website, students are excited and engaged as they embark on this learning adventure.*

## Engaging Student Curiosity

It's the best time to be a learner, as digital technologies offer more access to content than ever before. Nearly any topic can be studied at the click of a button! We celebrate that we have access to so much information in a variety of formats and complexity levels we can bring to students.

In today's multifaceted, digitized world, we teach comprehension across the day and the curriculum. Social studies, science, math, language, civics, and the arts all benefit from multimedia content that inspire students to think and learn. When comprehension strategies are at the core of science and social studies, kids learn and understand more deeply, engage more completely, and build knowledge over time (Harvey & Goudvis, 2016). Even when we have a packaged curriculum program or are departmentalized and don't specialize in content area studies, we can support all students in reading to learn.

New content offers new opportunities to tap into a young person's curiosity, engage students to care about the curriculum, and differentiate for student needs and interests. Print and digital texts, video, audio, and virtual reality bring differentiated content to students as learners who can read, view, and listen. Search engines and chatbots can guide students and teachers to new information and additional resources. Real-world experts are accessible through social media and discussion boards. Passion is piqued as we lower the walls of our classrooms and schools and engage students to create content for each other and the world. As Costa and Kallick (2008) suggest, content literacy is about what kids do with their new knowledge—how they make sense of it and use it in their daily lives. New resources bring new challenges, as seemingly unlimited content can feel overwhelming.

With information overload being a very real thing, we support young people with organizational structures that help them curate their questions and thinking. We recognize that all content is not created equal and, as a result, introduce students to only the highest quality sources. We teach lessons on where to go to find information and how to evaluate sources. We support learners with thinksheets, notebooks, graphic organizers, and a variety of digital tools for them to hold their thinking. Often, we help students slow down the pace of information access so they can engage deeply.

Across the day, we teach them to monitor their comprehension, ask questions, track new learning, summarize their findings, and offer time for them to develop these skills independently. We focus on strategies that are transferable and that can be used across the curriculum and in the world. Ultimately, we teach thinking. In doing so, we create a generation of students who are knowledge ABLE not merely information-FULL (Hammond, 2024).

## Creating Content for Readers

Every teacher understands the struggle of not having a book or resource needed for a particular lesson or student. We look for it in the library. We ask a colleague. And then we go down the rabbit hole of the internet, only to realize two hours later that we didn't find a resource that met our needs. Instead of paying for low-quality content on the internet or resorting to tears, I've learned that I can quickly create a resource that meets the needs of my lesson and students by simply writing an article about the topic.

I begin with a quick internet search. What do I need to know about the topic I will write about? Are there any fun facts that will surprise or excite my students and hook them into reading more? Once I have a little information, I can write up a short article that I can use for the lesson. I've found the best part of authoring articles for my students is that I can add a variety of features that I want students to know. For example, if we've been working on nonfiction features in second grade,

I can add words in bold print, photos with captions that tell a little bit more, or a map to show where something is located. For fifth-grade students, I might insert a footnote, share pertinent information in a graph, or embed a hyperlink for them to follow. When creating my own content, I can double-dip on my instructional goals as students are reading to learn while learning how to read deeply.

I take the information I have learned and use a simple publishing tool like Google Docs, Canva, Pages, or Word to craft the resource. All of these applications have a newsletter, brochure, or recipe template that lays out text, images, and graphics in a beautiful format. Since this is just a short article and not a dissertation, it takes 6–8 sentences to craft the article for students. Using an image search provided within the template or pulling from a site like Unsplash, I add photos and graphics to the template based on the skills I want students to employ while reading.

To differentiate for my learners, I can add a QR code that links to an audio recording of me reading the article. This provides access for students who may not be able to decode the text and includes them in the learning as they listen to the

**TIP:** You can wrap text around photos to make it look more like a newspaper article.

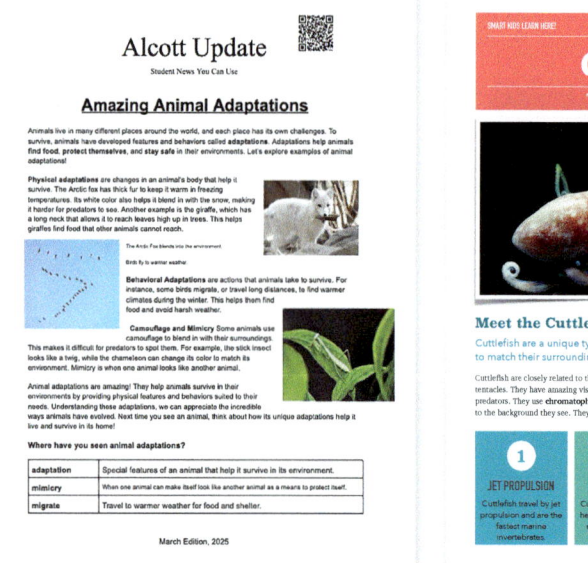

**Figure 5.1:** I create articles for readers that support their learning in science and social studies. Using a simple document or newsletter template, I am able to convey information, adjust the text for readers, and add text features. Because these articles mirror the features students study and use in ELA, time spent reading these content-specific texts feels like additional minutes spent practicing reading. Similarly, students in ELA can read these context-focused articles to build background knowledge and fluency with science text features, allowing us to double up our reading instruction across the day.

article read aloud. Once they've listened to the article, I encourage them to enter the learning where they are able—by independently reading a caption, a graphic, or another visual feature. An audio recording also provides layered access for all learners, inviting them to read and listen, which engages multiple comprehension systems to help them learn and understand even more.

## AI to Support Personalized Content Creation

This process is made even easier with AI. Artificial intelligence is a tremendous tool for classroom teachers: It can streamline our process and provide new learning opportunities for students. As with every new tool, we need to engage with it intentionally and cross-check the content it creates for accuracy, bias, and alignment with our curriculum. With a simple AI tool (MagicSchool, SchoolAI, Gemini), we can type in a prompt to generate the article content.

"Write a short article on animal adaptations for third-grade students and include how unique adaptations help animals survive."

After AI creates the content, I revise it to meet the needs of my students. That may mean:

- simplifying the vocabulary to make it more accessible for developing readers
- adding a sentence that matches the standards for the unit of study
- reducing the number of sentences in the article
- adding a sentence that includes information that AI did not suggest

AI also makes it easy to translate the article text into a language other than English. With the click of a button, I can adjust the language to make it more accessible for students or their caregivers.

Recently, I've been using AI to create content for older students who are still learning to decode and need additional phonics instruction. Many students dislike reading because it is difficult for them. They weren't taught the phonics and phonemic awareness skills needed to be proficient readers in the early years of their school career, and now they struggle as middle-grade students. While they need more explicit instruction in these skills and time to practice, they do not want to read the content typically designed to teach these skills.

I've been using AI to write short articles that these developing readers can and want to read. Using an AI tool, I can prompt it, "Write a short article about basketball player Giannis Antetokounmpo and include where he lives, what team he plays for, and his hobbies. Write the article at a second-grade reading level."

AI might produce something like this:

> Giannis Antetokounmpo is a famous basketball player who lives in Milwaukee, Wisconsin. He plays for the Milwaukee Bucks in the NBA. Giannis is known for being very tall and strong, which helps him score many points and win games. He has won important awards like the Most Valuable Player (MVP) twice! When he is not playing basketball, Giannis enjoys spending time with his family and playing video games. He also likes to help kids by supporting schools and charities. Giannis is an inspiring player both on and off the court!

And I may edit it for students to read like this:

> Giannis Antetokounmpo (Ah-deh-toh-KOOM-po) is a famous NBA basketball player who lives in Milwaukee, Wisconsin. He plays for the Milwaukee Bucks. Giannis is known for being very tall (6 feet, 11 inches) and strong. This helps him score many points. He has won important awards like the Most Valuable Player (MVP) twice! When he is not playing basketball, Giannis likes to spend time with his family and play video games. He also likes to support students and schools. Giannis is an exciting player in the NBA and someone you should watch.

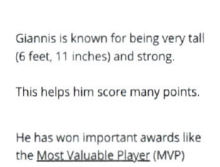

**Figure 5.2:** Book Creator is a wonderful tool for teachers and students to create content that is personalized and accessible. Speech-to-text, text-to-speech, and embedded audio can all be added to support readers with the touch of a button.

I might organize this as an article or add the information to Book Creator and publish it as an ebook for students to read. Book Creator is a fabulous tool that I've used for more than a decade to create content for students. It's an easy publication tool that embeds multimedia content and has many accessibility features. It's wonderful to use when teaching students how to read ebooks and, like authoring your own articles, allows you to embed the features you want students to know and use.

bit.ly/3FpYs01
Book Creator

When we create content for students, we personalize the reading experience and make the learning about them. We are responsive to their needs and differentiate so that young people can gain and practice the skills and strategies needed to become proficient readers. In doing so, we ensure that our learners have high-quality content at their fingertips.

## Accessing Content to Build Background Knowledge

For developing readers, vast content knowledge is foundational to future learning success. As students build schema for science and social studies concepts, young people connect new information to what they already know in order to construct knowledge. The more background knowledge students have, the more connections they are able to make, and the easier it becomes to build new knowledge. David Pearson says, "Today's new knowledge is tomorrow's background knowledge" (2008). We flood our classrooms with resources and strive to help kids gain background knowledge across the curriculum. When reading nonfiction, we teach lessons on how to gain information from features such as photos, diagrams, captions, and maps; when accessing digital content, we extend those features to include video, audio files, closed captions, and transcripts. We encourage kids to enter the thinking and learning wherever they can and use all features—big or small—to access information.

> **TIP:** AI can also offer students support outside the classroom. For middle school students, AI chatbots can make learning more accessible by reading a text aloud, explaining a process through video or translating ideas into a different language. You can customize chatbots with MagicSchool or SchoolAI to support your students as needed. As Ken Shelton and Dee Lanier write, "AI should light the way for those long left behind" (2024, p. 48).

In Debbie Plemons's kindergarten classroom on the southeast side of Chicago, joyful learning is at the heart of the curriculum. Each day, students bounce into her classroom filled with energy and curiosity. Debbie is masterful at how she helps her five- and six-year-olds channel their energy to build skills and independence. Using a class set of Chromebooks (trackpad, not touchscreen!), Debbie teaches her students to log on to their devices and access a Padlet wall she's created featuring their most used sites.

**Debbie Plemons**
Debbie Plemons is a kindergarten teacher at Our Lady of Guadalupe School in Chicago. Debbie finds joy in being a part of her students' stories; she celebrates that students become part of her story, too.

## Debbie Plemons - Reading Video for New Information

My students enter kindergarten with various skills; some have no previous school experience, others are reading at a second-grade level, a few speak only Spanish, and all need to become more independent. I believe it is my responsibility to teach my students new skills and strategies so they can guide their own learning adventures.

To launch a video lesson on view to learn, I gather students on the rug to introduce the new skill.

"Good morning, Room 201! I am super excited about what we're going to do today. Do you remember how we used a thinksheet to document our new learning and questions in the book *Tigers*? And how we tracked our learning and questions in *Surprising Sharks*? Today,

Debbie believes her kindergarten kids can do anything, and she empowers them to do so with tools and time.

What I noticed in Debbie's article was how she:

- Models what students are to do, keeping it short and focused.
- Uses familiar tools and common icons to support independence.
- Builds background knowledge and provides developing readers access to new information.

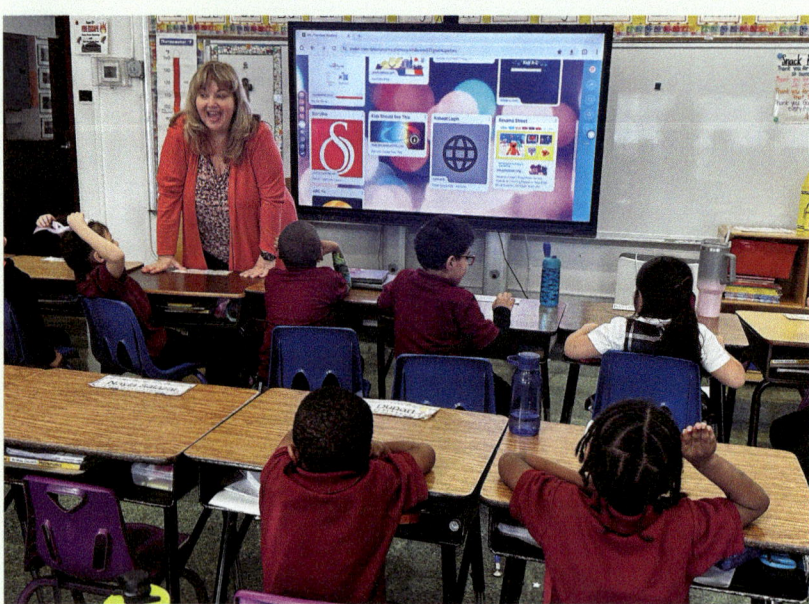

**Figure 5.3:** Debbie uses a digital bulletin board to curate the sites her kindergarten students access. From here, they link to Epic!, Seesaw, iReady, and other resources they use regularly.

you're going to do the same type of thinking, but this time, with a video! We call this type of work View to Learn."

Students excitedly cheer about this new opportunity and discuss what they will do.

"Let me show you quickly, and then you'll try it."

We use Padlet as our one-stop-spot to link to all other content, and I show students where the videos are linked on the class Padlet wall. I click the post to launch a video about grizzly bears. I view the video for about thirty seconds, and then I exclaim, "Whoa! Did you hear that? Grizzly bears weigh 700 pounds! Did you know that? That is a piece of new learning for me, so I'm going to write that in the learning column."

I quickly sketch a few circles to represent a bear and then write the number 700. When learning a new strategy, the modeling component is an important scaffold to show students what we want them to do. They observe my process and can adapt what I do to make it their own.

"Let's keep watching," I say. We watch a few more seconds and then I stop the video once again.

"Did you notice how big that bear's foot was? Did anyone see that? Let me go back so you can see. If you want to go back in a video, you can tap the ball on the line and drag it back a little bit. Watch me drag it back. See? Now, let's watch this section again. Take a close look at the foot."

I replay the section and push pause. "Did you see it?"

My students squeal with excitement:

"It was huge!"

"Big, big, big!"

"Awesome!"

I whisper to gain their attention. "So now, a wonder popped into my head. I'm wondering why a bear's foot is so big? I'm going to write that on the question side."

I sketch a foot and write "why" next to it. "Did you see how I wrote down my question about the bear? You can do this, too! Also, did you see how I pressed the two little lines to stop the video? Who remembers what that button is called?"

Multiple kids shout, "Pause!"

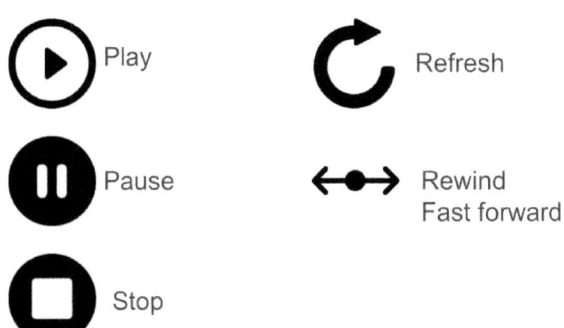

**Figure 5.4:** Early in the school year, I teach students fundamental truths about digital technology (Ziemke & Muhtaris, 2020). Giving them a high-level introduction to digital navigation promotes independence and endures across platforms and devices. They enter this lesson knowing how to press play and pause.

Again I whisper, "Now, here's what you're going to do: you're going to get a clipboard from the box. Next, you'll grab a thinksheet from the supply table. Then you'll pick up your Chromebook, log on to your computer, and go to the Padlet. Odd numbers, you may go get started."

I send my twenty-two students off in two waves. Students calmly get a clipboard, thinksheet, marker, Chromebook, and headphones. They independently choose where to sit, and then they begin to organize their materials.

"Give me a thumbs up when you get to the Padlet page." Around the room, thumbs pop up.

"On the Padlet, you'll see I gave you two videos to choose from: one is about grizzly bears, and the other is about polar bears. You choose which video you'd like to learn from and then document your new learning and questions as you go. Have fun!"

A buzz fills the room as kids excitedly discuss which video they will choose. Students put on their headphones and start to view to learn. Moments into the lesson, learners begin to track their new learning and questions on a two-column thinksheet. I walk around the room and can see students draw and sketch to document understanding. Others add labels and initial sounds to their drawings

**Figure 5.5:** A kindergarten student tracks her learning and wonders about grizzly bears using a two-column chart. Notice how she navigates her Chromebook, headphones, clipboard, thinksheet, and pencil to document her learning. When we offer space and time for kids to engage in ongoing thinking work, they show us how capable they are.

to signify their questions. Some use pictures and inventive spelling. Learners navigate between their device and their thinksheet.

A few minutes into their practice time, students start calling out to each other to tell or teach about a question they have or something they learned. Their energy is contagious, and collectively they begin to feel that learning is fun. Suddenly, Antonio jumps up from his desk, toppling over his seat. He whips off his headphones and says, "Guys! Did you see the part where they track grizzly bears by following their poop? They follow their poop to find where they are!"

Immediately, students run to Antonio's computer to see this spectacle in action. Applying the skills he's learned, Antonio drags back the cursor on the video to rewatch the section where the tracker shares how a bear's poop can be very informative.

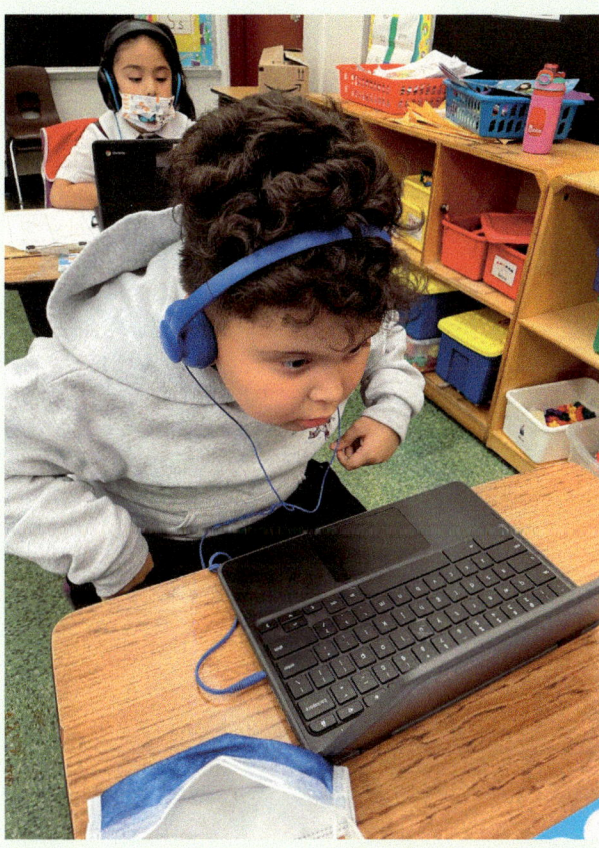

**Figure 5.6:** Antonio at the moment he learns how scientists track grizzly bears. This is the face of engagement!

This lesson is so much more than watching a video about bears. It's about providing developing readers access to information. It's about teaching young learners that they can find research topics they are curious about. It's about building background knowledge and using high-level vocabulary for kids who may not reside in a literacy-rich environment. It's about building autonomy so learners can keep thinking even when I'm not there to support them. When I see their expressions and hear their joyful squeals in response to learning, I am constantly reminded that kinder CAN.

## Critical Thinkers across Digital Contexts

Debbie's classroom shows us how ease of use and access to digital content can change the learning conditions for many. However, not all content is created equal. While mobile devices have democratized who can create and share messages, new lessons are needed to help students understand the content creation process so that they can evaluate the sources they encounter online. Lessons on content and contexts, mis- and disinformation, and author's perspective in text, photos, and video all become fundamental mini-lessons to developing critical thinkers today. To address students' misconceptions about content they accessed online, Angelique Trevino adjusted her nonfiction unit and made time, and new lessons, to teach information literacy.

**Angelique Trevino**
Angelique is a third-grade ESL educator in Austin, Texas. She is an educational technology specialist and is passionate about teaching students to navigate the world on- and offline. She loves to share her interests and curiosity with students as she learns about them.

### Angelique Trevino - Evaluating Sources

The wonderful thing about the internet is that pretty much ANYONE can put something up for others to view and read. It's a beautiful concept: a free(ish) and open space where you can share your thoughts, ideas, artwork, etc., with as many people as who want to access your contributions. However, because ANYONE can post their own thoughts, there is not necessarily anyone there to point out biases or mistakes. At times, content created and published online can seem very convincing but can still be inaccurate. This includes videos and podcasts (and even more so now with the advancement of AI and deepfakes). If adults sometimes have trouble discerning fact from fiction online, it's not surprising that a child would also struggle with the concept.

Angelique cares about how her students interact with and use information. She carefully responds to their misconceptions and misunderstandings of online content.

It's important how Angelique:
- Models with a digital think-aloud using a website and the projector in her classroom.
- Engages students to understand the authorship of content creators.
- Guides students to identify quality sources for students.

When I realized my students needed support evaluating online content, I decided to change the ways I taught nonfiction to include a bit of information literacy. When we move into writing or reading nonfiction in the curriculum, one of the things we discuss is what makes something a nonfiction piece. We explore the difference between fiction and nonfiction: Fiction is created and may have some elements of truth/real life, but nonfiction is factual and can be researched or proven. We learn about fact versus opinion, and we learn to recognize the difference between them—facts can be proven while opinions are based more on emotions and feelings.

During this unit, I set aside a bit of time to talk about what we might see online. There are plenty of ways to demonstrate this for students, and I am sure there are premade lessons you can follow, but what I find particularly powerful is to show students what it

> **Opinion** – how someone feels or believes
> ★ Superman vs. Batman
>
> **Fact** – something true, can be proved
> ★ Penguins are birds
>
> | Opinions (I think... I believe... The best...) | Facts |
> |---|---|
> | • Llamas are weird. | • Llamas are mammals. |
> | • Chocolate is the best candy. | • Chocolate is a popular candy. |
> | • I believe there are 9 planets. | • There are 8 planets in our solar system. |
> | • Mars is the best planet. | |
> | • Fiction books are funnier/better. | • Fiction means something that is not real - it is made up. |
> | • Fiction is more exciting. | |

**Figure 5.7:** An example of a fact versus opinion discussion. Some examples are mine, and some are from the students.

means: ANYONE can create content and put it online (including myself) and make themselves appear to be an expert source even when they aren't.

I start with a simple question: "Where do you go online for information?"

Most of them answer: "Google."

I ask further: "And what do you do from there?"

They answer: "I click the link of what's there."

At this point, we can pull up an example on the screen, something like our school mascot or a famous soccer player. As we look at the links that come up, we notice some common sites: Wikipedia, websites for zoos, sports magazines, etc. We also look at some of the sites we might not recognize: fan sites or videos Google is promoting that are related to what we searched. The conversation goes something like this:

I ask: "Who do you think made these videos?"

They answer: "TikTok! Google! YouTube!" (Usually, at least one student will answer with the username of the video creator.)

I ask: "Is this person an expert? Do they know absolutely everything about this football player?"

And at this point, students start to throw out responses or stay quiet, because they are not sure.

I ask: "Who can record a video for YouTube?"

They answer: "Anyone!" (Or, inevitably, "Oh, me! I can!")

I follow up with: "So, even if you know ABSOLUTELY NOTHING about our school mascot, you can still record a video about it and upload it for everyone to see?"

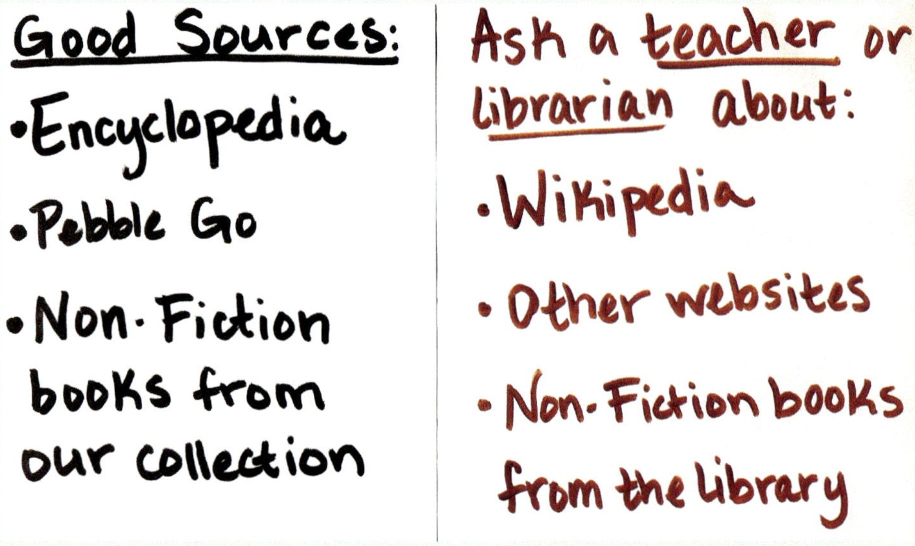

**Good Sources:**
- Encyclopedia
- Pebble Go
- Non-Fiction books from our collection

**Ask a teacher or librarian about:**
- Wikipedia
- Other websites
- Non-Fiction books from the library

**Figure 5.8:** What sources can we use?

I then share the website I created during the COVID-19 pandemic, when we were virtual teaching and I needed a way to communicate with parents and help them get set up with the online tools we would use. I tell students that this is a website that I made—I purchased the domain name, I set up the site using WordPress, and I recorded the videos and typed the content to fill it up. (I normally get oohs and ahhs or surprised Pikachu faces when I show them that I created this site myself.) So anyone, with a little money and a little know-how, can create content and publish it to the internet for other people to see. If anyone can upload to the internet, we have to really pay attention to who is creating the media we are watching or reading and think, *Is this person an expert? Are they someone who is knowledgeable about the topic and what they are saying? Can I trust this source?*

As I reflect on this unit, I know I need to begin to add a segue into AI—how it's a great tool but it's not an expert either, because it just synthesizes the information available online. That AI answer you get to a question you ask in Google might look professional but is sometimes wrong because it's not a person and it's not checking itself for accuracy.

As we continue our nonfiction unit, we note the difference between sources we can trust and sources we might be wary of. When we read about historical figures, we look for sources that are more trustworthy: encyclopedias, Wikipedia, and PebbleGo, and we can get help from a teacher or our librarian to find books that are good sources. The library conveniently has a section labeled nonfiction, which is also a great place to look for more information about the people and concepts we're learning about in class.

Throughout the year, we frequently revisit this lesson and update it with new sources. As kids become better readers and researchers, we introduce new sites and sources that are developmentally appropriate and will lead students to the information they seek. By the end of the school year, I want all my kids to know at least 4–6 terrific resources they can access independently, as well as know when and why to turn away from a source that might not be a good fit for young people.

Angelique's students gained new sources and skills for interacting with digital content and now can approach their informational reading from a more informed stance. Her curious learners have the skills needed to research independently, and safely, as they know good sources to turn to when evaluating online content.

## Create to Learn

One of the best ways to teach students to understand digital content is to have them create it. When students create content, they learn how to use new tools and interact with information in a variety of modes and formats. Students read, take notes, and research. They ask questions, identify the key details of the concept, and summarize what they've learned. Often, students develop project plans and discuss their new learning and their process with peers. All these layers amplify interaction and strengthen comprehension as kids learn content deeply in order to teach it to others. As students learn to create, they create to learn.

Contrary to direct instruction methods, where students are passive receptors of information that is presented by the adult in the room, embodied learning or, as it's more familiarly referred to, multimodal learning, encourages students to manipulate the content and encode information via multiple neurological routes, establishing a richer web of connections leading to deeper understanding (Mathias & von Kriegstein, 2023). Often, students create entirely new representations to demonstrate understanding that is personalized to their learning style and unique preferences. By actively engaging with content in multiple ways over extended periods of time, students maximize retention and comprehension.

When kids create content that mirrors what they see beyond the school day—podcasts, informational videos, memes, animations—we liberate them from the mundane work that only lives in school contexts and inspire them with work that lives in the real world. Products with purpose promote agency and motivate students to learn even more as they work to create learning artifacts that matter to them.

In central Iowa, Stacy Hansen supports educators and students to comprehend, create, and teach others. With an inquiry stance and a learner mindset, Stacy develops innovative experiences that invigorate the school setting. Layering kinesthetic learning with print and digital tools, Stacy looks to the learning sciences to help students build knowledge.

**Stacy Hansen**
Stacy is a technology and innovation coach for the Waukee Community School District. She supports educators across her district and was recently named Waukee Community Schools Teacher of the Year.

### Stacy Hansen - Animation to Support Science Learning

As a technology and innovation coach, I'm passionate about fostering purposeful digital learning. I believe in being intentional about students' device usage, balanced learning experiences, and I believe in a focus on quality tasks over tools. By combining physical activities, such as reading physical books and writing on paper, with digital experiences, we can activate essential neural connections and create a well-rounded learning environment. Working closely with incredible students and teachers across the district, I strive to implement these principles to enhance teaching and learning.

Cornelius Minor explains that when introducing a new tool, it is important to let learners explore it within a familiar context. This

Stacy leverages creativity in the content area curriculum to bring joyful learning to the students she works with. Using simple tools to build skills over time, she helps students to document their learning in new modalities.

I recognize the importance of how Stacy:
- Plans for instruction using the learning sciences to strengthen comprehension and retention.
- Uses familiar tools to create something new.
- Creates authentic audiences for students' work.

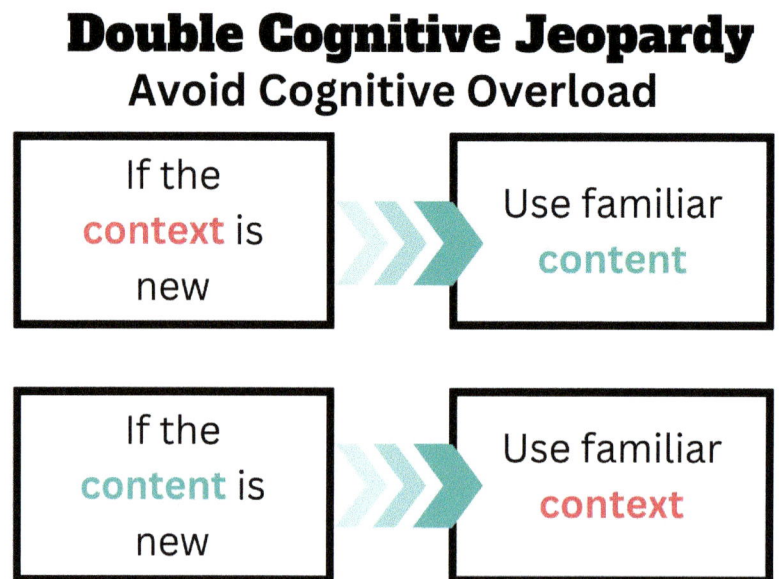

**Figure 5.9:** Enhance learning and retention by introducing new content within familiar contexts, making concepts more meaningful and memorable.

approach builds familiarity with the tool so that by the time they use it to demonstrate their learning, their focus can remain on the new material. If the tool and context are new, it can create what Minor calls "double cognitive jeopardy" (2018). When this happens, learners struggle to show their knowledge and comprehension while trying to navigate an unfamiliar tool.

To avoid this, I introduce new technology tools by having students explore freely and then use them to create something on a topic they already know well. This strategy helps build confidence with the tool, paving the way for deeper engagement when applying it in new learning contexts.

While collaborating with the fifth-grade teachers at Eason Elementary in Waukee, Iowa, an opportunity arose for their students to explain their science learning visually while incorporating nonfiction writing standards. We planned for the students to use Apple's Keynote app (it could easily be Google Slides—remember, task over tool) to create animation videos that showed a food web or ecosystem.

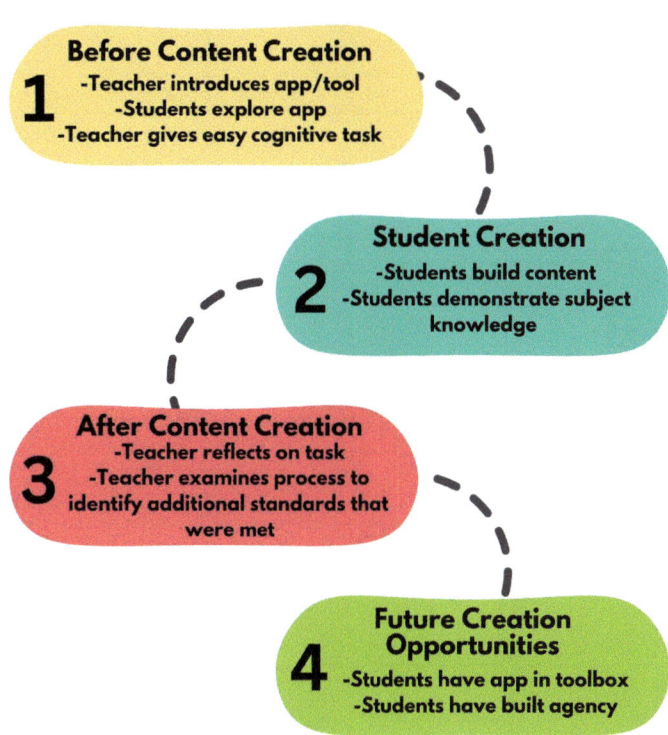

**Figure 5.10:** Encourage exploration when introducing new digital tools, empowering students to build confidence and take ownership of their learning.

The first time I went into their classrooms to teach, I provided students with an introduction to the Keynote app; we explored how to add shapes, build-ins, and animations, and how to record their voices. They were then set free to explore the app. The task was to create an "All about Me" with a familiar context (avoiding double cognitive jeopardy).

I returned to their classroom a few days later, and this time students focused on conveying their learning to an audience. They used the tool to add shapes and animations to create a scene that showed their understanding of the science standards (Next Generation Science Standards, https://www.nextgenscience.org/). Students had written about an ecosystem, but it didn't end there. They were able to show how producers and consumers impact their ecosystem. Students created scenes showing a squirrel eating an acorn produced by an oak tree and how wildflowers and prairie grass grow from the sun's energy. After making their scene and reading their written narrative as a voiceover, they exported it as a movie and uploaded it to Seesaw to share with others.

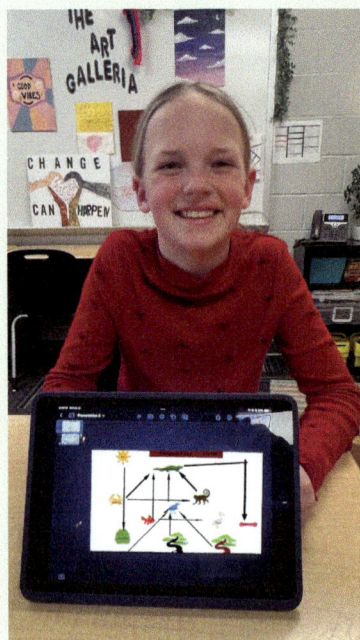
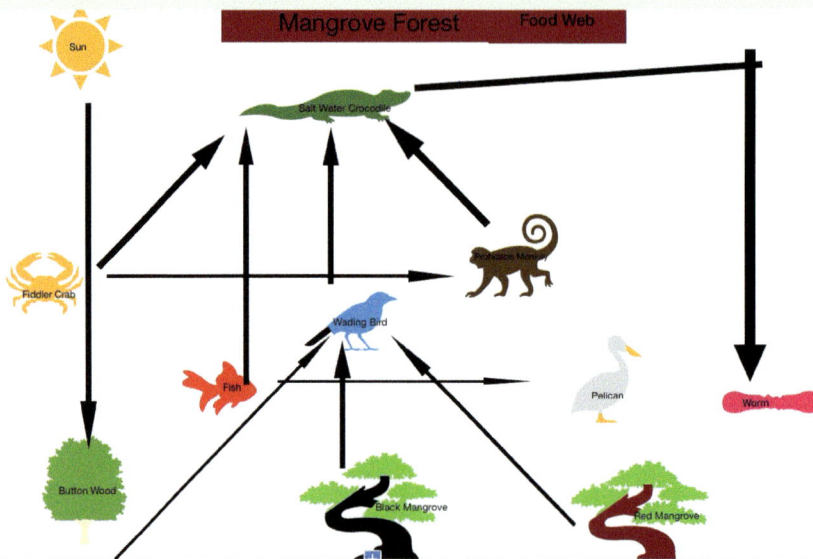

**Figure 5.11:** Students brought ecosystems to life by creating visual food webs. Using animations, they illustrated how different parts of the ecosystem interact with and impact one another.

If this project was on a Chromebook, I would use Google Slides. Students can use free online icon resources like CocoMaterial, Flaticon, and the Noun Project to build their scenes. With Keynote, all of the animations can be done on one slide; with Slides, multiple slides are needed. The students build their scene on the first slide and then duplicate the slide and make the icons move with two or three taps of the arrow key. They repeat this multiple times to create a flipbook-like experience that shows the action happening. The final slide is their typed written narrative explaining their ecosystem. Adding and exporting audio on Google Slides is not as easy as Keynote, so the typed narrative is in place of a voiceover. A short video can easily be over fifty slides with the small movements that are made. The presentation can be screen-recorded to create a movie to upload to Seesaw, Google Classroom, or another platform.

Limiting students to using built-in shapes in Keynote or searching for icons instead of using photographs puts creative constraints on them. This encourages them to think flexibly about how a shape or icon might represent an idea or how combining multiple shapes or icons can visually convey their concept. Working within these defined boundaries helps students channel their creativity to develop innovative and resourceful solutions.

Once students have familiarity with the app, it opens up additional opportunities for them to share their learning in creative ways. Their teachers know they understand how to use it and can let them create more innovative ways to share their learning. It is also a win that their initial exposure to a presentation app was not a traditional slideshow. Students will have already realized the creative potential beyond words on a slide to share their learning with others.

Stacy engages students to create to learn and helps educators prioritize time for student discovery and creativity. Digital technologies provide an easy opportunity to integrate the arts through digital drawings, animations, spoken word, or student-produced songs and videos. In addition to supporting cognitive science and multiple intelligence theory, increasing art opportunities in the classroom and making time for creative expression can lower stress, improve memory, and make students feel more socially connected (Warner, 2022).

Frequently, in education circles, I've heard teachers, librarians, tech coaches, and administrators debate how we should prioritize the time students spend on devices. Should students use their devices to consume new information and lessons? Or should kids create to show what they know? Again, the either/or question rears its ugly head as we try to simplify a complex idea by sorting it into binary categories. When will we learn that it's not that simple?

When I visit classrooms across the US and around the world, I observe students who spend way too much time consuming low-level digital worksheets and completing online busy work. Too often, I see young people doing computer-based "schoolwork" in the absence of instruction. I wholeheartedly believe that our kids are spending way too much passive time on devices doing skill-and-drill practice. And I *know* an online program can't teach your kids like you can. Instead, we need to teach students how to thoughtfully consume content that will help them seek information and build new knowledge.

For me, it's not a question of consume or create but one of consume *and* create. Learners need to know how to access the most up-to-date information. They need to know how to triangulate sources, read with a question in mind, and check for bias. They need to know how to ask the right questions, listen critically, and think independently. As with all things, we need to provide students with strategies for interacting with information and time to build fluency. Young people need time to read to learn.

Let's visit Stacy's school again as she offers guidance on how to help teachers and librarians organize their instruction with time for students to consume *and* create. Using podcasting as a vehicle for new learning, Stacy supports students in building skills in content consumption as a means to create a new product. First, students practice how to obtain information from a podcast. Next, they analyze the components of a podcast to see how bits of information are combined to create a story or teaching sequence. Finally, they plan and produce their own podcast authentically using the skills, strategies, and information they gained while studying a podcast and turn it into new knowledge.

**Stacy Hansen**

Stacy is a technology and innovation coach for the Waukee Community School District. She supports educators across her district and was recently named Waukee Community Schools Teacher of the Year.

# Stacy Hansen - Podcasting for Understanding in Social Studies

Podcasts provide a meaningful and engaging way for students to interact with content. When introducing podcasts to students, we begin by exploring their structure, purpose, and how to engage with them as active listeners. Like books, podcasts have titles, are often organized by seasons and episodes, and can serve as texts for entertaining or learning. To help students focus and organize their thinking, I provide a graphic organizer where they can record new information as they listen.

In this article, Stacy supports students as they create content that mirrors what they read, view, and listen to as they engage in the world.

I really love how Stacy supports students to:

- Consume content to understand the features before they create content.
- Leverage literacy skills to plan a podcast.
- Think with the end in mind and plan for what the listener will learn.

**Figure 5.12:** Stacy introduces podcasts to students using the site Brains On! Universe.

I introduced podcasts to a group of second graders using an episode on extreme weather. The sound effects and the hosts' energetic delivery captivated the students, sparking their curiosity. After listening, they reviewed their notes, and I asked for volunteers to share new learning. A boy raised his hand and explained how the earth's plates move and lava rises to cause volcanoes. His teacher approached me afterward, amazed. He was an English language learner who typically did not volunteer to share his learning out loud, but this opportunity unlocked a new way for him to attain content knowledge and gave him the confidence to share with peers. This moment highlighted the power of accessible, engaging content to empower students and give them confidence to participate in their learning community.

**Figure 5.13:** Learners write and plan for their podcasts. Pencils, iPads, and notebooks are all tools of technology that support content creation.

After students gain experience as podcast listeners, the next step is often for them to create their own. I collaborated with Josh Schoon, a fourth-grade teacher at Eason Elementary in Waukee, Iowa, to guide his students in creating podcasts connected to their social studies learning. The process included embedding literacy strategies like visualizing, persuasive writing, and creating for an audience. Some of these students had worked with me in second grade on podcasting, so building on their prior experiences and exploring more advanced tools and techniques was exciting.

**Figure 5.14:** Josh Schoon, fourth-grade teacher, works with a student to create a podcast about natural resources.

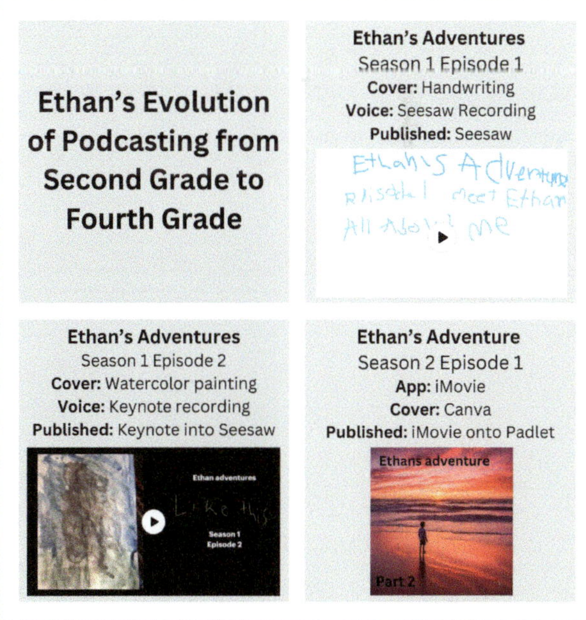

**Figure 5.15:** From second grade to fourth grade, Ethan's podcast journey shows growth in voice, creativity, and storytelling.

READING ACROSS CONTENT    163

**Figure 5.16:** Students move between print text, their notebooks, and an organizer as they read, write, and plan their podcast.

Active listening is an essential component when using podcasts for learning, but creating them shifts the focus to crafting an engaging and educational experience for others. Students begin by brainstorming using a graphic organizer similar to the one they used for listening, but this time, "What I learned" becomes "What I want my listeners to learn." This familiar structure helps students clarify their purpose while allowing space for creativity, such as naming their podcasts *Evan's Adventures* or *Bo's Stories*.

The fourth graders had been studying natural resources, so their podcast aimed to educate others on a resource, to promote sustainability, and to inspire action to protect these resources. Each student chose a specific resource to focus on, learned key ideas through inquiry to share, and crafted a call to action for their listeners. This structure helped them stay organized while developing their message.

**Figure 5.17:** Stacy helps students think with the listener in mind as they plan their podcast to explain the natural resource, discuss why it is at risk, and seek steps toward sustainability.

Incorporating digital creation skills with literacy standards offers many opportunities to assess student progress while fostering engagement. To help students manage the process, I often create a visual priority hierarchy. This pyramid anchor chart helps them focus on the necessary steps in a specific order. For instance, if a student is working on sound effects or font colors, part of the polishing stage, before completing their content and creation stages, I can gently redirect them to focus on the appropriate step. Even if students don't fully complete the polishing stage, the content and creation steps usually provide enough evidence to assess their progress effectively.

**Figure 5.18:** Anchor charts provide a visual guide that empowers students to navigate digital learning at their own pace and complete tasks independently.

After completing their nonfiction writing, students worked on two digital components: creating a podcast cover and recording their podcast. For the covers, we used Canva's AI image-generation tool. Crafting an effective AI prompt reinforced visualization strategies, as students had to determine the key details necessary to create a meaningful image. This guided use of AI under direct teacher supervision provided students with valuable exposure to emerging technology in an educational context.

To record their podcasts, students used iMovie, incorporating their Canva covers as the visual component. The built-in voice recorder empowered students to share their message and inspire action. While creating these podcasts was an expectation for all, many students took their projects further. They explored iMovie's audio options to add transitions and sound effects, while others used GarageBand to simulate a phone call from a listener, adding another creative dimension to their work.

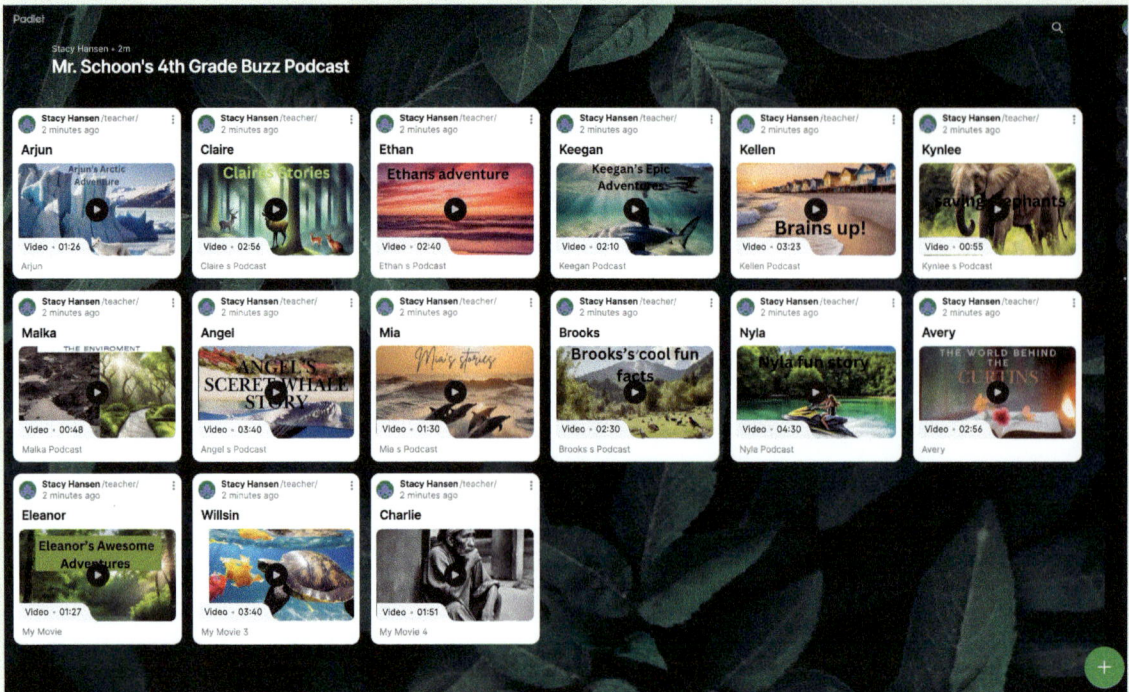

**Figure 5.19:** Students work independently to write and record their podcasts. They share their podcast to Padlet so others can listen to the finished product.

**Figure 5.20:** From script to spotlight, students publish their podcasts on Padlet, sharing their voices and learning with the world.

Throughout the entire process, from drafting scripts to designing covers and recording, students demonstrated high levels of engagement. They were fully immersed in their tasks, working with purpose and enthusiasm. No reminders or redirections were needed, as students were genuinely invested in their work.

Once their podcasts were complete, students uploaded them to Padlet, creating a shared space where they could showcase their work, explore their peers' creations, and provide feedback. This collaborative platform fostered a sense of community, allowing students to celebrate their efforts and learn from one another.

What we see in this article about podcasting is the layers of literacy that come into play as students consume and create. Yes, they're learning about extreme weather in science and natural resources in social studies, respectively, AND they're learning:

- The structure of podcasts and how they have many of the same organizational structures you find in books.
- To identify key details and write about scientific/historical concepts.
- To visualize learning so they can explain it to others.
- To write persuasively to inspire action.
- To plan for diverse audiences.
- Presentation and speaking skills.

When students are able to learn from and create work that lives in the world, they are engaged and inspired to access, create, share, and think. Once they enter the cycle of Consume → Learn → Create → Share, the loop becomes continuous as students keep seeking and creating to share with their peers, their teachers, and the larger community.

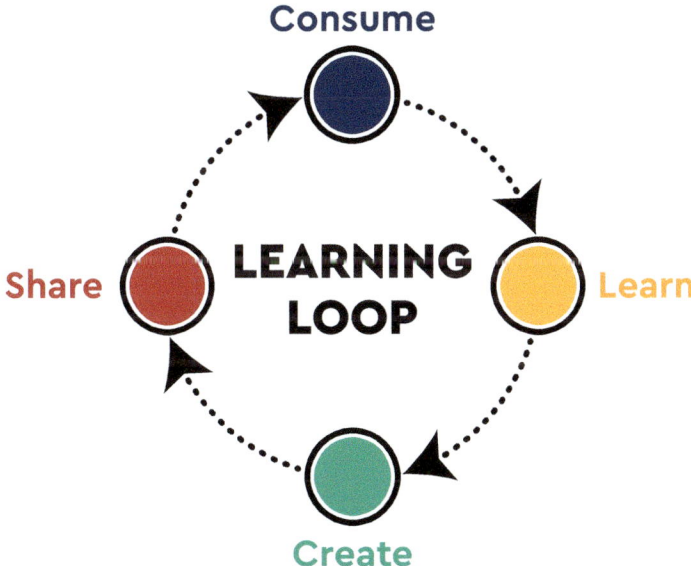

Even when our school or district presents us with a packaged social studies or science curriculum, we can easily adapt it to make it even more relevant for students. By adding authentic work products as Stacy did, inserting a video to give a concept real-world significance, or pulling out chart paper or a digital bulletin board to engage students in written conversation, we can leverage print and digital content to support students' comprehension.

At the Catherine Cook School in Chicago, Sara K. Ahmed invites students into the learning sequences with video. By projecting media content from the moment they walk in, she maximizes time on instruction and connects to kids' curiosity before the bell even rings.

**Sara K. Ahmed**

Sara is the director of curriculum integration and innovation at Catherine Cook School in Chicago. She works passionately to help students examine their identity and find humanity in others. She is the author of *Being the Change: Lessons and Strategies to Teach Social Comprehension* and is the coauthor with Harvey "Smokey" Daniels of *Upstanders: How to Engage Middle School Hearts and Minds with Inquiry*.

## Sara K. Ahmed - Click, Capture, Convert: A Science Conversation

As the fifth graders walk into their departmentalized science class, a time-lapse video is playing—a provocation that will pique their curiosities and get them thinking and talking from the moment they enter. Every minute counts, and we don't wait for the sound of the teacher's voice for the learning to begin.

The science teacher, Cara Davis, and I jot down what it looks like and sounds like when students see the video:

"Wait. What?"

Student standing nose-distance from the screen: "Is that Earth lighting up?"

"What's that light?"

Another student standing nose-distance from the screen: "Is that bioluminescent fish? I saw those once."

Background knowledge has entered the chat.

Big blank papers are already on their tables, ready for a written conversation and See, Think, Wonder—a visible thinking routine used widely across content areas. We hear the kids reading the questions aloud as they settle in, jot down their homework in their planners, and check out the agenda for the day.

We momentarily pause the video and revisit an idea they've explored a few times. There are different types of videos, just like there are different types of texts, and so there are different ways we watch and interact with videos. Ms. Davis is tuned into the kids and the idea that today's reader watches videos of people watching videos, videos of people playing games, videos of people reading a text and thinking aloud, narrating their experience all the way through. Sometimes, she notices that the kids mimic this behavior in class: She will play a video with an assigned narrator discussing the scientific phenomenon, and the kids engage in their own running commentary, even when she needs them to listen to the narrator.

Because our video was a silent time-lapse video, we decided to establish an intentional instructional move that bolsters students' ability to comprehend the text as individuals and co-construct knowledge as social beings simultaneously. We combined Kristin

It's awesome to see how Sara uses text, multimedia, writing, and students' innate curiosity to foster background knowledge and fuel written and verbal conversation. As students launch a new science unit, they're instantly hooked into the content and excited for the learning ahead.

I notice how Sara supports students to:
- Quickly build background knowledge for the unit of study.
- Write to process new information and thinking.
- Collaboratively construct meaning through peer-to-peer conversation.

Ziemke and Katie Muhtaris's "Read Video for Understanding" (2019) and another visible thinking routine like written conversation or silent dialogue to allow multiple pathways for students to process at their own speed and in their own ways.

In their coauthored book *Read the World*, Ziemke and Muhtaris invite students to consider what they See, Think, and Wonder when viewing a video: "Video allows students access and an entry point to content that they may not yet be able to decode or comprehend in print, thus inviting students to think and wonder at a higher level" (2019, p. 67).

The big blank papers on their desks already said: *What do you **see**? What do you **think** is happening? What do you **wonder**?* We ask for a quick turn-and-talk to describe a time-lapse video to a partner as we move around the room and listen.

We then set the intention with the kids that this time-lapse is a kind of silent video, like a silent or wordless book, and they will have time to silently view and read the video to allow everyone some think time, they'll have a chance to silently show their thinking on the big paper, then they will talk with their tablemates about what they think they see, what they think is happening, and what they wonder.

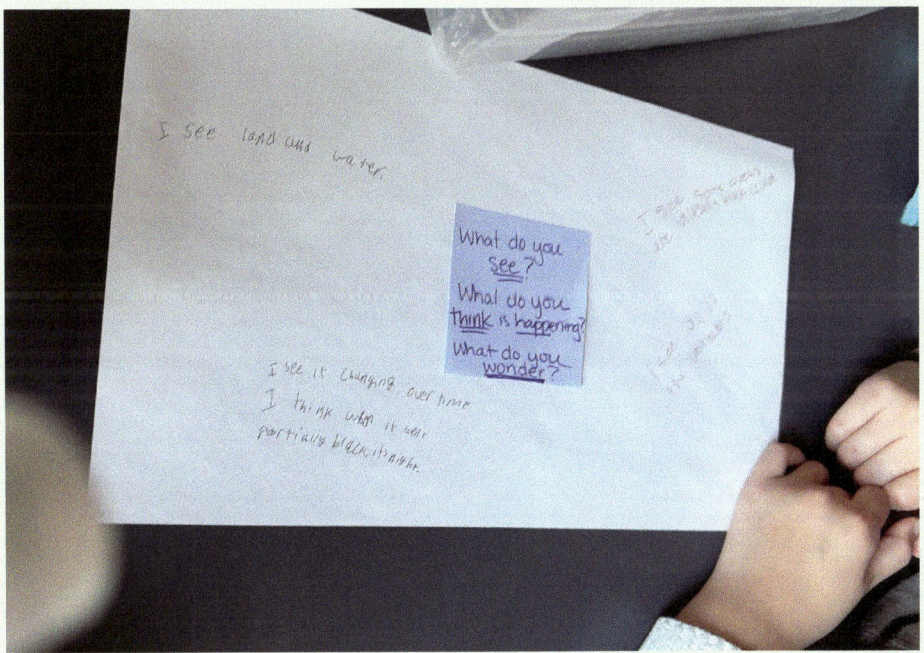

**Figure 5.21:** Student jots initial noticings about the video.

We start the video from the beginning, and they get to work observing and reading, thinking, making their thinking visible, and sharing their observations with partners. The first time, we pause the video, and I model my own writing on the board with what I see, think, and wonder, then we pause the video along the way to give all students time to get their thinking down on paper. By the second round, students are able to view and have written conversations almost simultaneously.

**Figure 5.22:** Students engage in written conversation with a partner where they share their noticings and questions.

After lots of great thinking and talking, we rewatch the video to answer questions, confirm hypotheses, and catch things a partner mentioned but maybe we missed on the first read. This time, we also reveal the title of the video before the rewatch: *Timelapse: Photosynthesis Seen from Space (Educator Version)* (California Academy of Sciences, 2021).

With the great reveal, they respond almost immediately:

"Ohhhhhhh! I get it now!"

"Wait, I think we learned about this in fourth grade when we grew our own plants!"

"But I still am not sure what the light is!"

"It must be that there's more photosynthesis when the video shows the summer months in North America. Are they showing seasons?"

Feeling that there is an urge to think aloud, we ask them to quickly turn and talk about what the term photosynthesis means to them.

We then layer an additional text into the learning that day, their chapter from their science curriculum. Now that they have built up their think-pair-shares—monitoring comprehension from the video, their silent conversations, and their shared table discussions—they are ready to read on their own and tackle the text and text structures of their curriculum.

**Figure 5.23:** Another layer of information is added as students use their textbooks to learn even more. As they read, they work with a partner to diagram the photosynthesis process.

Their task, after reading and answering a few end-of-section questions, is to revise their pair-share-visualize diagram they created after viewing the video with, now, even more knowledge they have from the printed text, nonfiction features, the video, and their conversations (out-loud and silently on paper).

**Figure 5.24:** Students have time to synthesize their understanding after accessing a variety of print and digital texts. They revise their diagrams to summarize their learning.

This results in a beautiful synthesis of co-constructing meaning-making. We felt they were on the road to understanding the big job of even the tiniest plants as energy architects for our world.

Teaching students to write in response to the video slows down learning, providing students time to think deeply. With layered opportunities to interact with the information in writing, through the textbook, by rewatching the video, diagramming, and revising their work, paired with the opportunity to discuss the text with a partner to question and clarify understanding, the structure of the lessons supported students across the comprehension continuum.

Let's take a moment to acknowledge all the ways that Sara and her partner teacher structured students' access and entry into the science unit:

- View a time-lapse video
- Question a piece of media
- Verbal conversation with classmates through turn-and-talk
- Written conversation on chart paper
- Reread the video a second time to answer questions and glean even more information
- Read their science text
- Diagram their understanding

With intentional planning, Sara and the science teacher were able to hook kids with curiosity, build background knowledge for photosynthesis, and engage students with writing, conversation, and informational text. This is a classic example of layering active literacy experiences to enhance comprehension. In one class period, students did all these things to monitor their comprehension, determine important information in the text and media, and ask questions to guide further learning.

My favorite source for accessing and extending learning in science and social studies is The Kid Should See This. It is my one-stop shop for nearly all video content that I share with students. Whenever I need to locate a video to support a concept, hook kids' curiosity, or craft a multimodal tech set, I start here. From their website: "7000+ kid-friendly videos, curated for teachers and parents who want to share smarter, more meaningful media in the classroom and at home."

bit.ly/4jA7Zk3
The Kid Should See This

Each video is accompanied by a detailed article that provides the reader with additional information about the topic. Throughout the article, images are used to support the reader and extend thinking, and hyperlinks are embedded to offer quick access to additional content. The article concludes with a list of additional videos on the site that cover the same topic and invites viewers to explore related content in a "If you liked this video, you may also like these…" format, suggesting six more videos on similar topics.

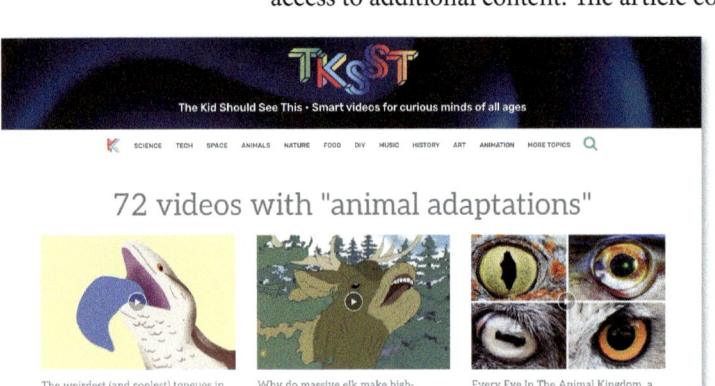

I teach students to use this site as a search engine when doing content-area research. It has several built-in supports that make it a perfect tool for elementary and middle school readers. Because the majority of the content is video, it is accessible to all and does not require a certain Lexile level to decode the content. Kids can view, listen, and learn. This site also gets students to the content they need quickly. Instead of searching endlessly on the internet for a site that meets student needs, The Kid Should See This curates high-quality content intended to help young people research and build knowledge. The site enhances active literacy as students read, listen, and view to comprehend new information.

There are many ways we can hook students into content-area reading. I like to support students by curating content around a unit of study and hosting it in a shared space like a classroom website, digital bulletin board, multitouch book, or slide deck. Curating a digital "tech set" for students ensures that all learners find content that they can and want to read so that they meet the learning goals and standards set forth by the curriculum. Of course, across the grades, students will also search for and locate their own content using developmentally appropriate sites and methods, but I like to create a central "hub" to launch the unit. Doing so also ensures that our initial conversations, research, and time spent building background knowledge is rooted in information that is accurate and student friendly.

> **TIP:** For students who may need additional visual support, I always start with an audio clip and an enlarged visual or piece of realia so they can build background knowledge by listening, viewing, or touching.

Starting with the sites above and then building upon that with a few other tried-and-true resources, I add images for students to analyze, articles from news sites, publications that are tailored to student readers, videos that will support their background knowledge or enhance their understanding, and a list of print books and resources for them to explore offline. I design the resource so that a student's first encounter is typically with an image or an audio clip; accessing images or audio is not limited by one's reading level, so it is a supportive entry point for most students.

For early years students, I offer scaffolded support as I model my thinking and how I move through the resources on the digital bulletin board. More experienced students determine how they would like to use the tech set and pace their own learning.

Throughout the unit, students come back to this tech set as a place to ground their thinking. Frequently, students add additional links and resources, create a

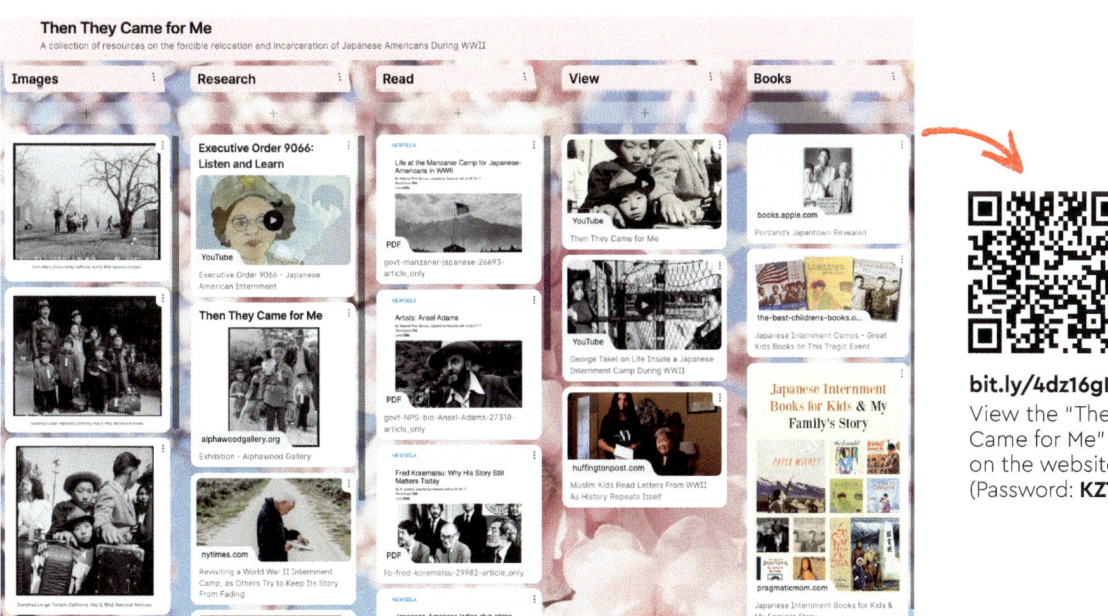

**Figure 5.25:** A tech set for a unit on the forced relocation and internment of Japanese Americans during WWII as a result of Executive Order 9066.

bit.ly/4dz16gl
View the "Then They Came for Me" Padlet on the website. (Password: **KZTandT**)

post to ask a question, or share a reaction to the information. Regularly, kids add posts to document their learning. With many high-quality resources available at the click of a button, students immerse themselves in the topic and read and research to learn more.

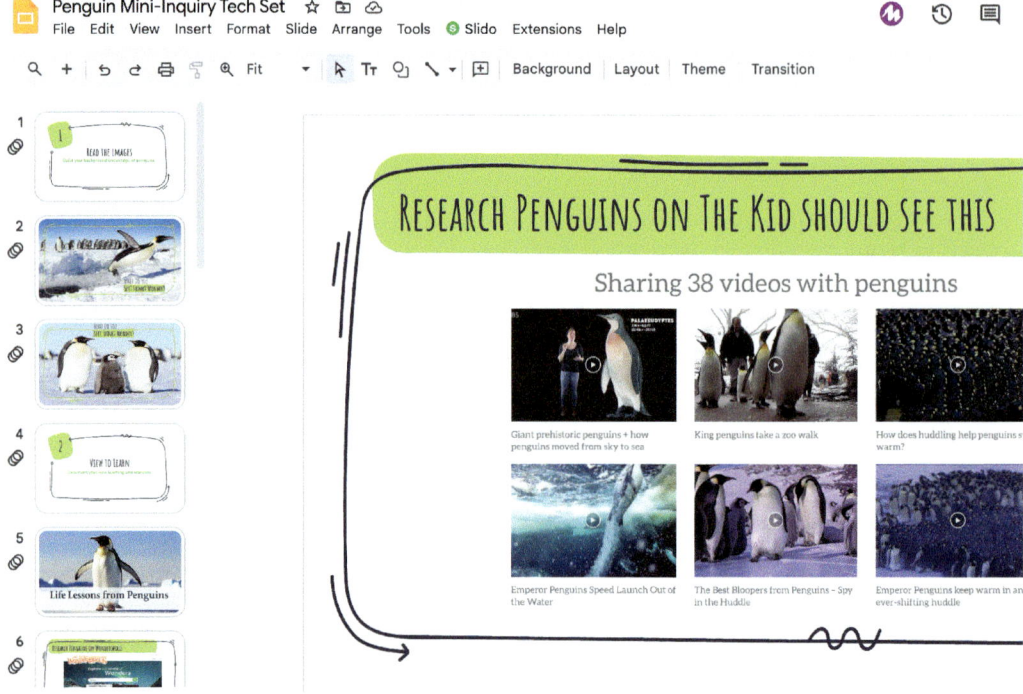

**Figure 5.26:** Google Slides is a great tool for curating a tech set for students. The Slide preview serves as a vertical workflow for students. They can progress from images to video to digital text with ease when you embed the content links on each Slide.

It's not just students who can be sucked into the vortex of exciting content—teachers and librarians can, too! In fact, as educators, we should explore our curriculum units with curiosity, passion, and the desire to learn something new! Even though we've all been to school for many, many years, each day we have the chance to keep seeking and keep learning. I love to discover new information as I prepare for a unit of study. It's even better when I can learn in the moment right alongside my students. I think it's critically important for students to see the joy we experience when discovering something new. I think it's even more important for them to see how we might experience cognitive dissonance when we encounter information we don't know.

I get excited when I don't know something in front of students because I want them to see what I do next as the teachable moment. What can we do when we don't know something? Rather than be embarrassed or ashamed, I want them to see that I embrace not knowing and that I have a set of strategies at the ready for how I can find out more. I can read a book. I can look up information online. I can ask a friend. I may not be able to learn more today, but I can come back to it another time. Not knowing is an important component of learning, and we have the responsibility to model what to do. Each day, our ability to model for students is one of the most powerful tools we have in our toolkit.

Katie Muhtaris is a tremendous model for what it looks like to go deep into the curiosity and content vortex. For years, she's been pulling me down the rabbit hole with her as we've written books, taught, and learned together. Katie will take you on her planning adventure and help you think through why and how to get curious about content.

## Katie Muhtaris - Planning for Content: Going Down the Rabbit Hole

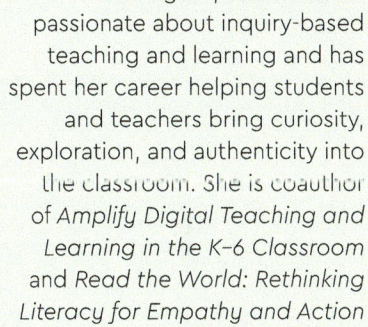

**Katie Muhtaris**
Katie is the elementary instructional facilitator in Barrington, Illinois. She is passionate about inquiry-based teaching and learning and has spent her career helping students and teachers bring curiosity, exploration, and authenticity into the classroom. She is coauthor of *Amplify Digital Teaching and Learning in the K–6 Classroom* and *Read the World: Rethinking Literacy for Empathy and Action* (with Kristin Ziemke).

How curiosity-driven teaching fosters deeper thinking and life-long learning.

To a passerby, it may have seemed like I was planning an adventurous vacation. However, my carefully curated Padlet of tourism articles, websites, maps, and videos was actually a road map for a different kind of journey. An inquiry journey. I've been writing curriculum units and lessons for the better part of nineteen years. Sometimes I wrote because I had no curriculum provided for me, other times because the provided curriculum was ineffective, dry, or lacking. Many times, I wrote as part of a team that wanted to build a curriculum that would inspire students and teachers to engage deeply, think critically, and connect to the world around them.

To the untrained eye, it may have appeared that I was filling my Padlet with a wide array of seemingly unconnected links. I was actually creating an "evidence board" of my thought process as I questioned, investigated, synthesized, analyzed, and reflected. My haphazard Padlet started with a need: create a geography unit for fifth graders. It eventually evolved into an inquiry journey for students that would challenge them to engage in a broad spectrum of literacy skills and, I hoped, find a seed of inspiration to begin building their own understanding. The secret sauce was my own curiosity.

Katie offers her personal curiosity a seat at the table and celebrates it as an essential force behind planning authentic and inspiring learning experiences for our students. When we gain excitement for our curriculum, so do our students.
I think it's important how Katie:
- Plans from two stances: curious inquirer and inquiry teacher.
- Names the many reading skills that go into content area reading and research.
- Identifies the learning assets and habits of mind for inquiry.
- Leverages AI as a thought partner.

**Figure 5.27:** A screenshot of Katie's Padlet as she started to plan a fifth-grade unit on geography.

**Get Curious**

Inquiry starts with curiosity, and as educators, we have the power to ignite that same curiosity in our students. It might feel like a challenge to allow our curiosity a seat at the planning table. In fact, it might be the last thing teachers consider as they balance standards, resources, student needs, and all of the other considerations of teaching and learning. The truth is, our own curiosity and our own ability to go down the rabbit hole might be the most essential part of planning authentic and inspiring learning experiences for our students. Why?

Teachers immersed in the inquiry process uniquely experience learning through the eyes of their students. They learn to meander through the forest of information we are bombarded with on a daily basis and begin to make sense of it in a way that helps us to develop a rich understanding of the world. In doing so, they wear two hats: curious inquirer and inquiry teacher. Kath Murdoch (2015) calls this split-screen teaching. This process of paying attention to how we are learning as much as what we are learning brings a deeply metacognitive aspect to the teacher's practice and the experience for the students. It's through this process that I was able to create a list of skills students would need to access resources, determine which resources would need to be adapted in order to be accessible, observe how resources worked together to build knowledge, and anticipate the possible directions that students might go in. I could see how a child might synthesize an article, map, and video to draw their own conclusions about an essential question. I was also able to anticipate where students might step into a much deeper rabbit hole, straying too far from the scope of our classroom work.

| SPLIT SCREEN INQUIRY | |
|---|---|
| **Teacher as Inquirer** | **Teacher as Inquiry Teacher** |
| Identifies relevant standards, overarching concepts, and essential questions during the inquiry process. | Revises essential questions in ways that spark student curiosity and invite deep thinking. Plans for how and when students will ask their own questions. |
| Takes note of what they are curious about and what questions they have about the topic. | Models curiosity by asking open-ended questions and demonstrating how to navigate resources, applying informational reading skills and disciplinary literacy. |
| Reads, views, and gathers diverse sources of information. | Selects and scaffolds resources to ensure accessibility and engagement for all students. Uses tools like AI to adapt resources for accessibility. |
| Organizes information to find patterns, connections, and gaps. | Guides students in using organizers, concept maps, or discussion protocols to structure and build thinking. |
| Revises questions based on new insights. | Coaches students in refining their own questions—narrowing or broadening as needed. |
| Analyzes multiple perspectives and evaluates credibility of sources. | Teaches and supports students to develop critical literacy skills by encouraging them to question sources and compare viewpoints. |
| Synthesizes information from multiple sources to construct new understanding. | Designs opportunities to prompt students to integrate information and form conclusions. |
| Draws conclusions and reflects on new learning. | Creates opportunities for students to share and apply their learning in meaningful ways. |
| Recognizes which lines of inquiry will support understanding and which are too far off track. | Helps students stay focused while allowing space for exploration. |
| Feels energized and excited to bring new learning opportunities to the classroom. | Models enthusiasm for learning and encourages a culture of curiosity in the classroom. |

**Create a Roadmap**

*Learners tend to learn more effectively when they are clear about their purpose. Knowing where you are going does not mean having to have every task mapped out in detail but it does mean clarity of purpose.*

— *Kath Murdoch*, The Power of Inquiry —

Fifth Grade Unit 2

**Unit Overview**

| | |
|---|---|
| **Essential Question** | What can we learn about the relationship between humans and their environment by studying how people adapt to, prepare for, and respond to potential geophysical events? |
| **Enduring Understandings** | • Scientists use tools such as data, maps, and models to study geophysical events, and their findings inform decisions that help communities in their decision making process.<br>• People make decisions about where to live based on a combination of environmental, economic, cultural, and social factors, even in areas prone to geophysical events or extreme weather events.<br>• Communities and governments play crucial roles in adapting to, preparing for, and responding to geophysical events, balancing immediate safety with long-term sustainability.<br>• Throughout history, human cultures have developed beliefs, traditions, and technologies shaped by their interaction with dynamic environments. |
| **Compelling Questions** | How can maps help us understand the relationship between people, places, and the environment?<br>Why would people live in areas that are impacted by geophysical activity or extreme weather events?<br>How do scientists and government officials work together to support communities living in close proximity to geophysical activity? |
| **Transfer Goal** | Students will be able to independently use their knowledge to draw conclusions about the relationship between people and the environment. |
| **Students will know** | • Students will understand how the physical geography of a place impacts the civic and economic decisions that people make.<br>• Students will understand different reasons (e.g. cultural, economic, environmental) why people choose to live in areas despite risks.<br>• Students will know how local communities and governments adapt to, prepare for, and respond to geophysical events, including specific examples like evacuation plans and early warning systems. |
| **Students will be skilled at** | • Students will be skilled at interpreting maps, charts, and data sets to identify patterns and relationships between human activity and geophysical events.<br>• Students will create maps and data visualizations to communicate information about geophysical events and their impact on communities.<br>• Students will be skilled at developing and investigating questions about human-environment interactions, using evidence to support their conclusions.<br>• Students will be skilled at using nonfiction reading strategies to understand, evaluate, and synthesize information about geophysical events from diverse sources.<br>• Students will be skilled at presenting their conclusions and recommendations through written, oral, or multimedia formats, tailoring their communication to different audiences.<br>• Students will be skilled at working in teams to explore compelling questions, share insights, and create cohesive presentations. |
| **Assessment** | • Inquiry self assessment<br>• Going public rubric<br>• Performance task |

**Figure 5.28:** The first page of the unit plan outlines our big ideas—essential and compelling questions, transfer goals, and what students will know and be able to do as a result of their inquiry throughout the unit.

Before diving down the research rabbit hole, I had a clear idea of what I was looking for. What initially started as "Let's create a geography unit that's not boring for kids" turned into the essential question, "What can we learn about the relationship between humans and their environment by studying how people adapt to, prepare for, and respond to potential geophysical events?" I started with one text that students would read in their literacy class as a spark point. The standards helped narrow down the topics we might address, but it was the essential question that I returned to again and again. This was an important reflection point and the beginning of my own split-screen planning process.

| Session Overview (15 days) ||||||
|---|---|---|---|---|---|
| **Compelling Question:** How can maps help us understand the relationships between people, places, and the environment? || **Compelling Questions:** Why would people live in areas that are impacted by geophysical activity or extreme weather events? <br> How do scientists and government officials work together to support communities living in close proximity to geophysical activity? ||||
| **Session 1 (2 days)** <br><br> How are maps created? <br> How has innovation impacted maps? | **Session 2 (2 days)** <br><br> What information can we learn from maps? | **Session 3 (1 day)** <br><br> How can we use maps to explain the locations of volcanoes? | **Session 4 (1 day)** <br><br> What are the human, economic, and natural costs and benefits of living in close proximity to volcanoes? | **Session 5 (7 days)** <br> **Student Inquiry** <br><br> What are the human, economic, and natural costs and benefits of living in close proximity to volcanoes? ||
| **Essential Question:** What can we learn about the relationship between humans and their environment by studying how people adapt to, prepare for, and respond to potential geophysical events? |||||| 
| **Session 6 (1 day)** <br><br> Why did people use myths to explain geophysical events? | **Session 7 (1 day)** <br><br> What have we learned about the relationship between humans and their environment by studying how people adapt to, prepare for, and respond to potential geophysical events? | | | | |

**Figure 5.29:** This session-by-session layout gives teachers a clear overview of the unit's flow, including the number of sessions and suggested timing. Teachers are encouraged to adapt the pacing and activities based on student needs and interests.

## The Joy and Practicality of Inquiry Learning

I genuinely enjoy this process. I want to read people's stories. I want to explore new types of resources and technology. I find it awe-inspiring to learn about something I once knew nothing about and exhilarating to challenge my own misconceptions. This isn't an innate skill—it's one anyone can develop. Anyone can find joy in inquiry. Like detectives solving mysteries, we find excitement in diving deep into topics and exploring different perspectives. The joy of learning grows as we create something meaningful—whether it's a project, a discussion, or an opportunity to make a real-world impact. Inquiry gives us the time and space to be more curious, engaged, and eager to keep learning.

And what of the practical benefits? I gained more than just knowledge during this process. I expanded my vocabulary, explored Geographic Information Systems, and synthesized information from videos, blogs, websites, scientific data sets, and maps. Watching documentaries offered new perspectives. I felt inspired to travel, eager to experience what I was learning firsthand, and, importantly, filled with a renewed sense of awe. Inquiry has a way of revealing what was once unknown or even inconceivable—those moments when understanding shifts in an instant, changing the way we see the world. Time and again, I found myself pausing, marveling at connections I had never made before. Most importantly, I considered how this learning applied to me, not just as an educator but as a lifelong learner. In the process, I engaged all of these literacy skills:

- **Multimodal Reading:** Engaging with a wide variety of resources such as websites, blog posts, videos, images, maps, graphs, and podcasts.
- **Comprehension and Critical Thinking:** Understanding complex texts, identifying main ideas, and making connections to prior knowledge.
- **Evaluating Sources:** Determining credibility, bias, and reliability when analyzing different types of information.
- **Investigating Multiple Perspectives:** Reading from diverse sources and viewpoints to gain a well-rounded understanding of a topic.
- **Making Inferences:** Reading between the lines to draw conclusions based on evidence.
- **Summarizing and Synthesizing:** Combining information from multiple sources to deepen understanding.
- **Formulating and Revising Questions:** Crafting open-ended, thought-provoking questions that guide research and discussion. Revising questions as needed to keep the inquiry flowing.
- **Organizing Ideas and Mapping:** Recording key information in a structured way that supports deep thinking such as concept maps.
- **Explaining Thinking:** Articulating reasoning and justifying conclusions based on evidence.
- **Asking Clarifying Questions:** Deepening understanding by seeking further explanations.
- **Active Listening:** Paying close attention to others' ideas and synthesizing them into one's own understanding.
- **Reflecting on Learning:** Assessing progress, identifying new questions, and refining inquiry paths.
- **Adapting Strategies:** Adjusting research approaches when faced with challenges or new insights.

As a teacher, I was able to reflect on my own process, consider what entry points existed for students, and curate resources in a way that would enable them to follow their own learning journey. I became more intentional about scaffolding experiences, anticipating where students might struggle and designing opportunities for them to make their own discoveries. My role wasn't to provide all the answers but to create the conditions for curiosity to thrive.

**Essential Learning Assets for Inquiry**
Every time I go down an inquiry rabbit hole, I'm reminded that the process is just as important as the outcome. The most powerful learning happens when we embrace curiosity, persistence, and the ability to adapt. Inquiry isn't just about research skills; it's about developing a mindset. Some of the most essential learning assets aren't about knowing the right answers but about having the habits of mind to navigate uncertainty and keep going when things get messy.

As inquiry teachers, we have to be keenly aware of how we engage our own learning assets, modeling the same skills we hope to cultivate in our students.

To support students in becoming confident, capable inquirers, our district has identified four key inquiry identities: Thinkers, Self-Managers, Collaborators, and Investigators. Each of these identities represents a different way students approach learning, helping them develop the mindset and skills to become confident, capable inquirers.

**Thinkers** embrace curiosity, critical thinking, and metacognition. Inquiry starts with curiosity—the drive to ask big questions, follow interesting leads, and explore beyond the surface. But curiosity alone isn't enough. Critical thinking helps learners evaluate sources, analyze biases, and sort through conflicting information to form their own well-reasoned conclusions. And then there's metacognition, learning to think about how we think. The best inquirers constantly reflect on what's working, what's not, and how they can refine their approach to learning.

**Self-Managers** persist even when inquiry gets challenging. Research is rarely a straight line, and it takes resilience to push through roadblocks, false starts, and frustrating dead ends. Flexibility is just as important—new information can challenge initial assumptions, and inquirers have to be willing to shift their thinking. Patience plays a role, too. Inquiry takes time, and deep learning doesn't happen overnight. Ultimately, students need opportunities to take ownership of the process. The most meaningful inquiry journeys happen when learners follow their curiosity rather than simply checking off boxes.

**Collaborators** know that learning is a social process. Inquiry thrives in discussion-rich environments, where people share ideas, challenge each other's thinking, and build new understandings together. Inquirers learn to articulate their ideas clearly, listen actively, and ask thoughtful questions that push conversations forward. It's not just about speaking—it's about engaging in meaningful dialogue, expressing complex thoughts, and adapting communication styles for different audiences. Whether discussing ideas with peers, presenting findings, or writing about their discoveries, effective communicators make their thinking visible and contribute to a deeper, collective understanding. Collaboration isn't limited to face-to-face conversations—it also happens in digital spaces. By using a variety of tools for communication and teamwork, students learn that collaboration can take many forms, each offering new ways to share and refine their ideas.

**Investigators** are naturally curious, but they also know how to dig deep. They look for patterns, connections, and evidence that help them form meaningful conclusions. They approach topics with an open mind, ready to explore different perspectives and make sense of complex information. Investigators don't just consume knowledge; they construct understanding by asking deeper questions and making meaningful connections across different sources.

Inquiry isn't just about finding answers—it's about developing the mindset and skills to keep asking better questions. When students (and teachers!) cultivate these learning assets, they don't just complete an inquiry unit; they build a way of thinking that serves them well beyond the classroom.

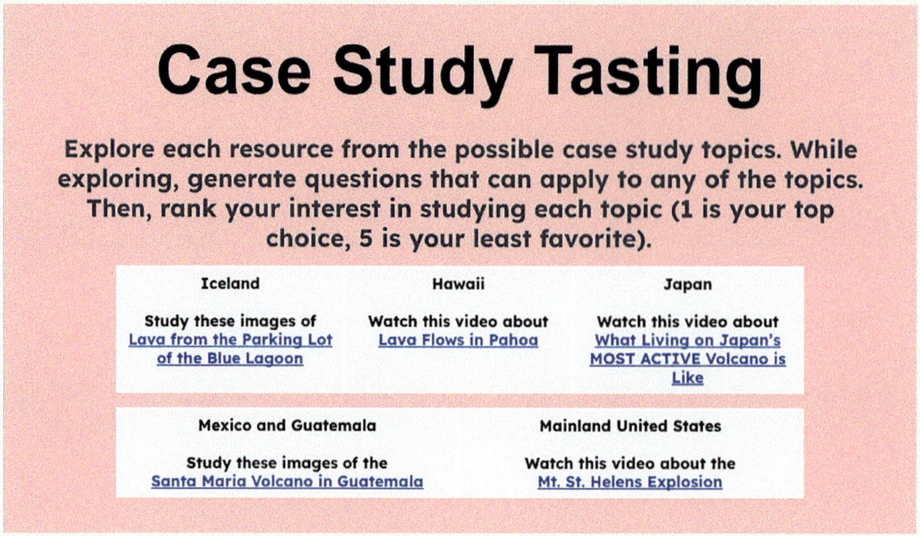

**Figure 5.30:** Prior to starting inquiry, we offer students a tasting menu so that they can see where they may be most interested in pursuing an inquiry. Students explore content for all the topics we have resources for, generate questions, and prioritize based on their interests.

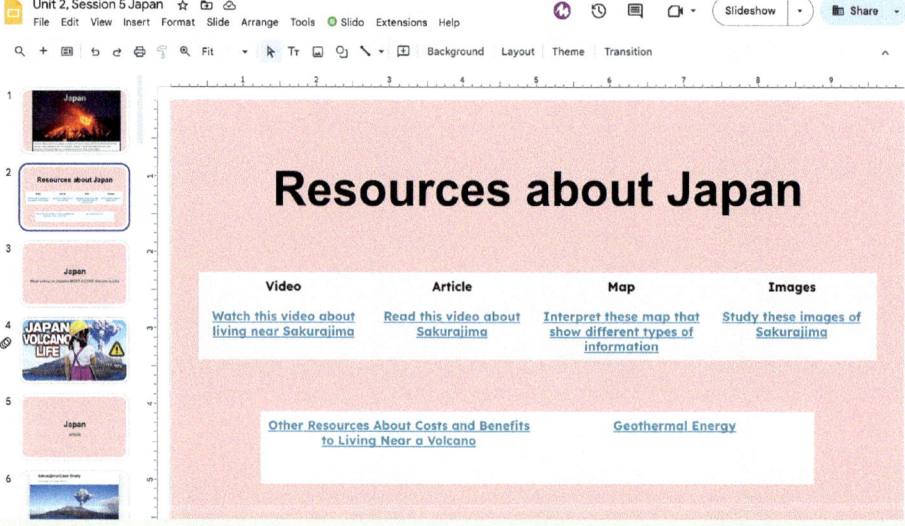

**Figure 5.31:** A Google Slide deck is one way we share resources with students, in addition to any research they may conduct in class or with the librarian. We also use Padlets, HyperDocs, and websites. A team of teachers makes this decision based on the age of the students and the nature of the resources.

### AI as a Thought Partner

As I ventured deeper into my inquiry journey and into curating resources, I introduced a new collaborator: artificial intelligence. At first, I saw AI as just another search engine. However, as I became more familiar with how to use it effectively, I realized its untapped potential. Here are some of the ways that AI helped me to develop and refine my ideas as I worked.

**Refining and Validating Ideas:** One of the main ways that I used AI was by bringing initial concepts to the discussion and asking for feedback on structures, resources, alignment with standards, and possible real-world connections. I would often ask for feedback about what was missing or what I might not have thought of. AI tools can help by generating a variety of possibilities for essential and supporting questions, providing feedback on initial ideas, and helping refine thinking by offering a variety of options. It was necessary to give it parameters, such as letting the tool know which standards and grade level I was planning for and giving the tool a gist of the unit.

Some helpful prompts:
- "How can I frame a compelling essential question about [topic]?"
- "Can you make this question more open ended and inquiry driven?"
- "Here is the essential question I'm considering. Can you write a few different versions for me?"
- "What supporting or follow-up questions might I or students ask to help students develop their own answer to this compelling question?"
- "Can you organize these supporting questions by the disciplines of economics, civics, geography, and history?"

**Generating Subtopics/Areas for Inquiry:** When I made the decision to focus the student inquiry on communities living in close proximity to volcanic regions, I realized that I had gaps in my own knowledge. AI helped me generate a list of different locations to start researching and was able to point me in the right direction for resources to begin with. It's important to note here that, as of writing this, I often found AI tools lacking in this area. Some links were active, relevant, and useful while others were broken, missing, or misleading. Teacher expertise and analysis are still very critical at this juncture. That said, AI was able to surface some resources that I wasn't otherwise able to find through other tools, and my inquiry brain took over from there.

Some helpful prompts:
- "Can you provide case studies or examples of communities that . . . ?"
- "What are some historical and modern examples of . . . ?"
- "Give me a list of subtopics/areas/places that I might want to explore."
- "Include links for each of the suggestions that you give me."
- "Can you give me real-world examples of [concept] in action?"
- "What are some case studies that illustrate [topic] in different cultures or time periods?"
- "How has [concept] evolved over time, and what are some key historical or modern-day examples?"
- "What are some communities that have successfully addressed [challenge]?"
- "How do different countries or regions approach [economic, environmental, or social issue]?"
- "Can you suggest texts, multimedia, or artifacts that support inquiry on [topic]?"

**Providing Suggestions for Framing Concepts:** I found AI a helpful partner in generating a multitude of ways to approach things with students. While I didn't always agree with some of the suggestions, it was helpful to have a menu to choose from. For example, I asked the tool to help me generate a list of ways to graphically organize key concepts in the unit. It was then able to further refine suggestions based on age. I found similar uses for getting ideas for instructional strategies, interactive ways to learn, and assessment tools.

Some helpful prompts:
- "How would you define [concept] in a way that is accessible for [grade level] students?"
- "What are some age-appropriate ways to explain [complex term] to elementary students?"
- "Can you provide multiple definitions of [concept] from different disciplinary perspectives (e.g., historian, geographer, economist)?"
- "Can you give me an engaging way to introduce [term] to young learners?"
- "What are some engaging metaphors or analogies to help students understand [concept]?"
- "How can I connect [concept] to something students encounter in their daily lives?"
- "What are some misconceptions students might have about [concept], and how can I address them?"

**Exploring Multiple Perspectives:** The AI tool was helpful in identifying other perspectives on the topics I was looking at. I found that to get the most from AI in this area, I needed to ask a variety of prompts to surface different aspects of the topic. This served to build my own knowledge while I considered which aspects would be most useful to bring into our unit. For example, one question on cultural perspectives led to an entire conversation about Indigenous beliefs, civic discourse, cultural stories, and ultimately asking for suggestions on picturebooks that students could read and consider.

Some helpful prompts:
- "How might a historian, economist, geographer, and civic scholar each approach [topic]?"
- "What are different cultural perspectives on [concept]?"
- "Can you compare how [concept] is viewed or applied in different parts of the world?"

**Organizing and Structuring Information**

Some helpful prompts:
- "Can you create a concept map of key ideas related to [topic]?"
- "What are the essential subtopics I should cover when teaching [concept]?"
- "Can you generate a timeline of key events related to [topic]?"
- "What are different ways I can scaffold this learning experience for students at different levels of understanding?"

AI is a valuable thought partner, but it cannot replace the interdisciplinary literacy and critical thinking skills essential for inquiry-based learning. It's important to verify sources and apply critical thinking. AI-generated information can sometimes be biased, outdated, or misleading, making human judgment essential in the inquiry process.

It was my own curiosity, skill set, and persistence that ultimately allowed me to structure the unit with clarity and purpose. AI provides broad insights, but only human expertise can adapt learning to the unique needs of students. Ultimately, inquiry-based learning isn't just about building engaging units—it's about fostering a mindset of curiosity, adaptability, and lifelong learning. When educators embrace the process themselves, they not only create richer experiences for students but also become more engaged, reflective, and inspired teachers. The journey of inquiry is ongoing. Where will your next rabbit hole take you?

Digital content is a terrific tool for sparking a young person's curiosity. When we engage students to read across the curriculum, we help them understand issues that matter. Content-area reading promotes critical thinking, perspective taking, and empathy. As students apply a lens of self, others, and the world, we help learners move from personal understanding to a multifaceted view, deepening their agency and ownership in their learning journey.

**bit.ly/4dz16gl**
Visit the website to hear Kristin share more about Chapter 5.
(Password: **KZTandT**)

# Putting It into *Practice*

**1.** *Listen and learn with a podcast.*

- Introduce a podcast as a tool for learning with students. For the first listen-and-learn experience, I like KidNuz or SquizKids. Both are current event news sites created for kids and have podcasts with a short run time—typically seven or eight minutes.
- Give students a blank piece of paper to sketch their new learning or guide them to fold their paper in half lengthwise and write an L for Learning at the top of one side and a ? for Questions at the top of the other side.
- Start the podcast by modeling for students. After thirty seconds of listening, pause the podcast and think aloud. Ask a question. State something you heard. Then model how to draw and write your questions and new learning.
- Play the podcast for 30–60 seconds more. Pause again. This time, invite students to draw and write in order to ask questions and document learning.
- Continue with this process for longer and longer time segments until the podcast is finished or students show you they are done for the day.

**bit.ly/4cXFiej**
KidNuz

**bit.ly/44feyUk**
SquizKids

## 2. Create a basic content area tech set for students.

- Think about an upcoming unit in which you would like to help students build background knowledge as they begin the unit.
- Using Slides, PowerPoint, or Keynote, prepare four slides that you will use with students.
- Locate two images that match your content study. Try to find photos that will invite discussion and questions. Google Images has some good options; I also like to use Unsplash. Place one image on slide one and the other on slide two. When you show these slides to students, ask them, "What do you see? Think? Wonder?" (Refer back to Sara's article on page 168 for support.)
- Go to the The Kid Should See This website. Using the search feature, look for a video that addresses your topic. Once you find a video that supports your unit, copy or embed it onto slide 3 of your deck. Before you show students the video, ask them to draw and write their thinking in a notebook or on a thinksheet. Feel free to pause the video as it plays to give students time to draw and write.
- On slide 4, have students do something with their new learning. Write, talk, make, or sketch are all great ways to have young people show what they know! You could also have them read something to keep thinking.
- When finished, reflect on the lesson structure. Ask students, "How'd it go with your learning today?" Their feedback will help you plan your next lesson.

## 3. Author an article for your readers.

- Instead of paying for an article that doesn't exactly meet your students' needs, make one!
- Using Docs, Word, or Pages, find a template or freestyle your own design (I typically use a newsletter or recipe template).
- Do a quick internet search to research your topic. Identify 4–5 key details that you will add.
- Use your research to write a short article, typically 5–6 sentences depending on the age of the students you work with.
- Locate images that support your text using your favorite Creative Commons site. Position the images within your doc.
- Add nonfiction features like words in bold print, italics, captions, maps, or cross-sections to enrich the reading experience.
- You can adjust the text complexity, language, or add a QR code to expand access to your readers.

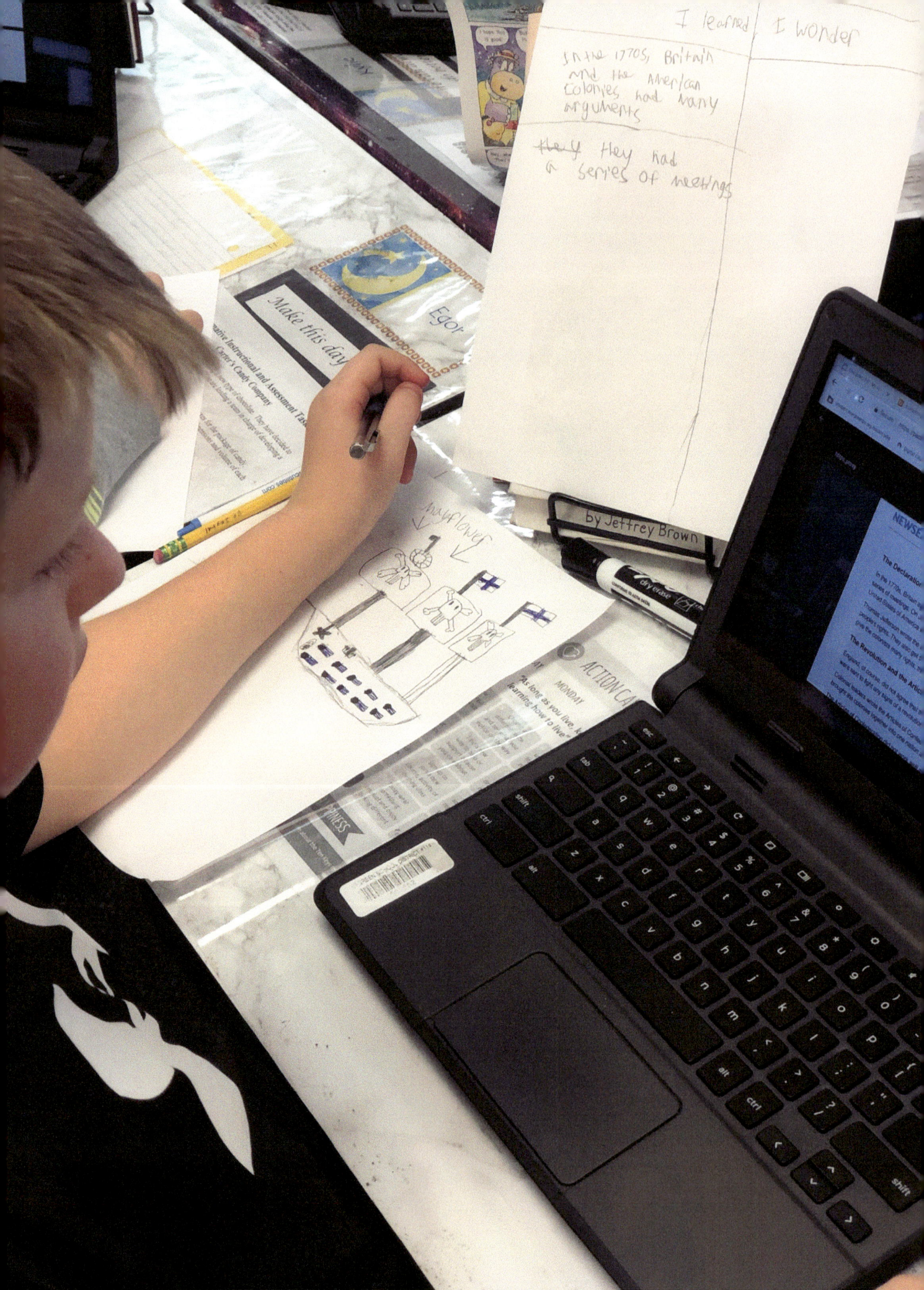

# Conclusion

As we pursue lifelong literacy, we keep learning. Literacy is a living and evolving practice. We recognize that all screen time is not equal; passive consumption does not result in high-level thinkers, nor does rote skill-and-drill practice. Losing oneself in an audiobook, creating a movie about one's learning, or collaborating with classmates to share with an authentic audience does. We learn and grow by moving beyond personal preference, one-or-the-other debates, simplistic dualisms, or even absolutism, and embrace new modes and formats to build knowledge.

It is text *and* tech.

It is print *and* digital.

It can be personal *and* collaborative.

It is embedded in all we do.

Yes, *and*. We guide students to access, craft, create, and comprehend all types of information and coach them to be adaptable and open to continued change.

We recognize that today, change occurs quickly. Campbell and Olteanu write, "We must develop new understanding of literacy in the face of rapid and widespread digital reconfigurations of how we learn, communicate, and exist" (2023, p. 572). Not only is the way we read changing, but so is the way we interact and exist. Digital is so enmeshed and entangled into everyday life that society can no longer separate the two (Lacković, 2020). As a result, literacy researchers and futurists claim we are now in the post-digital era, where text and tech are united and can no longer stand in opposition, let alone be independent of each other.

"As digital technologies permeate human existence, reading, writing, and other literacy practices occur in post-digital literacy ecologies" (Bhatt, 2023, p. 1). New tools have bred new modalities for interaction, resulting in new ways to communicate. Access to information is abundant, technologies advance rapidly, and literacy scales beyond print or digital. Learning, education, and literacy "need to 'reinvent' existing theories and practices for postdigital context" (Campbell & Olteanu, 2023, p. 573). Our lessons, our instruction, and our ecosystems of thought must evolve as the learning landscape shifts.

Learn. Unlearn. Relearn.

As conditions continue to change, we work to develop critical thinkers across mediums. We uplift student agency and liberate young people as they gain the knowledge, skills, and critical thinking abilities they need to keep learning without us. Learn how to learn. If we can teach our students that, they'll be prepared to interact with text, tech, and whatever comes next.

# References

**Introduction**

Hammond, Z. L. (2015). *Culturally responsive teaching and the brain.* Corwin Press.

Muhammad, G. (2020). *Cultivating genius.* Scholastic Inc.

Qarooni, N. (2024). *Nourishing caregiver collaborations: Elevating home experiences and classroom practices for collective care.* Routledge.

Shelton, K., & Lanier, D. (2024). *The promises and perils of AI in education: Ethics and equity have entered the chat.* Lanier Learning.

Toffler, A. (1970). *Future shock.* Random House.

**Chapter 1**

Clowes, R. W. (2018). Screen reading and the creation of new cognitive ecologies. *AI and Society, 34*(4), 705–720.

Coiro, J. (2020). Toward a multifaceted heuristic of digital reading to inform assessment, research, practice, and policy. *Reading Research Quarterly.* Advance online publication. https://digitalcommons.uri.edu/education_facpubs/21/

Erstad, O., Kucirkova, N. I., Mangen, A., Aarsand, P., & Blikstand-Balas, M. (2023). Reading in the digital age. *Nordic Journal of Digital Literacy 18*(4), 272–286. https://uis.brage.unit.no/uis-xmlui/bitstream/handle/11250/3119536/erstad-et-al-2023-reading-inthe-digital-age.pdf?sequence=2&isAllowed=y

Festinger, L. (1962). *A theory of cognitive dissonance.* Stanford University Press.

Freire, P., & Macedo, D. (1987). *Literacy: Reading the word and the world.* Bergin & Garvey.

Goodman, Y. M. (1978). Kid watching: An alternative to testing. *National Elementary Principal, 57*(4), 41–45.

Malafouris, L. (2013). *How things shape the mind: A theory of material engagement.* MIT Press.

Mangen, A. (2016). What hands may tell us about reading and writing. *Educational Theory, 66*(4), 457–477. https://doi.org/10.1111/edth.12183

Muhtaris, K., & Ziemke, K. (2015). *Amplify: Digital teaching and learning in the K–6 classroom.* Heinemann.

National Council of Teachers of English. (2019). *Definition of literacy in a digital age.* National Council of Teachers of English.

Singer Trakhman, L. M., Alexander, P. A., & Silverman, A. B. (2018). Profiling reading in print and digital mediums. *Learning and Instruction, 57,* 5–17. https://doi.org/10.1016/j.learninstruc.2018.04.001

Støle, H. (2018). Why digital natives need books: The myth of the digital native. *First Monday, 23*(10). https://doi.org/10.5210/fm.v23i10.9422

UNESCO. (n.d.). *Literacy.* https://www.unesco.org/en/literacy

van der Weel, A., & Mangen, A. (2022). Textual reading in digitised classrooms: Reflections on reading beyond the internet. *International Journal of Educational Research, 115,* Article 102036. https://doi.org/10.1016/j.ijer.2022.102036

**Chapter 2**

Albright, L. K., & Ariail, M. (2005). Tapping the potential of teacher read-alouds in middle schools. *Journal of Adolescent & Adult Literacy, 48*(7), 582–591.

Allington, R. L., & Gabriel, R. E. (2012). Every child, every day. *Educational Leadership, 69*(6), 10–15.

Bezemer, J., & Kress, G. (2016). *Multimodality, learning and communication: A social semiotic frame.* Routledge.

Cherry-Paul, S., & Johansen, D. (2014). *Teaching interpretation: Using text-based evidence to construct meaning.* Heinemann.

Clear, J. (2018). *Atomic habits: An easy & proven way to build good habits & break bad ones.* Avery.

Coustillac, R. (2020, June 30). *The ear reading advantage: Why students need audiobook access.* OverDrive. https://company.overdrive.com/2020/06/30/the-ear-reading-advantage-why-students-need-audiobook-access/

Deniz, F., Nunez-Elizalde, A. O., Huth, A. G., & Gallant, J. L. (2019). The representation of semantic information across human cerebral cortex during listening versus reading is invariant to stimulus modality. *Journal of Neuroscience, 39*(39), 7722–7736. https://doi.org/10.1523/JNEUROSCI.0675-19.2019

Ebarvia, T. (2017, December 13). Tricia Ebarvia: How inclusive is your literacy classroom really? *Heinemann Blog.* https://blog.heinemann.com/heinemann-fellow-tricia-ebavaria-inclusive-literacy-classroom-really

Fisher, D., Frey, N., & Lapp, D. (2008). Shared readings: Modeling comprehension, vocabulary, text structures, and text features for older readers. *The Reading Teacher, 61*(7), 548–556.

Gallagher, K. (2009). *Readicide: How schools are killing reading and what you can do about it.* Stenhouse Publishers.

Hammond, Z. (2024, June 11). [Keynote address]. ESC of Central Ohio Summer Literacy Institute, Columbus, OH.

Johansen, D. (2014, March 12). 10 ways digital bins spark engagement. LitLearnAct. https://litlearnact.wordpress.com/10-ways-digital-bins-spark-engagement/

Kittle, P. (2012). *Book love: Developing depth, stamina, and passion in adolescent readers.* Heinemann.

Lesesne, T. S. (2006). Reading aloud: A worthwhile investment? *Voices from the Middle, 13*(4), 50–54.

Moreno, R., & Mayer, R. (2007). Interactive multimodal learning environments. *Educational Psychology Review, 19*(3), 309–326. https://doi.org/10.1007/s10648-007-9047-2

Muhtaris, K., & Ziemke, K. (2015). *Amplify: Digital teaching and learning in the K–6 classroom.* Heinemann.

National Council of Teachers of English. (2017). *Statement on classroom libraries.* National Council of Teachers of English.

Nouri, J. (2019). Students multimodal literacy and design of learning during self-studies in higher education. *Technology, Knowledge and Learning, 24,* 683–698. https://link.springer.com/article/10.1007/s10758-018-9360-5

Phuong, A. E., Nguyen, J., & Marie, D. (2017). Evaluating an adaptive equity-oriented pedagogy: A study of its impacts in higher education. *Journal of Effective Teaching, 17*(2), 5–44.

Student Achievement Division. (2012, July). *The third teacher* (Capacity Building Series, Special Edition #27). Government of Ontario. https://www.education-leadership-ontario.ca/application/files/1714/9884/6979/Third_Teacher-Designing_the_Learning_Environment_for_Mathematics_and_Literacy_K-12.pdf

Trelease, J. (2006). *The read-aloud handbook* (6th ed.). Penguin Books.

**Chapter 3**

Baron, N. S., Calixte, R. M., & Havewala, M. (2017). The persistence of print among university students: An exploratory study. *Telematics and Informatics, 34*(5), 590–604. https://doi.org/10.1016/j.tele.2016.11.008

Baughcum, C. (2018a, March 17). *When they say, "I can't draw"* [Video]. YouTube. https://youtu.be/PWCJI-b-p_w?si=Pgnq28hPIDzqRseN

Baughcum, C. (2018b, March 24) *When they believe they can't draw* [Video]. YouTube. https://youtu.be/miuADyBxeqE?si=46NM1QR1ZcGlJbck

Baughcum, C. (2019). *My pencil made me do it: A guide to sketchnoting.* Proving Press.

Duke, N., & Pearson, P. (2002). Effective practices for developing reading comprehension. In A. E. Farstrup & S. J. Samuels (Eds.), *What research has to say about reading instruction* (3rd ed., pp. 205–242). International Reading Association, Inc. https://www.researchgate.net/publication/254282574_Effective_Practices_for_Developing_Reading_Comprehension

Edmiston, B., & Enciso, P. (n.d.). *Dramatic inquiry and collaborative meaning-making.* [Unpublished manuscript].

Edwards, C., Gandini, L., & Forman, G. (Eds.). (1998). *The hundred languages of children: The Reggio Emilia approach to early childhood education* (2nd ed.). Ablex Publishing.

Ferguson, R. F., Phillips, S. F., Rowley, J. F. S., & Friedlander, J. W. (2015, October). *The influence of teaching beyond standardized test scores: Engagement, mindsets, and agency*. The Achievement Gap Initiative at Harvard University.

Freire, P. (1970). *Pedagogy of the oppressed*. Herder and Herder.

Freire, P. (1985). Reading the world and reading the word: An interview with Paulo Freire. *Language Arts, 62*(1), 15–21.

Grotzer, T. A., Gonzalez, E., & Forshaw, T. (2021). *How fast fish sink or swim: Adopting an agentive view of learners* [Research brief]. Next Level Lab: Applied Learning Sciences for Access, Innovation, and Mastery at Harvard Graduate School of Education.

Harvey, S., & Goudvis, A. (2000). *Strategies that work: Teaching comprehension to enhance understanding*. Stenhouse Publishers.

Hillesund, T. (2010). Digital reading spaces: How expert readers handle books, the web and electronic paper. *First Monday, 15*(4). https://doi.org/10.5210/fm.v15i4.2762

Johnston, P. (2004). *Choice words*. Stenhouse Publishers.

Krechevsky, M. (2021). *Documenting children's learning – an interview with Mara Krechevsky*. Harvard Project Zero.

Malafouris, L. (2013). *How things shape the mind: A theory of material engagement*. MIT Press.

Mangen, A. (2016). What hands may tell us about reading and writing. *Educational Theory, 66*(4), 457–477. https://doi.org/10.1111/edth.12183

Organisation for Economic Co-operation and Development. (n.d.). *The OECD Learning Compass 2030*. https://www.oecd.org/en/data/tools/oecd-learning-compass-2030.html

Pillars, W. (2015). *Visual note-taking for educators: A teacher's guide to student creativity*. W. W. Norton & Company.

Rohde, M. (2012). *The sketchnote handbook: The illustrated guide to visual note-taking*. Peachpit Press.

Rosenblatt, L. M. (1978). *The reader, the text, the poem: The transactional theory of the literary work*. Southern Illinois University Press.

Street, B. V. (2003). What's "new" in New Literacy Studies? Critical approaches to literacy in theory and practice. *Current Issues in Comparative Education, 5*(2), 77–91.

Thorn, K. (2013, January 15). *What are sketch notes?*. NuggetHead Studioz. nuggethead.net/2013/01/what-are-sketch-notes/

Vasquez, V. M. (2004). *Negotiating critical literacies with young children*. Lawrence Erlbaum Associates.

Ziemke, K., & Muhtaris, K. (2020). *Read the world: Rethinking literacy for empathy and action in a digital age*. Heinemann.

**Chapter 4**

Bishop, R. S. (1990). Mirrors, windows, and sliding glass doors. *Perspectives: Choosing and Using Books for the Classroom, 6*(3), ix–xi.

Center on the Developing Child at Harvard University. (2019, August 9). *Play in early childhood: The role of play in any setting* [Video]. https://developingchild.harvard.edu/resources/videos/play-in-early-childhood-the-role-of-play-in-any-setting/

Daniels, H. (2017). *The curious classroom: 10 structures for teaching with student-directed inquiry.* Heinemann.

Foundation for Young Australians. (2017). *The new work smarts: Thriving in the New Work Order* (New Work Order). https://www.fya.org.au/app/uploads/2021/09/FYA_TheNewWorkSmarts_July2017.pdf

LEGO Group. (2024, September 10). *Unleash the fun! The LEGO Group is encouraging families to build more play into every day and join its global "Play is Your Superpower" campaign.* LEGO Newsroom. https://www.lego.com/en-us/aboutus/news/2024/september/play-is-your-superpower-campaign?locale=en-us

Neuman, M., & Freschi, E. (2023, October 3). *Putting the fun in fundamental: How playful learning improves children's outcomes.* Federation of American Scientists. https://fas.org/publication/playful-learning-improves-childrens-outcomes/

Ross, E. M. (2023, May 17). *Embracing learning through play: A new book encourages playful learning in classrooms — for all ages.* Harvard Graduate School of Education. https://www.gse.harvard.edu/ideas/usable-knowledge/23/05/embracing-learning-through-play

Scholastic Parents Staff. (2025, February 25). *How to help your child find just-right books.* Scholastic Canada. https://www2.scholastic.ca/scholasticblog/2025/02/25/how-to-help-your-child-find-just-right-books/

TEDx Talks. (2014, June 13). *The decline of play | Peter Gray | TEDxNavesink* [Video]. YouTube. http://www.youtube.com/watch?v=Bg-GEzM7iTk

Udemy Business. (2022). *2022 Udemy workplace learning trends report.*

Vincent-Lancrin, S., González-Sancho, C., Bouckaert, M., de Luca, F., Fernández-Barrerra, M., Jacotin, G., Urgel, J., & Vidal, Q. (2019, October 24). *Fostering students' creativity and critical thinking: What it means in school* (Educational Research and Innovation). OECD Publishing. https://doi.org/10.1787/62212c37-en

Wells, R. (2024, February 19). Soft skills vs. power skills—is there a difference? *Forbes.* https://www.forbes.com/sites/rachelwells/2024/02/19/soft-skills-vs-power-skills-is-there-a-difference/

World Economic Forum. (2023). *Defining education 4.0: A taxonomy for the future of learning* [White paper]. https://www3.weforum.org/docs/WEF_Defining_Education_4.0_2023.pdf

Zosh, J. M., Gaudreau, C., Golinkoff, R. M., & Hirsh-Pasek, K. (2022). The power of playful learning in the early childhood setting. *Young Children, 77*(2). https://www.naeyc.org/resources/pubs/yc/summer2022/power-playful-learning

**Chapter 5**

California Academy of Sciences (2021). *Timelapse: Photosynthesis Seen from Space (Educator Version)* [Video]. YouTube. https://www.youtube.com/watch?v=Nsmdzd2NSjQ

Costa, A. L., & Kallick, B. (Eds.). (2008). *Learning and leading with habits of mind: 16 essential characteristics for success.* Association for Supervision and Curriculum Development.

Hammond, Z. (2024, June 11). [Keynote address]. ESC of Central Ohio Summer Literacy Institute, Columbus, OH.

Harvey, S., & Goudvis, A., (2016). Content literacy: *Building knowledge through thinking-intensive learning.* Stephanie Harvey Consulting. https://www.stephanieharvey.com/sites/default/files/ContentLiteracyArticle_fromPDCJ.pdf

Mathias, B., & von Kriegstein, K. (2023, January). Enriched learning: Behavior, brain, and computation. *Trends in Cognitive Sciences, 27*(1), 81–97. https://doi.org/10.1016/j.tics.2022.10.007

Minor, C. (2018, January 12–15). [Keynote speech]. Heinemann Multi-Day Institute: Teaching with Student Directed Inquiry, Santa Fe, NM.

Murdoch, K. (2015). *The power of inquiry: Teaching and learning with curiosity, creativity, and purpose in the contemporary classroom.* Hawker Brownlow Education.

Pearson, D. (2008, May 4–8). *Today's new knowledge is tomorrow's background knowledge* [Keynote address]. International Reading Association Annual Conference, Atlanta, GA.

Shelton, K., & Lanier, D. (2024). *The promises and perils of AI in education: Ethics and equity have entered the chat.* Lanier Learning.

Warner, A. (2022, August 30). The benefits of arts education for K–12 students. *US News & World Report.* https://www.usnews.com/education/k12/articles/the-benefits-of-arts-education-for-k-12-students.

Ziemke, K., & Muhtaris, K. (2019). *Read the world: Rethinking literacy for empathy and action in a digital age.* Heinemann.

**Figure 5.2**

Keith Allison from Hanover, MD, USA. CC BY-SA 2.0. https://creativecommons.org/licenses/by-sa/2.0 via Wikimedia Commons.

Erik Drost, CC BY 2.0. https://creativecommons.org/licenses/by/2.0 via Wikimedia Commons.

Michael Barera, CC BY-SA 4.0. https://creativecommons.org/licenses/by-sa/4.0 via Wikimedia Commons.

**Conclusion**

Bhatt, I. (2023). Postdigital literacies. In P. Jandrić (Ed.), *Encyclopedia of postdigital science and education,* 1–5. Springer Nature Switzerland. https://doi.org/10.1007/978-3-031-35469-4_15-1

Campbell, C., & Olteanu, A. (2023). The challenge of postdigital literacy: Extending multimodality and social semiotics for a new age. *Postdigital Science and Education, 6,* 572–594. https://doi.org/10.1007/s42438-023-00414-8

Lacković, N. (2020). Thinking with digital images in the post-truth era: A method in critical media literacy. *Postdigital Science and Education, 2,* 442–462. https://doi.org/10.1007/s42438-019-00099-y

# Biographies

**Kristin Ziemke**

Kristin Ziemke is a lifelong teacher and curious learner who has worked in service to young people for more than two decades. Recognized internationally for her expertise in literacy, inquiry, and technology, she partners with educators and organizations around the world to design learning experiences that redefine school. An expert kid-watcher and active listener, Kristin centers her work around students—amplifying their voices, nurturing agency, and honoring their stories. A resident teacher for the Big Shoulders Fund in Chicago, she is a National Board Certified teacher and the coauthor of *Read the World: Rethinking Literacy for Empathy and Action in a Digital Age*, *Amplify: Digital Teaching and Learning in the K–6 Classroom*, and *Connecting Comprehension and Technology: Adapt and Extend Toolkit Practices*. Learn more about her:

- web: KristinZiemke.com
- BlueSky: @kristinziemke.bsky.social
- Instagram: @Kziemke22

## Contributors

**Sara K. Ahmed**

Sara K. Ahmed currently serves as the director of curriculum integration and innovation at Catherine Cook School in Chicago. She has taught and coached in public, private, local, and international schools where her classrooms were designed to help students examine their own identities and see the humanity in others. When she is not in the classroom or meeting with teachers, you can find her coaching the soccer (football) teams at school.

She is the author of *Being the Change: Lessons and Strategies to Teach Social Comprehension* and coauthor with Harvey "Smokey" Daniels of *Upstanders: How to Engage Middle School Hearts and Minds with Inquiry*. She is an international speaker and staff developer in schools around the world— bridging literacy, inquiry, and social identity work through curriculum development, professional growth meetings, and lab classrooms. She has also served on the Teacher Leadership Team for Facing History and Ourselves and currently serves on the Re-Imagining Migration educator ambassador team.

Before moving back to the States in 2020, she lived in Bangkok, Thailand, where she served as a literacy coach and consultant-in-residence at NIST International

School. These days, you can find her running, playing tennis, reading, or writing her way through a rediscovery of her sweet home, Chicago.

You can find her on BlueSky: @sarakahmed.bsky.social, or Instagram: @SaraKAhmed2.

### Carrie Baughcum

Carrie Baughcum (she/her/hers) is a mother, mismatched sock wearer, a self described inspiration junkie, learning enthusiast, and, most of all, a passionate believer that all children can learn, we just need to find out how. As a teacher of twenty-six years of students who receive support and services through IEPs, she aims to integrate technology, creative thinking, a fearless attitude, and endless doodles into her classroom. She strives every day to enhance her students' learning while empowering them to achieve things they never knew they could do or be a part of. She is also the mother to two children, seventeen and nineteen years old. At home, she encourages her children to explore, learn, and try anything they want to be. She shares her experiences from her classroom, her adventures, and reflections on her time with students by presenting at conferences, sharing on her YouTube channel, and at carriebaughcum.com. She shares her deep passion for the power of doodles, visual thinking, and sketchnoting in her books *My Pencil Made Me Do It: A Guide to Sketchnoting* and *Stanley and the Very Messy Desk: An Adventure in Sketchnoting,* and on her weekly YouTube Live! show, hosted with Dr. Mandi Tolen, called *Doodle and Chat with Friends.* Follow her at carriebaughcum.com; youtube.com/carriebaughcum/, and at @carrie_baughcum.

### Shameer Bismilla

Shameer Bismilla is an experienced early childhood and primary school educator, literacy coach, and passionate advocate for children's literature. With over twenty-five years of experience in curriculum planning, English as a second language (ESL), coaching, teacher mentoring, and classroom management, he is dedicated to fostering a love of reading and writing in young learners. A firm believer in the power of books to shape children's identities, he strives to create meaningful literary experiences that help children see themselves in stories. His expertise lies in the readers' and writers' workshop method of instruction, where he nurtures young voices to become confident readers and storytellers. He has coauthored two picturebooks, *The Boy and the Box* and *The Girl and the Box,* and is an active picturebook reviewer. He is currently working on a new picturebook, set to be released soon. Follow him at www.shameer-reads.com and on Instagram: @shameer_reads.

### Lynsey Burkins

Lynsey Burkins is a proud educator, social worker, and advocate who has worked on behalf of children for over two decades. With twenty-one years of experience as an elementary teacher in Dublin, Ohio, she is deeply committed to creating antiracist, liberatory spaces where children feel free, have agency, and know they are loved. Lynsey recently earned her second master's degree in social work from The Ohio State University and now serves as a school social worker in Dublin, where she brings together her passions for literacy, mental health, and justice to support students and families. Her work is grounded in the belief that healing and transformation begin in community, and that schools can be powerful sites of both.

A fierce believer in the power of stories, Lynsey presents nationally on using literature to help students make sense of their world and nurture both their spirits and intellects. She is the coauthor of *Classroom Design for Student Agency* and *In Community with Readers: Transforming Reading Instruction with Read-Alouds and Minilessons*. Whether in the classroom or the counseling office, Lynsey's work is rooted in care, liberation, and the radical belief that every child deserves to be seen, valued, and free.

### Ann Marie Corgill

Ann Marie Corgill has been a classroom teacher in grades 1–6 for the past thirty years. She's currently teaching and learning with fifth graders in Alabama. Ann Marie has served on NCTE's Nominating Committee, Elementary Section Steering Committee, and as the Elementary Representative-at-Large on NCTE's Executive Committee. She served as the co-chair for the 2025 NCTE-NCTM Joint Conference for Elementary Literacy and Mathematics. She served as Alabama's Teacher of the Year in 2015 and was named one of four finalists for National Teacher of the Year. She is the author of *Of Primary Importance: What's Essential in Teaching Young Writers*.

### Kathleen Fox

Kathleen Fox is an educator who has served in St. Louis and Chicago. She has served as a teacher, assistant principal, and principal at St. Ann School over the past eleven years. She earned her master's degree in education from Loyola University Chicago and her master's degree in educational leadership from the University of Notre Dame.

### Sophia Garcia-Smith

Sophia Garcia-Smith is an educator and library media specialist who loves to create, collaborate, and share her love of teaching and technology. She currently works at a suburban Chicago school district. She has presented at many educational tech conferences across the United States. She has connected with schools from around the world, looking to give her students an authentic audience. Follow her on Bluesky: @garciasmithteach.bsky.social.

### Gary R. Gray Jr.

Gary R. Gray Jr. is a Black Canadian educator and author from Preston, Nova Scotia, home to Canada's oldest indigenous Black community. With over eleven years of international teaching experience, he holds an MEd in early elementary pedagogy, specializing in culturally responsive teaching. Outside the classroom, he enjoys coaching basketball, storytelling, and traveling with his wife. His debut picturebook, *I'm From,* illustrated by Oge Mora, was released on September 19, 2023, and his second book, *Spendin' Time,* is slated for release in 2026. Follow him at garyrgrayjr.com.

### Stacy Hansen

Stacy Hansen is a technology and innovation coach based in Waukee, Iowa. Passionate about integrating creativity into the classroom, she works closely with teachers and students to design innovative, purposeful learning experiences. Outside of work, she enjoys traveling with family and friends, embracing new cultures and experiences. Follow her: @stac34.bsky.social.

### Katie Keier

Katie Keier (she/her/hers) has been a public school educator in grades preK–8 for over thirty years. She is currently a kindergarten teacher in a public Title I school near Washington, DC. Katie is passionate about play, literacy learning, equity, and access for all learners, arts integration, and Reggio Emilia-inspired pedagogy. She is the coauthor of *Catching Readers before They Fall,* writes on the www.catchingreaders.com blog, and posts as @bluskyz on Instagram, Threads, and Bluesky. You can also reach her at katieannkeier@gmail.com to continue the conversation.

### Clare Landrigan

Clare Landrigan's work as an educator started over thirty years ago, teaching in a preschool mixed-aged group and a first- and second-grade classroom at the Eliot Pearson Children's School of Tufts University in Medford, Massachusetts. She is a part-time lead teacher at the Clinton Path Preschool and leads a professional development business, partnering with schools to implement best practices in literacy. She believes that effective professional development includes side-by-side teaching, analysis of student work, mutual trust, and a good dose of laughter. She also speaks at state and national conferences. She coauthored the books *It's All About the Books: How to Create Bookrooms and Classroom Libraries That Inspire Readers* and *Assessment in Perspective: Focusing on the Reader behind the Numbers.* Her forthcoming book, *Poetry Is Love: A Collection of Possibilities to Liberate the Hearts and Minds of Young Readers,* is coauthored with Aeriale Johnson. When she's not working, you can find her running, hiking, gardening, skiing, cooking, adding books to Little Free Libraries, or cozying up with a good book.
www.clarelandrigan.com
@clare.landrigan
www.facebook.com/ClareLandriganLLC

### Chrissy Moore

Chrissy Moore has taught first and second grade for the past seven years. She's a University of Missouri graduate with a bachelor's in elementary education, a DePaul University graduate with a master's degree in education, and a reading specialist. She has studied educational settings and philosophies in other cultures around the world, believing that we do our best when we learn from one another. She believes that every child has the potential to succeed when given the right support and opportunities. At school, she creates a safe, nurturing, and inclusive classroom where all students feel valued and empowered to reach their fullest potential. She holds students to high expectations, believing that with the right guidance, they can overcome challenges and achieve great things. She ensures that all students have the tools they need to thrive academically and personally. She hopes to inspire a love of learning while fostering a growth mindset in every student.

### Nessy Moos

Nessy Moos has spent her career as a special educator in Chicago Public Schools, teaching K–8 students across all subjects and grade levels. She is passionate about independent reading and ensuring that math is accessible to every learner. Her goal is to contribute to inclusive, engaging learning environments where all students feel both supported and autonomous. She believes literacy opens doors to opportunity, and she works to instill a love of books and reading while breaking down barriers to math instruction. Committed to student agency and equity in education, she continues to support students, families, and fellow educators in building a future where every child has the tools to thrive and be happy.

### Katie Muhtaris

Katie Muhtaris is the elementary instructional facilitator for Barrington 220 School District in Illinois. With over nineteen years of experience in education, she has served as a classroom teacher, instructional coach, and district leader. She is passionate about inquiry-based teaching and learning and has spent her career helping students and teachers bring curiosity, exploration, and authenticity into the classroom. She leads the Elementary Social Global Studies Steering Team in her district, where she helped design an award-winning, original inquiry-based curriculum. A longtime advocate for professional learning, she has provided professional development for educators across the country on topics such as literacy, technology integration, and authentic, student-centered instruction. She is also the coauthor of three professional books that support teachers in creating engaging, responsive learning environments.

### Debbie Plemons

Debbie Plemons is a kindergarten teacher at Our Lady of Guadalupe School in Chicago. She grew up nearby and loves working in the community. She's "always been a teacher," first with graduate students, then undergraduate, and elementary. She found her calling in early childhood, as she loves the opportunity to shape and learn from young minds. She believes there is no greater reward than to be a part of her students' stories and their successes; she celebrates that her students become a part of her story, too.

### Franki Sibberson

Franki Sibberson is a longtime classroom teacher, having taught elementary students in Dublin, Ohio, for over thirty years. She is a thought leader in literacy, with specific focus on literacy workshop, student agency, readers in grades 3–6, and digital literacy. She is a former President of the National Council of Teachers of English (NCTE), having served in 2018–2019. She has coauthored numerous publications and books, including *In Community with Readers* and *Classroom Design for Student Agency*. Currently, she is co-owner of OH What a Space, a play-based learning studio in Ohio. She also provides leadership and consulting to schools and nonprofits, supporting both local and national literacy initiatives.

### Angelique Trevino

Angelique Trevino is a third-grade ESL teacher in Austin, Texas. She has a master's degree in educational technology from Texas State University. She is passionate about teaching kids to navigate the world around them, both off- and online. One of the things she loves about teaching is that she can share her interests with students. She is very passionate about technology and art, so she loves that she can include both in various ways in her lessons and help children make connections with the content.

### Stella Villalba

Stella Villalba was raised and nurtured in a bicultural and bilingual household, born in Argentina to parents from Paraguay. Her family cultivated in her a love for stories at the dinner table. She believes that being multilingual is a tremendous gift, and it's through those lenses that she teaches, listens, writes, and leads every day. She has been working, learning, and dreaming alongside multilingual learners for more than twenty years. She is currently pursuing a PhD at The Ohio State University. You can find her online @stellavillalba.bsky.social or her blog: https://www.teachingcoachinglife.com/.

This book was typeset in Blackbird, Cera Pro, and Minion Pro by Jon Reigelman. The typefaces used on the cover include Blackbird and Cera Pro.